TO

FROM

Originally published by Christian Art Publishers
under the title *You Are Worth More Than Rubies*

Copyright © 2015 by Christian Art Publishers
PO Box 1599, Vereeniging, 1930, RSA

First edition 2017

Designed by Christian Art Publishers

Images used under license from Shutterstock.com

Scripture quotations marked NIV are taken from the *Holy Bible*,
New International Version® NIV®.
Copyright © 1973, 1978, 1984, 2011 by Biblica, Inc.®
Used by permission.
All rights reserved worldwide.

Scripture quotations marked NLT are taken from the *Holy Bible*,
New Living Translation®. Copyright 1996, 2004, 2007 by Tyndale House Foundation.
Used by permission of Tyndale House Publishers Inc., Carol Stream, Illinois 60188.
All rights reserved.

Scripture quotations marked NKJV are taken from the New King James Version.
Copyright © 1979, 1980, 1982 by Thomas Nelson, Inc. Used by permission.
All rights reserved.

Scripture quotations marked NCV are taken from the *Holy Bible*, New Century Version®
Copyright © 1987, 1988, 1991, 2005 by Word Publishing, a division of Thomas Nelson, In
Used by permission.

Printed in China

ISBN 978-1-4321-2497-7

Christian Art Publishers has made every effort to trace the ownership of all quotes
and poems in this book. In the event of any question that may arise from the use
of any quote or poem, we regret any error made and will be pleased to make
the necessary correction in future editions of this book.

17  18  19  20  21  22  23  24  25  26  –  10  9  8  7  6  5  4  3  2  1

# YOU ARE Blessed

## 366 DEVOTIONS

CHRISTIAN ART
PUBLISHERS

*Karen Moore*

Karen is the author of more than
60 books for both children and adults.
She has a Master's degree in education
and is a teacher, writer, speaker.
Karen is the mother of three grown
children and lives in sunny Florida.

## A WIFE OF

*noble character*

### WHO CAN FIND?
### SHE IS WORTH FAR MORE
### THAN RUBIES.

PROVERBS 31:10

## Learning to walk again

May your creed be for you as a mirror. Look at yourself in it,
to see if you believe everything you say you believe.
And rejoice in your faith each day.

St.. Augustine

That first time you toddled across a room was the beginning of you learning to walk. It helped you understand gravity and motion, and the certainty of landing safely in your mother's arms.

Since then, life has sent you out walking on your own and it still seeks to know what you really believe. Do you believe you have value and that you can become even more of what God intended? Do you believe you can land safely in His arms?

Today, walk over to your mirror and see the woman standing there. Remind her that each day of this new year she will be loved and valued by God. Once you believe that, you can walk worthy of the Lord. It will be a great year!

*What does the LORD your God ask of you but to … walk in obedience to Him,*
*to love Him, to serve the Lord your God with all your heart and with all your soul.*

Deuteronomy 10:12 NIV

Lord, thank You for seeing me right
where I am and for blessing my walk with You.
Amen.

## *You've got what it takes!*

Love not what you are, but what you may become.

Miguel de Cervantes

---

Most of us start a new year by creating some kind of resolution. We resolve that we will shape up and do things in a better way. We'll eat better, save more, and live more fully. Deep down, we know we can become more than we are right now. God knows that too.

God wants to encourage your walk with Him. That means He's fully prepared to help you with those resolutions as long as you're willing to put Him in the midst of them. He wants your mind, your body, and your spirit to become fully alive and fully engaged in all you can be.

As a woman of worth, you're alive in the Spirit of the Living God. You are a force to be reckoned with because your strength comes from Him. Grasp His hand everywhere you walk today.

*If we live in the Spirit, let us also walk in the Spirit.*

Galatians 5:25 NKJV

Lord, I resolve to be more aware of
You in every aspect of my life.
Amen.

# Feeling good, feeling God's love!

Martin Luther was once asked, "Do you feel
that you are a child of God this morning?"
And he answered, "I cannot say that I do,
but I know that I am."

---

As women, we tend to give a lot of credit to how we feel about things. We often decide what we will or won't do, solely based on how we feel. The problem is that our feelings continually change. One day we may feel very worthy of God's love and the next day, wonder why He cares about us at all. Fortunately for us, His love is the same yesterday, today, and forever. That means we can count on it all the time!

Emotions are a beautiful God-given thing and they serve us well. The beauty of God's love though is that it is based on fact, not feelings. He loves us! Doesn't that make everything in life more worthwhile?

*We have known and believed the love that God has for us. God is love,
and he who abides in love abides in God, and God in him.*

1 John 4:16 NKJV

Lord, help me to feel Your love each day,
and when I don't, help me to know for
sure that it is still there.
Amen.

## *Walking in the right direction*

> O Lord, forgive what I have been,
> sanctify what I am, and order what I shall be.
>
> Thomas Wilson

Thomas Wilson's prayer may well be our own. After all, as we begin a new year and strive to walk in the right direction, we recognize that we may well need some forgiveness. The kind of forgiveness we need may come from shattered dreams, or harsh words. It may come from a lack of good judgment or simply not doing the right thing. The fact is that we can start again and forgiveness helps us get there.

God sees you right now, right where you are and nothing pleases Him more than when you come close to Him and seek His guidance and His blessing on your life. He wants to give you the tools you need to build a stronger character and become the woman He knows you to be.

Change your shoes, change your pace, step out in faith in a new way and give God a chance to help you walk more closely with Him today.

> *Let us walk properly, as in the day.*
>
> Romans 13:13 NKJV

Lord, I will follow You! Help me to seek
Your guidance in all things this year.
Amen.

## *If you've been walking on the wild side*

*We all want progress, but if you're on the wrong road, progress means doing an about-turn and walking back to the right road; in that case, the one who turns back soonest is the most progressive.*

C. S. Lewis

One of the lessons we all need to learn when it comes to becoming a woman of worth is to stop looking at where we've been and start looking at where we want to be. The life of a Jesus follower is not about being perfect, but about being forgiven. It's not about getting it right every time, it's about getting back on track as quickly as possible when we take the wrong turn.

We all make wrong choices or do foolish things. That doesn't change God's love for us. When we seek His help, what changes is our love for Him. With greater love comes the desire to transform our lives and try to do better next time. If you've been walking on the wild side, step up your game and ask God to help you change. He's there for you, always has been … always will be!

*God has said, "Never will I leave you; never will I forsake you."*

Hebrews 13:5 NIV

Lord, I know I've made some pretty poor choices in my life.
Please help me get back on the path You want for me.
Amen.

## Not quite walking on air

*When you put your hand in God's hand,
you will never walk alone.*

Woodrow Kroll

No matter what we hope to become, we have to start with where we are. We can wonder what it really means when we hear others talk about their "walk" with the Lord. We can imagine they must have something we don't, or that God must prefer them over us. We can feel simply like we're limping along. We want to become more, but it seems like too big a job.

As you begin this new year and this new chapter of your life, imagine yourself holding God's hand. Picture yourself walking side by side with the Creator of the Universe, sharing your stories, loving each step you take together. If you can simply let your imagination soar, it may not be long at all until you truly are walking on air. God always imagines the very best for you and that's all He sees.

*God can see what is in people's hearts. And He knows what is in the mind of the Spirit, because the Spirit speaks to God for His people in the way God wants. We know that in everything God works for the good of those who love Him.*

Romans 8:27-28 NCV

Dear Lord, I know I just seem to be limping along the path of life,
not really up to speed with what You want from me.
Please help me to desire to walk on air with You.
Amen.

# If it seems like you're walking backwards

> Behold Solomon, the wisest of men, yet the greatest fool who ever lived. Even Job fails in patience, and Abraham, staggers as to his faith.
>
> Charles H. Spurgeon

There are times when you simply seem to take one step forward and two steps back. You decide to work out at the gym three times a week, and then you have to work too much, or the kids get sick, or the demands on your time are so over-whelming, you don't get a chance to work out. So, you feel defeated and you go ahead and have the chocolate mousse anyway, and before you realize it, your effort and motivation is gone.

It can be the same way in the life of your spirit. You can make great plans to read your Bible more often, go to church more regularly, or simply pray consistently. Somehow the routine doesn't get established, and before you know it weeks go by and you realize you've been starving your spirit. You haven't nurtured your soul in some time. You've actually taken a step backwards.

Try a new routine. One step backwards, two steps forward. Eventually you'll get where you and God wanted to you to go.

> Fight the battle well, holding on to faith and a good conscience,
> which some have rejected and so have suffered shipwreck with regard to the faith.
>
> 1 Timothy 1:18-19 NIV

Lord, I've been slipping backwards lately and I ask that You would hold on to me and help me find my way to move forward again.

Amen.

# It's going to be worth the wait!

Let us step into the darkness and reach
out for the hand of God. The path of faith and darkness
is so much safer than the one we would choose by sight.

George MacDonald

Most of us would have to admit that waiting is not our strongest suit. We don't like waiting in traffic or waiting for a job promotion or even waiting for payday. We like things to happen when we want them. Sometimes we're waiting in the dark, wondering about the medical test results or wondering if the bank will approve our loan. Waiting fills us with anxiety.

What about waiting for God? If we're truly walking in the darkness, there can be no better place to wait than in the Presence of God. He offers the only true light for the world. He offers the promise that He is with us always, no matter where we are, whether we're walking, running, or patiently waiting. If we wait on God's perfect timing, we can see His hand at work and we can see that the outcome was well worth the wait.

The One who holds you up in such high esteem sees you and is doing everything possible to assist your needs right now. Trust in Him and wait with confidence.

*The Lord is good to those who wait for Him, to the soul who seeks Him.*
*It is good that one should hope and wait quietly for the salvation of the Lord.*

Lamentations 3:25-26 NKJV

Dear Lord, I'm not very good at patient waiting. Please draw near to
me today and help me trust totally in You.

Amen.

# JANUARY 9

## The weight of waiting

Either He will shield you from suffering,
or He will give you unfailing strength to bear it.
Be at peace then, and put aside all anxious thoughts.

Francis de Sales

---

One of the problems with waiting for nearly anything is that it gives us time to create stories in our heads. When we're not sure whether God is hearing our prayers or whether God will even answer those prayers, that waiting time becomes a weight, an anchor around our shoulders. Sometimes the waiting can even paralyze us and keep us from doing the things we could do in the process of it all.

Becoming a woman of worth means that you are ready to turn your anxieties over to God. You're willing to wait for His direction because you know that going out on your own won't help the situation. The best practice is to change the stories in your head to prayers. Affirm your willingness to wait in spite of difficulty and uncertainty. Give God a chance to bless you even in the waiting. He does not want your heart to be troubled.

*"I am leaving you with a gift – peace of mind and heart. And the peace I give is a gift the world cannot give. So don't be troubled or afraid."*

John 14:27 NLT

Dear Lord, my heart is so heavy. Sometimes I simply cannot bear the waiting. I ask for Your strength and Your peace as I wait for Your answers.
Amen.

# *Waiting until you've got it all together*

*Nothing would be done at all if one waited until one could do it so well that no one could find fault with it.*

John H. Newman

We often are told that timing plays a big part in the success of anything, whether it's meeting the man of your dreams, or walking in on a one-day sale at your favorite store. At the right time, things come together.

When we're waiting for something important to happen to us, we sometimes assume that means we can't really do anything, that life is on hold, or we imagine that we just don't have all the pieces together yet for God to drop the checkered flag so we can get moving. Waiting on the Lord is a great place to begin, but sometimes, God is already with you simply agreeing that the time is right for you to act.

May God speak to your heart and direct your steps in all the things that matter most to you. May He help you to know when to act and give you His favor.

*I will bless the Lord who guides me; even at night my heart instructs me. I know the Lord is always with me. I will not be shaken, for He is right beside me.*

Psalm 16:7-8 NLT

Lord, I pray that You will be with me as I wait for Your timing and help me to take action according to Your will and purpose.

Amen.

## Do we wait and see what happens?

*Let us not be content to wait and see what will happen,*
*but give us the determination to make the right things happen.*

Peter Marshall

---

It can be tricky to figure out what it really means to wait for God's timing and what it means for us to have the determination to help move things along. The good news is that even when we don't know what to do, even if we're ready to wait, or to act, we cannot go too far in the wrong direction if we take our concerns to God first. Resting in Him is a bit different than simply waiting to see what happens.

When you've taken your concerns to Him, you can be assured that He seeks the best options for you right away. He alone knows all the outcomes and never has to resort to a "wait and see" attitude. The psalmist reminds us to "taste and see that the Lord is good." When we get a taste of how God works in our lives, we're more willing and more prepared to wait with expectation. We trust Him to work out what happens in the best ways.

*Taste and see that the Lord is good;*
*blessed is the one who takes refuge in Him.*

Psalm 34:8 NIV

Lord, help me to know the difference between waiting
for You and simply waiting because I don't dare to move
forward. Help me to seek Your timing in all that I do.
Amen.

## Waiting takes courage

Courage is what it takes to stand up and speak;
courage is also what it takes to sit down and listen.

Winston Churchill

---

Waiting takes courage. Some women have bravely waited while their soldiers have gone to battle, using every ounce of courage they could muster to maintain a sense of a normal life in the process. Others have had to wait in hospital rooms at the bedsides of those they love, or wait for the freedom to act and know the right direction for their lives. In the best and the worst of circumstances, waiting takes strength of purpose and courage.

Sometimes you have to stand up and be counted. Other times you have to have the courage to be still. When you wait for God's direction, you can be sure that He is right there with you, strengthening your heart and mind for the work that must be done. May He lead you and give you a courageous heart for all that is ahead.

*Wait patiently for the Lord. Be brave and courageous.*
*Yes, wait patiently for the Lord.*

Psalm 27:14 NLT

Lord, thank You for being with me during the long hours of endless
waiting. Give me the courage to trust and believe
that You are working everything out for me.

Amen.

## *Waiting for your plans to succeed*

It is not your business to succeed, but to do right.
When you have done so, the rest lies with God.

C. S. Lewis

We sometimes imagine that having a fancy title in a corporation, or becoming the chairman of the committee at school or in the community, will help us look successful. We have attached value to those titles and positions in our culture.

The fact is that God isn't looking to see if you're the CEO of a corporate entity. He's not trying to help you create a status position, because you already have a status position. You are a woman of worth! You are His design and He has great plans for you to help you succeed in all ways that are truly right for you. Wait for His plans to unfold and He'll surprise you with opportunities you never even knew existed.

Don't spend too much time or energy watching others who may only "look" successful, spend time with God and He will guide you into all the ways you can succeed in life.

*Wait and trust the Lord. Don't be upset when others get rich or when someone else's plans succeed. Don't get angry. Don't be upset; it only leads to trouble.*

Psalm 37:7-8 NCV

Lord, help me to keep it straight in my mind that
I am always valuable to You. Guide me and direct
my work according to Your purposes for me.
Amen.

## Waiting for dreams to come true

*Dreams do come true, if we only wish hard enough. You can have everything in life if you will sacrifice everything else for it. "What will you have?" says God. "Pray for it and take it."*

James M. Barrie

---

Dreamers recognize the hard work involved in getting their longings fulfilled. Dreams require lots of work, planning and waiting, and lots of believing. Any one of those things is not easy and all of them together can seem impossible. The good news is that God is the God of the possible. He takes everything we might imagine to be too hard or too far out of reach and says, if we work together, we can make that happen.

The start of a new year often motivates us to consider our dreams and where we want to be by the time the year is over. Where do you want to be? How can God help you now to understand how incredibly valuable you are to Him and how much He wants to help you follow your dreams? Pray and God will go ahead of you to open the doors and pave the way for you. He is indeed the Author of dreams.

*A longing fulfilled is sweet to the soul.*

Proverbs 13:19 NIV

Lord, I do have dreams and I pray they are worthy of what You would have me do. Help me to put my dreams before You and to trust You to work them out in the best ways for me.

Amen.

## Wise women have "uncommon" sense

*Common sense is genius dressed in its working clothes.*

Ralph Waldo Emerson

—◦◦◦❈◦◦◦—

Do you ever feel like common sense has simply gone out the window? Somehow, our culture has become so programmed to rely on computers and calculators and tablets that we have forgotten how to put two and two together for ourselves. We've lost the ability to make common sense decisions and we are perplexed about how it all happened.

Folk wisdom provides us with wonderful "old wives' tales" and many of those sage bits of advice were born out of common sense. They were the little things that helped our grandmothers and great-grandmothers stay content. As women who want to be worthy in the sight of God, we want to be wise, and more than that, we want Him to know that we approach life with the common sense He built into us. The more you operate with "uncommon sense," the more God can guide you into great wisdom. It's okay to add things up for yourself.

*Treat wisdom as a sister, and make understanding your closest friend.*

Proverbs 7:4 NCV

Lord, grant me the wisdom to use my own good sense
in the things I do and say. Help me to trust myself to make good
decisions because I have put all my choices in Your hands.
Amen.

## *God knows you're brilliant!*

Once you realize how valuable you are and how much you have going for you, the smiles will return, the sun will break out, the music will play, and you will finally be able to move forward in the life that God intended for you with grace, strength, courage, and confidence.

Og Mandino

When you think about women you admire, you may look at those in leadership roles or celebrities who support great causes. You might admire writers or advocates for social justice and reform. You might also admire women who are excellent mothers and caretakers. One woman to add to the list of those you admire should be you.

After all, God admires you very much. He sees your finest qualities and appreciates your efforts to use your gifts and talents wisely and well. He knows how hard you work and how much you do to take care of the people around you. God loves you because of everything you are and everything He knows you are yet to be. Your knowledge of many things is truly impressive, but your wisdom comes from living a life of mercy, grace, and trust in God.

*I want you to be wise in what is good and innocent in what is evil.*

Romans 16:19 NCV

Lord, I do admire some of the women I know
and some that I've just read about. Help me to see myself
as a woman that You and others admire as well.

Amen.

# *Wise and wonderful you*

The world will never starve for want of wonders,
but only for want of wonder.

G. K. Chesterton

Science and technology have challenged and changed the world bringing innovations we never imagined and opportunities for men and women alike. Our culture has witnessed explosions in the arts and the natural sciences and yet we are still baffled by the wonders of our ancient ancestors who created the Pyramids. Knowledge and wisdom are God's gifts to all who are willing to use them to His glory.

Becoming a woman of worth means that you are part of the wonders of the present age, and yet God wants even more from you. He wants you to maintain your sense of awe and wonder in Him. He wants you to understand all He has done to design you so well, to create you wonderfully and in His image. The more you see His hand in everything about you and around you, the more you please Him. Give God the glory that you have been fearfully and wonderfully made.

*I praise You because I am fearfully and wonderfully made;*
*Your works are wonderful, I know that full well.*

Psalm 139:14 NIV

Lord, I am truly in awe of You and the wonders of the world
that You've created. Thank You for making me just as I am.

Amen.

## The wisdom of free will

Why did God give them free will? Because free will,
though it makes evil possible, is also the only thing that makes
possible any love or goodness or joy worth having.

C. S. Lewis

Though God could have created us with simple blind obedience in our DNA, He chose something better. He chose to create us so we could choose to have a relationship with Him. He chose to give us the freedom to follow Him or to walk the earth without Him. Either way, we receive His gift of life, but by His grace, He offers us life eternal.

The freedom to choose takes wisdom and awareness. It is woven together with insight and understanding and made strong by God's own Spirit. Yes, He didn't create us with a choice and then just back away. No, He placed a portion of Himself within us so that we would be able to hear His call and respond to His voice. Within that framework, He gave us free will. He wants us to love Him as He loves us, but He gives us the chance to make that choice on our own. Choosing Him makes everything else worthwhile.

*Now the Lord is the Spirit, and where the Spirit of the Lord is, there is freedom.*

2 Corinthians 3:17 NIV

Dear Lord, thank You for giving me the
choice every day to love You and serve You.
Help me always to choose to be by Your side.
Amen.

## *The wisdom of the heart*

The right kind of heart is a kind heart like God's.

Anonymous

Women are sometimes faulted for leading with the heart, instead of the head. Chances are that most women are adept at leading with both of these faculties and doing so wisely. God gave you a heart in a physical way to keep every aspect of your body strong and healthy. He gave you a heart in a metaphorical way so that you could keep every aspect of life feeling strong and healthy. Your heart is always called upon to be strong and wise.

As you grow in your relationship with Christ, you may find that your heart becomes enlarged, perhaps even overwhelms you. The more you see Him, the more you will see Him in everyone around you and the more your heart will go out to others in sympathy and compassion. Your understanding of God's grace and mercy will cause your Spirit to overflow with a certain kind of joy that deepens your intimate relationship with the Savior. You'll have a heart for others and God will bless you for it.

*Keep your heart with all diligence, for out of it spring the issues of life.*

Proverbs 4:23 NKJV

Dear Lord, please grant me a heart of wisdom so that all the works of my hands will reflect a willing and loving heart.

Amen.

# *Wisdom for today*

*She is a wise woman who does not grieve for the things which she has not, but rejoices for those which she has.*

Epictetus (adapted)

As women, we sometimes wander back into the past more often than might be healthy for us. We grieve for the things we've lost, the moments we've missed or would hope to do over again. For some of us that grief is such a strong magnet to what once was that we're missing what is. We're unable to rejoice in the present moment or even look forward to the future without the weight of the past always being dragged along with us.

The more we come to understand all that God has for us, the more we can let go of yesterday. God is changing us. He is working with us and creating in us new hearts that are best kept in the moment He's giving us right now. He wants us to be content with what we have today, so that He can continue to bless us in the days to come. Walk with Him today and ask Him to keep you in the present moment. Your joy will overflow.

*Give me neither poverty nor riches – feed me with the food allotted to me.*

Proverbs 30:8 NKJV

Dear Lord, forgive the past moments where I was
not wise or aware of You, and bless me today,
right where I am, and keep me close to You.
Amen.

## *Dare to be wiser today!*

Dare to be wise: begin! She who postpones the hour
of living rightly is like the peasant who waits for the river
to drain away. Yet on it glides, and will glide forever.

Horace (adapted)

Of course, we would choose to live more wisely if we were fully conscious of the choices to do so. Yet, that may well be where wisdom shows itself, looming in front of us as decisions must be made. It presents options and offers to wait with us, work with us, and help us cross the rivers of life as soon as we are ready. Wisdom is not at a standstill, nor is there a shortage available to you, so embrace it.

God has called you to be His and as His child, offers You infinite wisdom to handle situations from day to day, infinite grace to make mistakes, and endless possibility to try again or to try something different. He knows with each effort you make that you'll become wiser. He longs to instill the secrets of the universe and the wisdom of the ages to you, His beloved and gracious woman.

*I am as happy over Your promises as if I had found a great treasure.*

Psalm 119:162 NCV

Lord, I don't always realize that it takes courage to do
the wise thing, to live according to what You most
want from me. Help me to be wiser this very day.
Amen.

## God doesn't make an inferior anything!

There is about us, if only we have eyes to see, a creation of such spectacular profusion, spendthrift richness, and absurd detail, as to make us catch our breath in astonished wonder.

Michael Mayne

When we stop to think about it, the glorious visions surrounding us are a continual reminder of God's handiwork. If we examine such mundane things as the petals on a flower or the colors of a butterfly's wing, we see His amazing attention to detail. How much more then, should we be awed by the human body?

When God made you, He knew exactly what He was doing. He knew every detail about who you would be and the purpose you could serve in the lives of others. He created you with love, seeing the perfect and beautiful you before you were even born. As you look in the mirror today, instead of noticing the things you might not be fond of about your appearance, note the things God did to make you exquisite.

*You made all the delicate, inner parts of my body and knit*
*me together in my mother's womb. Thank You for making me so wonderfully*
*complex! Your workmanship is marvelous – and how well I know it.*

Psalm 139:13-14 NLT

Lord, I know that You created me with love and placed me in a family where I could grow and learn. Bless all those who have helped me become more of what You want me to be.

Amen.

## *Let your light shine!*

When you own something beautiful, let's say a painting or a flower vase with an intricate design, you put it somewhere so others can see it and admire it. That's what God did too. He put you in the midst of others so that they could see His amazing handiwork and offer Him praise and thanks.

You're His light in the world. You're the one who helps others discover His presence in their own lives. You're His ambassador wherever you are. Sometimes, you'll light up the darkness because you'll be in the midst of people with such great need of God's love. Other times, you'll simply add to the light and the joy around you as you mingle with people who are also willing to shine.

You are a unique design, infused with the light of God's Spirit, and God always sees that great light when He looks at you. Give Him thanks and praise and step into His light even more today.

*"You should be a light for other people. Live so that they will see the good things you do and will praise your Father in heaven."*

Matthew 5:16 NCV

Lord, help me to be a brilliant and awesome
light just for You today.
Amen.

## Letting God lead!

And I said to the man who stood at the gate of the year: "Give me a light that I may tread safely into the unknown." And he replied: "Go out into the darkness and put your hand into the hand of God. That shall be to you better than light and safer than a known way."

Minnie L. Haskins

As human beings, we sometimes manage to get ahead of ourselves, or maybe we get ahead of God by taking actions before we know the way. Sometimes we drag our feet and lag behind, so that we lose sight of where God wanted us to go.

This year you can make a conscious choice. You can choose every morning just how you'll spend the day. You can step out on your own and hope for the best, or you can put your hand in the hand of the One who is more than willing to lead the way, and walk in joy and confidence.

Whatever you were going to do today, stop for a moment, and see if you are following the Leader!

*Your Word is a lamp to my feet and a light to my path.*

Psalm 119:105 NKJV

Lord, please forgive me when I walk ahead of You or lose sight of You. Help me to always stay close by Your side.

Amen.

## God's faith in you

*I may not be who I want to be, and I may not be who
I am going to be but thank God, I am not who I was.*

Anonymous

God has always believed in you. He knows who you are at this very moment and He is excited about who you are going to be five years from now. You're a work in progress and He couldn't be more delighted about that. He has total faith in you.

Sometimes though, it's hard to have faith in yourself. It's difficult to look at where you are today and even imagine a stronger, brighter, better you in the days ahead. Always remember, that you are a child of God's promise, an heir to His estate and so He will always believe in you.

As you trust Him to help you change, to become even more of what He designed you to be, you can enjoy the process and keep walking toward the goal. Be confident and steadfast in all you do today.

*No matter how many promises God has made, they are "Yes" in Christ.
And so through Him the "Amen" is spoken by us to the glory of God.*

2 Corinthians 1:20 NIV

Lord, it actually overwhelms me to realize that You
have faith in me. Help me to trust Your faith and grow
that same faith in myself for Your glory.

Amen.

# Created to make a difference

*You must be careful how you walk, and where you go, for there are those following you who will set their feet where yours are set.*

Robert E. Lee

Did you know you make a difference to everyone around you? You have unique skills and gifts that you share, that only have your imprint, and have an impact because of your love and your style. You are a leader at home, at church, and in your community even if you've never chaired a committee. You are a leader because God designed you to show others the way.

As you consider those who observe your life to see the light of Christ, imagine where you want to take them. Imagine what you might offer them so they can turn up the light in themselves and shine on. Whether you have a passing conversation with someone in the grocery store aisle, or you lead a Bible study, you impact the lives of those who know you. God is proud of your efforts and no matter what difference you are able to make in the lives of others, you always make a difference to Him. May God bless your day with great desire to shine.

*"But indeed for this purpose I have raised you up, that I may show My power in you, and that My name may be declared in all the earth."*

Exodus 9:16 NKJV

Lord, thank You for enriching my life with Your presence and creating a unique purpose for me. Help me to truly make a difference in the lives of others.
Amen.

# *Being authentically you*

Believe in yourself! Have faith in your abilities!
Without a humble but reasonable confidence in your
own powers you cannot be successful or happy.

Norman Vincent Peale

It's important to believe in your own worth, that is to know the truth of yourself. God has no desire for anything about you to be lost or destroyed. He wants you to live abundantly and well and to stay true to the woman He created you to be. He wants you to be totally authentic.

If you can think of anything in your life that does not ring true, that is not authentic for you, it is a good time to let it go and to discover a new path. In your effort to change, to become of great worth to yourself, to others, and to God, it is essential that you live in as much of your truth as possible.

It's okay to throw out the old stuff that no longer serves you. You can let go of the plastic, and the temporary, and the disposable. God wants only what is real, only what is truly from your heart. He'll help you get there.

*"What do you benefit if you gain the whole*
*world but are yourself lost or destroyed?"*

Luke 9:25 NLT

Lord, I want to be the real me in every area of my life.
I especially want to be authentic in my relationship with You.
Amen.

## You are a masterpiece

*Do not grudge the Hand that is moulding the still too shapeless image within you. It is growing more beautiful, though you see it not, and every touch of temptation may add to its perfection.*

Henry Drummond

———◆——◆✕◆——◆———

When God creates, everything He does is a masterpiece. He doesn't make mistakes and He doesn't have to do His work over and over again to get it right. It is completely perfect from the start. That's how you know you are a brilliant work of His hand and a woman of great worth.

In honor of the beauty He's placed within your soul and your spirit, He's inspired artists of all possible media to continue to emulate His effort. He offers us their unique talents and skills to make our lives a more beautiful experience. That is precisely what He did with you as well. He's offered you as some of His greatest work so that others may enjoy the experience of getting to know you and getting to see life in a more delightful way because of you. You are indeed His special masterpiece.

*Keep on working to complete your salvation with fear and trembling, because God is working in you to help you want to do and be able to do what pleases Him.*

Philippians 2:12-13 NCV

Lord, please keep working with me, shaping me,
molding me into the woman You already know I can be.
Amen.

## You're a warrior woman!

*We're in spiritual combat – cosmic combat for*
*the heart and soul of humankind.*

Chuck Colson

The beauty of becoming a stronger woman of worth in God's sight is that He can use you in more situations and circumstances. He can prepare you to hold up the light for others who are battling the depths of despair and darkness. He can strengthen you for spiritual combat because it is going on everywhere around you. God needs you to stand up to the faith He has given you and use it as a shield to protect yourself and your loved ones.

You're His warrior woman! He counts on you to be there in those moments when someone needs a strong voice, or a kind heart, where someone needs to see that God is real. You're His hands and feet in this world and He has equipped you in every way to do His work. He'll never leave you unprotected because He is your strength and your shield in every life circumstance.

*Take up the shield of faith, with which you can*
*extinguish all the flaming arrows of the evil one.*

Ephesians 6:16 NIV

Lord, I don't really think of myself as a warrior, but I am certainly a woman who wants to share Your love with others. Thank You for protecting me and equipping me for this task.
Amen.

## *Putting on the armor*

Christ tells us plainly, and without any qualifications, that we
are involved in a war in which there is no room for neutrals.

Hugh Redwood

One of the reasons, God has equipped you to share His love with others is because He knows your heart. He knows that you are His all the way and that you are totally connected to each other. That connection means that you are never in neutral territory because you're always certain of which side you're on. He trusts you to do what you've been called to do and He knows you have what it takes.

He has not only equipped you for the job, He has provided His own armor to protect you, to shield you from the slings and arrows of insults and obstacles. His truth guides you and you never have to guess when He needs you to stand your ground for Him because He makes each circumstance very clear. Your team may not have a mascot and a jersey, but it is always victorious. Hooray for you!

*Stand your ground, putting on the belt of truth*
*and the body armor of God's righteousness.*

Ephesians 6:14 NLT

Lord, I don't know if I always am aware of standing
my ground, but help me to know any time You
need me to do my part for the sake of someone else.
I want to spread Your love everywhere I go.
Amen.

# *Standing for a cause*

The foundation stones for a balanced success are honesty,
character, integrity, faith, love and loyalty.

Zig Ziglar

You know you were designed for a purpose. You may have figured out some of what that purpose is as it pertains to the things of God. You may still be wondering if you'll ever stumble across that one thing God may really want you to do. God has placed a portion of Himself within your heart. Because of that, you are drawn to Him and to the things that He wants to accomplish through you.

He always has a cause, the cause of getting more people to know His Son, Jesus. He also wants to shout out His love for human beings. You're His emissary, His ambassador. You're the woman He called to stand up for Him and to share His love. He may work through you in the job you do, within your family, or simply by social action, a cause you are drawn to because of His guidance.

Never fear that His purposes will be accomplished. He delights in knowing that He can count on you.

*Speak up for those who cannot speak for themselves; ensure justice for those being crushed. Yes, speak up for the poor and helpless, and see that they get justice.*

Proverbs 31:8-9 NLT

Lord, please help me to be willing to stand up for You and
for the needs of others in any way You might guide me.
Amen.

# HER HUSBAND CAN
*trust her*

## AND SHE WILL
## GREATLY ENRICH
## HIS LIFE

PROVERBS 31:11

## *You're outstanding in every way!*

Women are the real architects of society.

Harriet Beecher Stowe

God blessed you with a lot of unique abilities and strengths. He caused you to be able to lead and to follow. He created you with brilliance and charm. Your sensitivity to cultures and people, your compassion for those less fortunate than yourself, your willingness to pitch in and do what needs to be done in any situation, are just a few of the ways He has blessed others through you.

Though your achievements may be without end, the only thing God wants in return is your love and devotion. He wants to know that you recognize His handiwork so that you can fulfill His purposes for your life. You have so many roles to play in business, in family, and in friendship, and even in faith.

Let God continue to be your strength no matter what role you play today and where you go. Turn to Him in praise and gratitude for all that you are and all that you will be.

*Charm is deceptive, and beauty does not last;*
*but a woman who fears the Lord will be greatly praised.*

Proverbs 31:30 NLT

Lord, help me to be the best woman I can
be no matter what job I have to do, or what person
I have to share a conversation with today.
Amen.

# *It's a matter of self-control!*

*Self-control is the mother of spiritual health.*
John Climacus

Did you start the new year with a resolution to do one thing better this year than you did last year? Do you even remember what it is you resolved to do? Many of us start out so well when a new calendar year begins and we make promises to ourselves to exercise more, to eat more healthily, to take that class we've been meaning to take, and yet, somehow just a few short weeks into the year, we give up.

The real issue is self-control. It's not easy to break habits that may not serve us very well. It's not easy to choose a green smoothie over a milkshake. It's not easy, but with God's help it's possible. You can start today to seek God's guidance to help you do things better. He wants you to be strong and healthy. He wants you to have an abundant and successful life.

Think of one thing today that you would change if you had an accountability partner … yes, even God!

*Let us who live in the light be clearheaded …*
1 Thessalonians 5:8 NLT

Lord, I know I'm not good at the follow-through of my own intentions.
Help me to start again and stick with the plan.
Amen.

## *Everything about you matters to God!*

Above all the grace and the gifts that Christ gives
to His beloved is that of overcoming self.

Francis of Assisi

---

We live in a culture that encourages our independence, strokes our egos, and seeks to remind us how important we are. All of that is good … to a degree. God certainly wants us to be independent and capable of managing the world around us and He wants us to understand our value, but not to the exclusion of all other things. Every aspect of our lives matters to God, both the things He has given us for ourselves and the gifts He gave us to share with others.

In our efforts to become more of Him, it stands to reason that we have to get out of our own way. We have to seek more of Him and less of ourselves and that is a matter of self-control. You have been given gifts designed to be used for the good of others. All God asks, is that you use those gifts to His glory. You were blessed to be a blessing and sometimes it's a simple matter of self-control.

*Each of you should use whatever gift you have received to serve others,*
*as faithful stewards of God's grace in its various forms.*

1 Peter 4:10 NIV

Lord, I know You have blessed me. Help me to step out
of the way and be willing to share my gifts and talents
with others according to Your will and purpose.
Amen.

## Persistence and determination

*Never give in, never give in, never, never, never, never –*
*in nothing, great or small, large or petty – never give in*
*except to convictions of honor and good sense.*

Winston Churchill

Part of growing and changing and becoming more of what God designed you to be is about persisting in the effort. You may have some old habits to break or some struggles to overcome. Hold tightly to the hope you have in Jesus and He will bless you. Some days, your ego will taunt you and try to convince you that all this changing doesn't really matter. It may even cause you to take a step backwards.

As soon as you recognize it, stop where you are, pray, and take God's hand once again. He is always there! Gather with others who are seeking to grow in the same ways that you are and encourage each other. All of this together will help you become the woman of worth you long to be. It just may take a little persistence and determination.

No problem! God will strengthen and renew you every day.

*Let us hold tightly without wavering to the hope we affirm, for God can*
*be trusted to keep His promise. Let us think of ways to motivate*
*one another to acts of love and good works.*

Hebrews 10:23-24 NLT

Lord, sometimes I wonder if I can really grow in the ways
You might hope. I get started and then I fall backward. Help me to
move forward again and let me never, never give up.

Amen.

## The sister of patience

*Perseverance is the sister of patience, the daughter
of constancy, the friend of peace, the cementer of friendships,
the bond of harmony, and the bulwark of holiness.*

Bernard of Clairvaux

You've probably long understood why patience has been deemed a virtue. It seems that the more you sense an inability to really be patient, the more opportunities you get to practice. Patience is all about self-control. It's the one thing that tests you nearly every day of your life. Can you be patient when your spouse isn't listening to you? Can you be patient when there's a long line at the bank, but you simply must do a transaction today?

Imagine, if you can, what it must be like for God to be patient with human beings. If you dare, imagine what it takes for Him to be patient with you. Patience may coincide with perseverance because it is an attitude. Adopting a patient attitude, may not only help you grow, it may also save your heart a lot of stress.

Embrace those moments when you are called upon to be patient. Stand back and observe them. You'll get better at being patient each time you try.

*We also have joy with our troubles, because we know that these troubles produce
patience. And patience produces character, and character produces hope.*

Romans 5:3-4 NCV

Lord, help me to be aware of those moments when I'm not
willing to be patient. Thank You for being so patient with me.
Amen.

## *His banner over me is love*

You aren't loved because you're valuable.
You're valuable because God loves you.

Anonymous

You might think of a banner as something that you hang up in a room to make an announcement, like the type we often put up in churches at Easter or Christmas time. Or, perhaps you think of a banner expressing "Congratulations" to someone or? "Happy Birthday!"

A "banner" moment, however, denotes something that is excellent or noteworthy or exceptional. It is something unique and out of the ordinary. When God created you it was a "banner" moment and He was delighted with His work. He saw you as exceptional and extraordinary. He saw you as some of His best work ever!

Imagine then that He has declared His love to you for all the world to see. He holds you in such esteem that He welcomes you at His table all the time. His banner for you always declares His great love.

*He brought me to the banqueting house,*
*and His banner over me was love.*

Song of Solomon 2:4 NKJV

Lord, I can't always imagine Your love for me. I know that
it is because I have not yet grasped what it means for You to
value me so much. Thank You for loving me all the time.
Amen.

# I love to tell the story

Little self-denials, little honesties, little passing words
of sympathy, little nameless acts of kindness, little silent
victories over favorite temptations – these are the silent
threads of gold which, when woven together, gleam out
so brightly in the pattern of life that God approves.

Frederick William Farrar

---

Being God's witness in the world is not always about declaring His name aloud in public places or sharing your faith with an acquaintance. Sometimes, being His witness is about the things you do, the ways you act that help others to see His light.

When you make choices that show your self-sacrifice, your kind heart, and your willingness to put others before yourself, you show His love. You tell His story loud and clear and others are drawn into the tale.

If you feel a bit shy about sharing your faith, you don't have to be. Simply live in those ways that you know please God, and you'll be one of His heroines wherever you are. Your story and His are connected with love.

*"You are the light of the world."*

Matthew 5:14 NIV

Lord, bless the opportunities I may have
today to share Your love with others. Let me always
be willing to tell Your amazing story.
Amen.

## Your compassionate heart

*It is the duty of every Christian to be Christ to his neighbor.*

Martin Luther

The beauty of being a compassionate woman is that it is a natural part of who you are. You were nurtured in being compassionate from the time you were a little girl. You loved your pets, fed strays when you could get away with it, and spoke kindly to the sweet little ladies who sat alone at church.

Your compassion for others shines through every time you become aware of another person's need and respond in some way. Of course, you can't take care of the whole world, but you do take the "love your neighbor" command seriously and you help everyone you possibly can.

God loves your kindness and your sympathy toward others. He needs you to be His hands and feet in this world. Someone needs you today.

*All of you should be of one mind. Sympathize with each other. Love each other as brothers and sisters. Be tenderhearted, and keep a humble attitude.*

1 Peter 3:8 NLT

Lord, help me to never be too busy, or too unwilling
to bring comfort or sympathy to someone who needs me.
Amen.

## You can lead the way

*Remember, a small light will do a great deal when it is in a very dark place. Put one little tallow candle in the middle of a large hall, and it will give a good deal of light.*

Dwight L. Moody

Some of us imagine that we aren't leaders. We aren't the chairman of the board somewhere or the leader of a women's group. We tend to think it's better to leave that kind of leadership to others. We don't really welcome the limelight.

You don't have to be a recognized leader in any social or professional arena to lead the way for Christ. If you think of John the Baptist, eating locusts and honey and living in the wilderness, you might not have picked him out as a leader. He was, though. He was called to lead the way for the Lord. He was called to open other people's eyes to the kingdom that was coming.

Happily, you don't have to change your diet or move to the desert to be Christ's advocate. You can stay right where you are and be His example. You can lead the way for one person to see Him differently and you can do that any time the moment presents itself. God couldn't have a better person than you are to help lead others His way.

*"You did not choose Me, but I chose you."*

John 15:16 NKJV

Lord, bless me when I strive to share Your love with others.
Help me to be a good example of Your loving kindness.

Amen.

## When others see you

*We are the Bibles the world is reading;*
*we are the creeds the world is needing;*
*we are the sermons the world is heeding.*

Billy Graham

———————

Pastors will tell us that one of the biggest problems in the church today is a lack of Bible literacy. Though most people own Bibles, it appears that few people actually read them on a regular basis. What that means is that people are not learning about God's love from His Word nearly as often as they are learning about God's love from His children.

You may be the only peek into the Bible that some of the friends and neighbors in your circle will ever see. You may be the only reference they have to what it means to be a child of God.

The beauty of that is it means you are free to be authentic. You are free to be the woman of worth God created you to be because He can use you right where you are. Sometimes you may speak of Him to others, but most of the time, others will simply see Him through you.

*"Let your light shine before others, that they may see*
*your good deeds and glorify your Father in heaven."*

Matthew 5:16 NIV

Lord, thank You for the privilege to share
Your love with others. Help me to always be willing
to shine as an example of Your grace, mercy, and peace.
Amen.

## Standing firm in your faith

We share our faith because the love of God is shed abroad
in our hearts and not out of self-interest.

David Havard

An old adage says that if you don't stand for something, you'll fall for anything. It's a good one for all of us to keep in mind as we ponder what it means to stand up for our faith. As women, we're willing to stand up for our children, our families, and the things we believe in. We're willing to support the causes we feel will make a difference in the world.

As we become stronger women of worth in the sight of God, He wants us to be willing to stand strong for Him and for our beliefs. He wants us to stand firm in just one way and for just one reason, because we love Him! Love is our only motivation when it comes to sharing our faith. Love is what God promises to give anyone who walks in His direction. In matters of faith, it's not about us at all, it's all about Jesus.

Let your faith help you stand strong today.

*Be on your guard; stand firm in the faith; be courageous; be strong.*

*Do everything in love.*

1 Corinthians 16:13-14 NIV

Lord, thank You for giving me such a powerful faith and such a great desire to know more of You. Help me to be strong in You.

Amen.

## Little things mean a lot

*Accustom yourself continually to make many acts of love,
for they rekindle and melt the soul.*

Teresa of Ávila

---

You know how much it brings you instant joy when someone does some little thing to brighten your day. It may be as small as paying you a particular compliment or as big as bringing you an unexpected present or treating you to lunch. Little things mean a lot.

Most friendships blossom over time and an array of experiences that create warm memories. You discover the things you have in common or the ideas that you share with great enthusiasm and life feels better. The same is true for the little things that help your faith blossom, or the things you do to cause someone else's faith to grow stronger. You're the greatest witness to God's truth and love that many people will ever know. When you offer your kindness, your joy, and your generous spirit, you make hearts melt and souls come to life.

It's a great day to share a little of God's love.

*Your kindness will reward you.*

Proverbs 11:17 NLT

Lord, remind me to do whatever I can for others today.
Help me to seek opportunities to share Your love with others.
Amen.

## *When your heart speaks*

Preach the Gospel at all times, and when necessary, use words.

Francis of Assisi

---

You don't have to be a street-corner preacher to share the messages God has put on your heart. Sometimes you don't have to speak at all. You simply have to be the beautiful, positive, loving woman God designed you to be. Your heart speaks volumes to those closest to you and they soak in your goodness far more than you may even realize.

Whatever you are doing today, keep in mind that no matter how important it is, God will bless you even more when you share His truth with those around you. How? You become the woman they can count on, the one they can trust to be there when they are suffering or when they need a friend. You are the angel in their midst and each time you offer them a simple kindness, they see the gospel come to life anew.

*"I tell you the truth, anyone who welcomes My messenger is welcoming Me, and anyone who welcomes Me is welcoming the Father who sent Me."*

John 13:20 NLT

Lord, I pray that my heart will speak of You to
anyone who wants to see You today. Thank You
for sharing Your love through me.

Amen.

## God so loved you

*Spread love everywhere you go: First of all in your own house … let no one ever come to you without leaving better and happier. Be the living expression of God's kindness; kindness in your face, kindness in your eyes, kindness in your smile, kindness in your warm greeting.*

Mother Teresa

It's Love Day! It's the day where we send Valentines to those we care about and let them know in a special way how much they mean to us. It's the day when we pause to consider how important it is to experience love and how healthy it is for love to be shared with those around us.

We often say that "God is love." Sometimes we understand what that means, but much of the time, we don't? We are students of love. We're all learning what it means to love more fully or to love unconditionally as God does. We're women who want to give and receive the beautiful kind of love God intended.

Today is a great day to reach out to someone who holds your heart, and embrace them with the gift of love. Remember that each person you know is truly, honestly, and completely loved by God … even the person you see in your mirror.

*"God loved the world so much that He gave His one and only Son so that whoever believes in Him may not be lost, but have eternal life."*

John 3:16 NCV

Dear Lord, it's hard to imagine what it truly means
to have Your love. Thank You for knowing how much we
need You. I send You my love on this Valentine's Day.
Amen.

## It's a love triangle

With the one and with the other
There was equality,
So Three Persons, one Beloved,
Loved all, and they were three.

John of the Cross

Some of us struggle with trying to understand the concept of the Trinity. We can appreciate the idea that there is a Creator God, His beloved Son, Jesus who came to earth as an infant, lived long enough to give us a taste of God's plan and purpose, was put to death, and then rose again to go back to heaven where He had come from. When Jesus left, He said He'd send the Holy Spirit. We embrace the idea of this incredible Comforter who knows us so well and can pray for us when we can't find the right words.

We can take all that in, but we still have to imagine what it truly means that this Being, this God of the Universe is really all these Beings at the same time … Father, Son, and Holy Spirit. In whatever form we receive Him, He comes to us and loves us, three in one.

*There are three that bear witness in heaven: the Father,*
*the Word, and the Holy Spirit; and these three are one.*

1 John 5:7 NKJV

Lord, thank You for giving us so many ways to connect
with You and to understand You. Thank You for guiding us
through Your love, Your Word, and Your Holy Spirit.

Amen.

## *Love always serves its best*

When the people see that you truly love them,
they will hear anything from you.

Richard Baxter

"Becoming" almost anything means that we recognize there's work to be done. We may be good at something, but we're not there yet. We strive to get better and possibly even the best at things that matter. Sometimes, we have to admit we aren't all that interested in doing our best. We do what must be done because we're too tired or too overwhelmed by life to dig in much deeper. Sometimes we become apathetic and wonder why it even matters what we do.

As a woman of worth, of great value and beloved by God, His hope for you is that you'll be able to offer your best any time you act on His behalf. After all, you are His representative and so the way that you love others, is some indicator of how He loves others. God wants you to do all things in love and that kind of love serves its best.

When you're a bit too weary or you're not sure any more how to do that, spend some quiet time in prayer with the One who loves you and you'll get back on track.

*Love is what holds you all together in perfect unity.*

Colossians 3:14 NCV

Lord, thank You for loving me and teaching me what it means
to serve and to love others. Help me to give my best for You.

Amen

## Recipes for love

God created your soul with a capacity for loving – so much
so that you cannot live without love. Indeed love is your food.

Catherine of Siena (adapted)

If you could create a great recipe for love, what might you include? Perhaps you'd have a cup of kindness, a tablespoon of patience, a measure of forgiveness and even a pinch of humility. Whatever your recipe might be, the idea is to take all that you have and all that you are and stir them into the mix to share with others. God has poured out His Holy Spirit on you, filled with overflowing love and He always makes sure you have what you need. He feeds you a daily dose of love.

The beauty of a good recipe is that when you really like it, you write it up and print it out and share it with your friends. You want them all to enjoy the same delight and goodness you experience with that recipe. That's what God wants too. He wants you to share His recipe for love and to offer it to starving people everywhere. After all, He is the bread of life.

What do you have cooking today?

*Better is a dinner of herbs where love is, than a fatted calf with hatred.*

Proverbs 15:17 NKJV

Lord, help me to change my recipe, so that
I'm always able to serve others with genuine love.

Amen.

## Second-chance love

O God of Second Chances and new Beginnings, here I am again.

Nancy Spiegelberg

Most of us believe in getting a second chance or even third chances if we need them. That's what God gives us. He gives us a new chance with each sunrise. He looks at us with love and hopes we'll understand more fully what He expects with each passing day, with each step of becoming more.

Though we all want God to give us a number of chances, we aren't always as willing to give those same chances to other people who disappoint us or who do something we feel is unforgiveable. We have a pretty short leash for errors that those around us might make.

Unfortunately, the "errors" someone else makes may only be errors to us. Perhaps they have a different method for getting something accomplished than we do. Maybe they don't agree with our assumptions and so we walk away when they don't meet our standards. Love gives second chances.

*Wisdom rests in the heart of him who has understanding,*
*but what is in the heart of fools is made known.*

Proverbs 14:33 NKJV

Lord, help me to have the kind of wisdom that sees into the motivations of another person, leaving the door open even when mistakes are made and gives a second chance.

Amen.

## Another helping of love

*We can do no great things, only small things with great love.*

Mother Teresa

---

When you were younger, you may have aspired to do something extraordinary, something the world would recognize as really great. It was a lofty goal and a good idea because it's always good to strive to become more than we are at one moment in time. Big goals require dedication, courage and a willingness to fail. They also require greater love.

Love gets you started on a path that seems especially right for you. Another helping of love is needed though when you understand the realities of the work involved and the effort it takes to get where you want to go. The second helping of love that truly sparks greatness though is the kind that includes others, that is motivated by the outcome of your goal and how it makes life better for those around you. When we're truly motivated by love, then anything we do, big or small becomes a great thing in the eyes of God.

Keeping your heart in tune with His goals, designed with love, will help you to achieve worthy things every day.

*"Do to others what you want them to do to you."*

Matthew 7:12 NCV

Lord, help me to strive to achieve the things that are great in Your eyes. Help me to desire to be more like You in all that I do.

Amen.

## When you worship

A woman of worth worships with her whole heart and mind and soul. She pours all that she has and all that she is into her praise and adoration of God. Whether we're at home or at church or driving in the car, we can take the time to worship. We can turn our hearts over to God for some precious moments of quality time, connecting with Him in every way.

The psalmist reminds us that the "world and all its people belong to Him." That means that worship happens in every little hamlet, every community, every place where the heart of someone is turned toward the Creator. We are spiritual beings, intended to live in relationship with the most powerful Spiritual being that could ever be. We are part of a greater whole and it all belongs to God.

"The earth is the Lord's, and everything in it." This statement isn't open for discussion or negotiation or an understanding of different belief systems. It's a simple truth and one that we can embrace to bring us more joy. Praise the Lord!

*The earth is the LORD's, and everything in it. The world and all its people belong to Him. For He laid the earth's foundation on the seas and built it on the ocean depths.*

Psalm 24:1-2 NLT

Lord, I praise You and thank You for all
You are and all You allow me to be.
Amen.

## We love because God loves us

The history of the world suggests that without love of God there is little likelihood of a love for others that does not become corrupt.

François Fénelon

On any given day, news headlines and newspapers shout out the corruption and darkness in the world. They remind us in no uncertain terms that we have yet to understand what it means to "love one another." It's staggering to think about what the world might be like if there were not some who honor God, who revere His name, and who offer His light.

We are the women who choose to make a difference. We are the ones who want to hold up the light and offer another solution to the darkness, bring a balance to what the world is experiencing. This is one of the primary reasons we seek to become women of more worth, so that we can be God's hands and feet and voices of love and compassion.

It's not easy to shine all by yourself, but when you know that you are part of a network of millions of others who seek to share God's love, it helps. The future is in need of whatever light we have to offer so let us keep loving God with all our hearts and minds.

*This is the teaching you have heard from the beginning:*
*We must love each other.*

1 John 3:11 NCV

Lord, help me to be a light in the world in every possible way.
Amen.

## Love and doing what God wants

One loving soul sets another on fire.

St. Augustine

What God wants from you is for you to start a little fire. He wants you to set a flame going inside the heart and mind of someone else. Oh, He's already put everything there to get a fire going, He just wants you to strike a match that keeps the fire burning.

When you do what God wants, He blesses your life in every possible way. He seeks to provide for you and to give you more of your heart's desires. He does this because He sees the motivations of your heart and He knows that you do the good things you do out of love for Him.

Some people collect things and when they do, they always want one more thing to add to their collection. They may collect material things, or friends, or travel brochures, but whatever it is, the wanting never ends. As a woman of worth, you want what God wants for you and that's the best possible direction for your life.

*The world and its desires pass away,*
*but whoever does the will of God lives forever.*

1 John 2:17 NIV

Lord, I confess that sometimes I want things just because it feels like some new "thing" will make a difference in my life. Help me to recognize the things that truly make a difference and desire those more than anything else.

Amen.

## Love and forgiveness

We are too ready to retaliate, rather than forgive, or to gain by love and information. Let us try what love will do: for if others see we love them, we should find they will not harm us.

William Penn (adapted)

That little desire to retaliate comes up more often than you like to think. It's evident when someone takes your parking spot even after they saw you had your blinker on, or in your mind over the person who gossiped about you when you were in the seventh grade. You think you have it all under control and then, someone else gets the job promotion you were sure would be yours, and it rears its ugly head again.

We like to think we're pretty forgiving, but chances are we get a lot of opportunities to test that theory. We get to see how the slights of life here and there add up and how they affect our thinking and our attitudes.

When we find it difficult to forgive or to let go of slights from the past, we have only one choice. We have to stop, pray, and relinquish those feelings. We have to let God know how we feel and ask His help. Forgiveness takes a lot of love. God knows because He forgives each of us over and over again.

*"I tell you that her many sins are forgiven, so she showed great love.*
*But the person who is forgiven only a little will love only a little."*

Luke 7:47 NCV

Lord, help me to forgive others when little things they do annoy me.
Help them to forgive me when I also do irritating things.
Amen.

## Love and respect

*Without respect, love cannot go far or rise high;*
*it is an angel with but one wing.*

Alexandre Dumas

---

What is it that causes you to respect someone else? Is it because they have a strong character quality you admire or because they have overcome great obstacles to succeed, or have moved on in spite of numerous setbacks? We usually think of people "earning" respect because of something they accomplished, something they did that brought honor to their name.

Most of us grew up with the admonition that we should respect our elders. Respect then, brings honor to the other person and admiration and love to the relationship. We are grateful when we know our children respect and honor us. Like the woman in Proverbs 31, we love the idea that our children would call us blessed.

Knowing how grateful you feel when you know that others respect you, pray for greater wisdom in coming to know and respect others. You just may give them wings to fly.

*Her children stand and bless her. Her husband praises her: "There are many virtuous and capable women in the world, but you surpass them all!"*

Proverbs 31:28-29 NLT

Lord, thank You for teaching us to honor
and respect the people in our lives. I ask Your blessing
on each of those people today.
Amen.

## *Love hurts*

It is possible to love your friends, your competitors,
and even your enemies. It is hard, bitterly hard,
but there is a long distance between hard and impossible.

Herbert Welch

Sometimes love hurts. It hurts when you and the person you love don't see eye to eye and have a major communication breakdown. It hurts when your teenager walks out the door without sharing what might be troubling them. It hurts when your loved one is ill and there is nothing you can do, but be nearby and pray.

Sometimes you even struggle with past hurts in friendships, letting misunderstandings and personal egos get in the way of forgiveness and love. You lose each other in the process and wonder why. It feels impossible to repair the lost relationship.

When you read the story of the prodigal son, you get a glimpse of what it must be like for God when we continually hurt Him by our poor choices and unkind ways. He invites us to return every time and He embraces us with joy.

Perhaps there's a relationship in your life that you'd like to repair, one that you might embrace with renewed joy.

*A wise child brings joy to a father; a foolish child brings grief to a mother.*

Proverbs 10:1 NLT

Lord, when I'm hurt by loved ones, help me to remember that I have also hurt them and that all of us need forgiveness sometimes. Thank You for being the one who heals every hurt and every breaking heart.
Amen.

## Love one another

To love another person is to see the face of God.

Victor Hugo

Perhaps you're not a list maker, but it might be interesting to try to make a list of all the ways you are known for being a disciple of Jesus. List those things that show your love for others and see if the list offers you any insight about how you might grow in the ways of loving others.

"Love one another" sounds like an easy request and yet, we often struggle with simply loving the people in our own households or the people we work with each day. We allow the people that attend our church to remain perfect strangers to us week after week and we ignore all those requests that come in the mail to make another charitable donation.

How can you develop more skill in the ways of loving others? Jesus certainly offered many examples of what that would look like. He suggested that we might help support widows and orphans or be hospitable to strangers. Challenge yourself to become a better woman in the ways you truly love others. God will surely support your loving efforts.

*If we love one another, God abides in us, and His love has been perfected in us.*

1 John 4:12 NKJV

Lord, please help me to learn more about what it means
to love others. Expand my list of ways that I might show
my love to You and those You've placed in my life.

Amen.

## When love fails

*Love is swift, sincere, pious, joyful, generous, strong, patient, faithful, prudent, long-suffering, courageous, and never seeking its own; for wherever a person seeks his own, there he falls from love.*

Thomas à Kempis

---

If you've never failed at love, you can probably pass over this section. If you have failed at love, then you're in the majority and are probably on guard against such a thing happening to you again. How can you protect yourself from a love that fails?

Chances are, you can't. The only unfailing love that will ever be is the love God has for you. He will never stop loving you. If you start from there, the best you can do is to try your best to love others in the ways that help to keep love strong.

Perhaps if we took careful inventory of what love is, what it means to us, and then applied 1 Corinthians 13, we'd have more joy in matters of love. Just for today, think about the people you love, and practice this one thing … "love is patient and kind."

Once you've mastered that one, move on to "love is not jealous, it does not brag, and is not proud." Your love for others will surely grow stronger.

*Love never ends.*

1 Corinthians 13:8 NCV

Dear Lord, please protect my love relationships. Help me to be the kind of person that makes it easy for others to relate to me in loving ways. Help me to be patient and kind to everyone today.

Amen

## What love isn't

*If you judge people, you have no time to love them.*

Mother Teresa

---

You've probably thought a lot about what love is or what it is meant to be. Perhaps you haven't given as much thought to what love isn't. Some of the things on the list would be: Love isn't jealous or rude, it isn't judgmental or controlling, it isn't self-centered and "me first." Love doesn't keep track of all the things others have done to offend or disappoint or insult it. Love doesn't lie about others or shirk responsibility for everything from spoken words to inappropriate actions.

Love comes with mercy. If it didn't, we'd all be in trouble. Sometimes we struggle over love because all we can see are the obstacles. We focus on the difficult things and the disappointing things and before we know it, love disappears along with our hopes and desires for something beautiful and fulfilling.

Love isn't about having absolutely everything the way we want to have it. It isn't about always being right. It is about a relationship and the more you cultivate the relationship, the more it will grow.

*Three things will last forever – faith, hope, and love –*
*and the greatest of these is love.*

1 Corinthians 13:13 NLT

Lord, forgive me when I do not know how to love.
Help me to strive to be more about what love is than
what it is not. Bless the people I love today.
Amen.

## *There's no one quite like you*

*Go measure the heavens with your span; go weigh the mountains in the scales; go take the ocean's water and calculate each drop; go count the sand upon the sea's wide shore; and when you have accomplished all of this, then you can tell how much He loves you! He has loved you long! He has loved you well! He will love you forever!*

Charles H. Spurgeon

There is no one else quite like you. You're a unique design, a one-of-a-kind, hand-made, hand-picked by God woman of worth. You are a fabulous original and priceless in every way.

Have you ever stopped to grasp what it means to know the Creator of the whole universe loves you? Imagine yourself standing against a giant redwood tree or climbing the mountain near your home. Watch the stars as they illuminate the night sky or the birds as they sing through the trees. Not one of these things, as impressive as they are, compares with you. Not one of these things brings out God's love and desire to do His best like you do.

Now take a look at the people around you. As you look at each one, see them as God does. See them as His masterpieces, the children of His heart and love them as He does.

*I will sing to the LORD all my life; I will sing praises to my God as long as I live. May my thoughts please Him; I am happy in the LORD.*

Psalm 104:33-34 NCV

Lord, thank You for this incredible love You offer me with such grace and mercy. Help me to be forever worthy of You.

Amen.

# SHE RISES WHILE IT IS YET NIGHT

*and provides*

## FOOD FOR HER HOUSEHOLD

PROVERBS 31:15

## *Moving on*

Live your beliefs and you can turn the world around.

Henry David Thoreau

---

Do you ever find yourself wondering what is happening in the world? You wake up every day to a new tragedy, or a military disturbance somewhere. You hear of children sadly abused and teenagers killing their friends. What is going on?

Part of the joy of knowing who you are as a woman of worth is that you can stand firm in your beliefs. You can offer to help in little ways and big ways and all those ways make a difference. Your beliefs truly can help to turn the world around.

All you need to do is trust your heart and the ways that God leads you. Trust that He'll be with you when you take a stand. Trust that He wants you to speak up on behalf of others. You are a mover and a shaker, someone moving ahead to shine the light of Christ, and someone ready to shake up the apathy and indifference that keeps repeating itself.

Go ahead and boldly shine!

*"All things are possible for the one who believes."*

Mark 9:23 NCV

Dear Lord, help me to be brave and stand strong for You and the things I believe. Be with all those who trust in Your name.

Amen.

## Becoming perfect worshipers

We should dedicate ourselves to becoming in this life the
most perfect worshipers of God we can possibly be,
as we hope to be through all eternity.

Brother Lawrence

Close your eyes and picture yourself standing around the throne of God. You're connected to Him in every way and your heart nearly breaks with love for Him. Worship is not something you feel you have to do, it's something you are thrilled to do. You're so honored to be able to give God utter love and thanks and praise.

It's hard to imagine the experience of that kind of heavenly worship. We get a glimpse of it here now and then when a song of praise inspires us anew, or a great sermon makes us want to shout for joy. We participate in worship, but someday, worship will flow through us without concern for who might be looking when we raise our hands or what anybody else might think.

Worship the Lord today with your whole heart and mind. Get out of your own way and let Him know how much you love Him.

*"The time is coming when the true worshipers will worship
the Father in spirit and truth, and that time is here already."*

John 4:23 NCV

Lord, I bow my head to worship You and my spirit
weeps with the joy of knowing You hear my heart.
Amen.

# More than feelings

*We must not trust every word of others or every
feeling within ourselves, but cautiously and patiently
try the matter, whether it be of God.*

Thomas à Kempis

You've probably had a chance to reflect on actions you've taken before because you "felt" certain that you needed to take those steps. Later, when you discovered more of the truth of a situation, you probably wished you hadn't acted in haste.

Sometimes we can't rely totally on how we feel about something. Feelings can deceive you and cause you to make mistakes. God has certainly given women a strong intuitive spirit, but He often seeks our greater wisdom to come from waiting patiently for Him. He wants us to trust His Word and His Spirit more than any feeling we might have.

When you're feeling an impulse to go and do something, stop yourself. Wait until you are clearly directed to take a step. There are few situations where a bit more quiet reflection will not be worth the effort. God strengthens you when you bring everything you feel to Him.

*"It is the Spirit who gives life; the flesh profits nothing."*

John 6:63 NKJV

Lord, help me to wait for You before I take an action
in any situation. Lead me to seek Your truth in all I do.
Amen.

## Outstanding moments

*You will find, as you look back upon your life, that the moments that stand out are the moments when you have done things for others.*

Henry Drummond

When you donate to a good cause, you feel good. When you help someone in great need by sharing what you have, you rejoice. Doing good things for each other causes the Spirit within us to celebrate. God designed us to do good deeds because His greatest joy is that we learn to love and take care of one another.

Most of us are better at giving a compliment to someone else than we are at receiving a compliment. When someone does something nice for us, we appreciate it and share in the joy of the moment. As good as it feels though, the better part of sharing is being the giver. God loves a cheerful giver in every way because it means your heart is fully engaged in the process.

Give what you can to someone else today and tomorrow your happiness will surely reflect in your face and in everything you do. God bless you as you bless others.

*"Freely you have received; freely give."*

Matthew 10:8 NIV

Lord, please help me to have a willing heart
whenever I'm called upon to give to others. Help me
to demonstrate Your love by the things I do.
Amen.

## Turning up the light

*Words which do not give the light of Christ increase the darkness.*

Mother Teresa

---

Words are powerful things. Whether you're reading the Bible and taking in the truths that God would have you know, or you're actively engaged in conversation with a friend, the words being shared are powerful indeed. God created a whole universe by speaking and reminded us to be aware of any time we might choose to make a vow that it was a matter of great importance.

Be aware of your words. Some words can be so destructive that they cause someone else to suffer for months to come. Some words do not shine a light of truth. Some words do not echo any kind of love.

As a woman of worth, you want to shine the light of Christ. You want to make the world a brighter place and bring joy to those around you. Speak from the heart, with truth and love, and you will always help to turn up the light.

*Good people's words will help many others.*

Proverbs 10:21 NCV

Lord, help me to weigh the words I speak. Help me
not to jump to conclusions or hastily voice opinions
that are not grounded. Help me to shine Your light.

Amen.

## Doing what works

*Work with all your might, but never trust in your work. Pray with all your might for the blessing in God, but work at the same time with all diligence, with all patience, with all perseverance.*

George Müller

You probably know people who are defined by their work. They are known as your accountant or your waiter. They are your hair stylist or your dentist. Whatever their role, you probably know them best for what they do. They may work hard and they may be wonderful people, but chances are you don't really know much more about them. You don't know what makes life work for them.

It's important to strive to be good at the work you do, but not to trust that the work is the only definition of you. At the same time, you must work diligently, even when you're praying for God's blessings, because He wants you to live fully and abundantly. He wants you to excel.

You can appreciate the people you know who take on various tasks around you. You can love the work you do, but you must rely solely on the grace of God to put it all together. God knows what works best for you.

*Make every effort to give yourself to God as the kind of person He will approve. Be a worker who is not ashamed and who uses the true teaching in the right way.*

2 Timothy 2:15 NCV

Lord, bless the work that I do according to Your will and purpose for my life. Help me to trust only in Your providence.

Amen.

## Just as I am

*Jesus accepts you the way you are,*
*but loves you too much to leave you that way.*

Lee Venden

---

Isn't it amazing to know that you can stand before the Creator of the whole universe, puny woman that you are, and radiate? You can come to Him just as you are, no need to buy new shoes or find the right outfit. You can simply arrive and bask in His presence.

He sees you and though He thoroughly loves everything about you, His heart breaks for the things you've yet to learn and understand. He sees you are making a great effort to get closer to Him and He wants to reward you as much as possible.

On the other hand, He knows that there are things you have not yet learned, attitudes that would change your life for the better, people that will help guide and shape you, and so He rejoices in that as well. He loves you, and not just the one standing before Him now, but the one He already recognizes will be there some time in the future. He applauds what you are becoming at every stage.

*Pursue righteousness, faith, love, peace with those*
*who call on the Lord out of a pure heart.*

2 Timothy 2:22 NKJV

Lord, thank You for loving me just as I am.
Thank You for giving me a desire to become even more
of the woman You already know I can be.
Amen.

## Stop or go!

*Set yourself earnestly to discover what you are made to do,
and then give yourself passionately to the doing of it.*

Martin Luther King, Jr.

Sometimes we wait for dreams to come true. Other times, we have to go out and create the circumstances that will make the dream possible ourselves. Helping with the creation process doesn't mean you're not waiting for God to act on your behalf. It simply means that you trust Him to walk with you through the details and guide you to the best results.

Faith is an active verb. It requires you to keep living and moving and working toward your own goals. It lifts you up in the process and it gives you hope. It's not always easy to make up your mind about something, especially when your decision impacts the lives of others, but at some point an action is required. You simply must trust God has your back and that He knows where you want to go and has already gone before you to ease the way.

Waiting is good, but acting in faith will get you where you want to go.

*In Him we live and move and exit.*

Acts 17:28 NLT

Lord, I do have a tendency to give myself excuses
and to put things off. Help me to step out in faith
and trust in You as I go forward.
Amen.

### *Drawing outside the lines*

*Stop worrying about whether or not you're effective.*
*Worry about what is possible for you to do,*
*which is always greater than you imagine.*

Archbishop Oscar Romero

When you were a child, you probably felt free to color outside the lines. Then one day, someone told you that your picture would be more beautiful if you kept within the borders of the black lines as you colored. You believed it and you stopped trying to imagine what could happen outside of those borders.

Sometimes life is like that too. We stop trying to see what else we could do. We never break the rules even when they are without merit. We don't imagine that we can be more than we are or do more than we do. Yet, all things are possible for the child of God. You have infinite possibility and when you imagine more for yourself, it can happen.

Becoming a woman of worth means that you recognize there's more that you can be. You know that with your willingness and God's design that great things can happen in your life, even now. It's time to create a new picture. It's sure to be beautiful!

*With God nothing will be impossible.*

Luke 1:37 NKJV

Lord, help me to imagine more for my life, for the work I do, and for the people I love. Give me a willingness to try new things and even to color outside of the lines.

Amen.

# Who holds tomorrow?

*We must face today as children of tomorrow. We must meet the uncertainties of this world with the certainty of the world to come.*

A. W. Tozer

There's something about uncertainty that keeps you on your toes. If you don't know for sure how someone will react to something you plan to do or say, you're more careful about how you make your approach. If you're not certain whether you'll get promoted in your job, you're more aware of doing a good job.

Sometimes we can compensate for life's uncertainties. The main goal though is to not allow potential risks to keep us from believing in possibility. We may not know the outcome of a given situation, but we know the One who holds us together and keeps us safely in His hand. We know that His plans for us will come to fruition as long as we're willing to keep believing in all that He wants for us.

The world may look uncertain and it may cause you to wonder what tomorrow may bring. But when you seek the One who holds tomorrow, you can be sure that new opportunities will present themselves just for you.

*Teach us to number our days, that we may gain a heart of wisdom.*

Psalm 90:12 NIV

Lord, when I get too fearful about things that I cannot control in any way, please remind me that You are still in control. Help me to trust in Your certainty and hope.

Amen.

## Jumping into your work

Set yourself earnestly to discover what you are made to do,
and then give yourself passionately to the doing of it.

Martin Luther King, Jr.

Do you get up every morning so excited about going to work
you can hardly wait to get there? Do you clean the house with
great enthusiasm or do the grocery shopping with great vigor?
You were made to do a lot of things! You were designed with
infinite possibility. The beauty of growing and changing and
becoming is that it means you are seeking new ways to define
yourself. You are earnestly trying to discover the best possible
you to share with the world.

Whatever you do, when you realize how important it is to
God and to those around you, you do with more gusto. You do it
because it is "your thing" to do and you love it. You do it because
somehow everything about it feels right to you. You have a lot of
gifts and talents. The ones that really make your light shine are
those that God meant for you to do.

You're doing amazing things!

*Every good and perfect gift is from above, coming down from the Father
of the heavenly lights, who does not change like shifting shadows.*

James 1:17 NIV

Lord, thank You for the gifts and talents You've given me.
Help me to discover more of what You know I can be so
that I can work to Your glory.
Amen.

# Thinking like a queen

*A woman who treasures, respects and honors the Lord is a queen in His eyes and will be respected and honored by those around her.*

Anonymous

You may appreciate the idea of being a princess now and then, but it's probably more difficult for you to think like a queen. After all, the queen rules! The queen gets to have everything her way, or so we like to imagine.

Under certain circumstances though, it may indeed be helpful to "think like a queen." You might wonder if you can possibly reach a particular goal, or if you can become the woman you long to be. The queen inside you wants to succeed. She wants to be respected and honored for her ideas and her abilities.

Give her the respect she is due. That means you must give yourself the respect you would give to others. You must trust your decisions and your intuition. You must trust in God's guidance for the choices that you have to make. The important thing to remember is that in some ways, you rule … as long as you keep the King of the Universe apprised of your plans. Don't be afraid to try something new.

*Honor her for all that her hands have done,*
*and let her works bring her praise at the city gate.*

Proverbs 31:31 NIV

Lord, I believe in You and I like knowing that You rule over my life, that You're in control. Help me to know when You want me to trust in my choices and move forward with confidence.

Amen.

## Don't rain on my parade

*If you spend your whole life waiting for the storm,*
*you'll never enjoy the sunshine.*

Horace

---

Some of us can only imagine the dark side of any opportunity. When good things happen, we choose to think that something not good is probably coming our way. When joy peeks through the window, we look to find the clouds that surely will turn the world upside down. After all, we're just not worthy of the good things that others enjoy. We do our best to prepare for the worst and never get a chance to experience God's best.

Why do we do that? Our God of goodness and steadfast love offers us a new chance every single day. We rise to possibilities beyond measure. We see His hand in places we never expected because He has gone before us to make sure all is safe and well for us. He is the light and He bids us to follow Him wherever we go. We don't have to sit in the darkness and wait for the thunderstorms to come rolling in.

Today, accept God's goodness! Alert yourself to moments when you can see His hand at work, chasing away the clouds.

*Hope deferred makes the heart sick, but a dream fulfilled is a tree of life.*

Proverbs 13:12 NLT

Lord, help me to see the good in every situation,
not giving up when the storms come, but rejoicing
always in the coming sunshine.
Amen.

## It's good to keep dreaming

*Far away there in the sunshine are my highest aspirations.*
*I may not reach them, but I can look up and see their beauty,*
*believe in them, and try to follow where they lead.*

Louisa May Alcott

Do you have some visual object that you can look to that reminds you of what you want to accomplish? Maybe you have a picture of yourself in a cap and gown at your graduation, or a picture of the house you hope to buy some day. You might have the travel brochure of the country you want to visit, or the list of your top five hopes and dreams for your life.

Whatever it is, it's good to have a reference point. It's good to give yourself a daily dose of where you want to go and keep your intentions and your focus strong. You have dreams that matter and God wants you to reach your goals.

Dreams are always just slightly out of reach. They inspire us to follow them and motivate all we do. After all, dreams are about becoming more than we are now, about participating in a treasure that God has already designed for us. Follow your dreams!

*"Keep on seeking, and you will find. Keep on knocking,*
*and the door will be opened to you."*

Luke 11:9 NLT

Lord, thank You for the dreams that fill my heart.
Help me to be strong and to wait patiently for them.
Help me to follow them wherever they lead.
Amen.

## *When you're feeling skeptical*

*The Holy Spirit is no skeptic. He has written neither doubt nor mere opinion into our hearts, but rather solid assurances, which are more sure and solid than all experience and even life itself.*

Martin Luther

The Holy Spirit can only give you one kind of counsel. He can only offer you the truth. The truth He offers you about who God is and what God wants for your life is absolutely sure. He doesn't ever get wishy-washy. He's never wrong. He doesn't plant any seeds that He doesn't expect will grow well.

If you have any doubts about your work or your life or what God wants from you, then embrace the Spirit of Truth and He will guide you. People who care about you, who love you and want good things for you, can only offer opinions. They can only give you their perspective on any situation. They cannot see everything or know everything.

God can! Commit your work to Him and to His guidance. Go to Him any time you feel overwhelmed by doubt and let Him comfort you with truth and love. He will never disappoint you. You have His word on it!

*Commit your actions to the LORD,*
*and your plans will succeed.*

Proverbs 16:3 NLT

Lord, forgive me when I doubt You, when I am not fully committed to the path You have ordained for me. Help me receive Your truth and to listen for Your Word with all my heart.

Amen.

*Think happy!*

Our happiness depends on the habit of mind we cultivate.
So practice happy thinking every day. Cultivate the merry heart,
develop the happiness habit, and life will become a continual feast.

Norman Vincent Peale

---

Have you ever noticed the difference in response of two people who have had the same experience? For instance, two different women are fired from their jobs through no fault of their own. The company didn't even give them a good reason for letting them go. The first woman looks at the situation and falls into a depression, weakened so much by the blow that she can't imagine what else she'll do with her life. The second woman is somewhat taken by surprise at the event, but decides that this is just one loss and that she'll start immediately to discover a better option for herself. She'll take the good things she learned from her old job and apply it somewhere else.

The difference is totally about attitude. Each woman suffered the loss of a job, but each one chose how to respond to it. You may not have had a choice in the experience of a loss, but you have a lot to do with the real outcome of it.

*The Lord Almighty says: "Give careful thought to your ways."*

Haggai 1:7 NIV

Lord, bless me with a positive attitude to face the circumstances
of life that are difficult. Remind me that You are near me and
know the future plans You have for me for my good.

Amen.

## Healing thoughts

A strong positive mental attitude will create
more miracles than any wonder drug.

Patricia Neal

Sometimes when we hear bad news, all we can do is think about it. We dwell on it so much that it makes us ill. We allow it to frighten us and cause us to want to hide away and not look out at the world. Sometimes we want to medicate it with drugs or alcohol. We just want the problem to go away and leave us alone.

The sad part is that with a response like that, we simply make the problem worse. We add another layer of difficulty on top of the circumstance we aren't able to face. We wonder why miracles don't happen and we imagine God just isn't in the miracle business anymore.

The truth is that we are part of the miracle. We have the ability to offer healing thoughts to the situation which will improve things right away. We can witness strength and renewal as it seeks to help us with each hopeful thought and prayer.

Heal your thoughts and you can heal your heart.

*"You cannot add any time to your life by worrying about it."*

Matthew 6:27 NCV

Lord, wash away the weary thoughts that hold me
back and fill me with your Spirit so that I might adopt
a positive attitude and discover your miracles.

Amen.

# *You are beautiful!*

Characteristics which define beauty are
wholeness, harmony and radiance.

Thomas Aquinas

———

Have you ever watched the women who compete in a beauty
contest? If they never said a word or shared a unique talent, you
might think they were lovely, but you wouldn't have any idea
about their real beauty. Truly beautiful women radiate from the
inside out. They share the strength of their ideas and the joy in
their hearts with ease. They are grateful for all that they are and
all that they are meant to be and so they are in harmony with life.

You are like that too. You may not be walking across a stage in
a designer gown, but you still radiate beauty. You still shine the
light of God's love with a wholesome spirit that is undeniable.
You express the natural harmony God intended every time you
smile with kindness, offer a helping hand, or encourage the heart
of another. You are a gift and a blessing that is truly beautiful.

*May the Lord bless you and protect you. May the Lord smile on you and be gracious
to you. May the Lord show you His favor and give you His peace.*

Numbers 6:24-26 NLT

Lord, I pray that I will always be beautiful in Your sight,
radiating the joy of Your Spirit to those around me.

Amen.

## *The blessing of beauty*

*Never lose an opportunity of seeing anything that is beautiful,*
*for beauty is God's handwriting – a wayside sacrament.*
*Welcome it in every fair face, in every fair sky, in every flower,*
*and thank God for it as a cup of blessing.*

Ralph Waldo Emerson

We are continually surrounded by beauty, the kind that only God could create. It's amazing that we don't go around wide-eyed and awed at everything we see with such glorious color and shape and design. God's artistry is everywhere.

Perhaps He could have created the world in black and white, making everything some shade of gray. He could have made a few general designs and then decided that was enough and not created anything more. The amazing thing is that He did not and, in fact, we have not even discovered the intricacies of the wonders of nature that there are to explore.

This same God who created all these beautiful things, also created you. He knew who you would be and what you would need to guide you through the world. He gave you everything and He is always willing to give you more. Praise Him!

*All things were made through Him, and without*
*Him nothing was made that was made.*

John 1:3 NKJV

Lord, thank You for blessing my life with beauty. I am truly
enchanted with Your work and hope to become even more
aware of all that You have provided for me to enjoy.
Amen.

# *Becoming a woman of worth*

Be dogmatically true, obstinately holy,
immovably honest, desperately kind, fixedly upright.

Charles H. Spurgeon

What would it mean for you to see yourself as "desperately kind"? Would you find yourself opting for kindness in any and every situation? If someone was rude to you, you would be kind. If someone hurt your feelings, you would retaliate with kindness, if someone lied to you, you would remain fixedly upright. You would not budge from doing the right thing, the honest thing, the obstinately holy thing, no matter what!

What a beautiful picture and what a difficult one to uphold. Yes, we can do our best to be honest, but those little temptations might still slip in that allowed us to cheat on our diets or spend more money than we know is good for us. We might go to church, but forget what we learned before we hit the parking lot. We might want to be kind, but turn our backs on someone who needs our help without even realizing we did. Yes, this is a difficult list of qualities and yet it is not impossible.

You're becoming more of these things every day.

*A person may think their own ways are right, but the Lord weighs the heart.*

Proverbs 21:2 NIV

Lord, if I'm going to be stubborn, then let me be stubborn for You.
Let me be obstinate in my efforts to become more holy,
more honest and more kind.
Amen.

## You do so many good things

*Do all the good you can, by all the means you can,*
*in all the ways you can, in all the places you can,*
*to all the people you can, as long as ever you can.*

John Wesley

There's a primary difference between the statements, "I can!" and "I will!" One of these sets up the opportunity to do good things, any way you want, any time you want and for any one you want to do good things for. The other one quits talking about what you can do and simply does it: "I will!"

As you look at your own day and your life, imagine those places where you can do good for others. Make a list if you'd like of all the things you can do. Once you've created the list, look at what stops you from taking the next steps. What prevents you from moving the "can" to the "will"?

God knows you can do it. What He doesn't know is if you will do it. After all, He gives you the choice, the freedom to do as you please. Show Him just how good you can be today.

*The LORD has told you, human, what is good; He has told you*
*what He wants from you: to do what is right to other people,*
*love being kind to others, and live humbly, obeying your God.*

Micah 6:8 NCV

Lord, I know I'm constantly doing things, but I'm not so sure
I can say I'm doing a lot of "good" things. Help me to be more aware
of doing good for others wherever and whenever I can.

Amen.

## My beliefs in the dark

*I believe in the sun even when it is not shining. I believe in love even when I am not feeling it. I believe in God even when He is silent.*

Anonymous

Sometimes we don't know what we believe when everything is good and the light seems to shine brightly all around us. We imagine that everything is okay and that we're okay and not much seems to be required of us. We don't always have to summon our beliefs until everything that makes us comfortable is taken away.

When we're sitting in the dark, feeling overwhelmed or uncertain, we start to call on our own beliefs. We start to identify the things that really matter to us. Yes, it might be terrible to lose our worldly goods in a flood, but we have not lost one thing we believe in. We have not lost our faith in God and His protection. We have not lost our understanding of all that is good about humanity. We have only gained new eyes that manage to see well even as we adjust to the dim light.

You may declare your beliefs in the light, but you'll hang on to them tightly in the dark.

*Jesus said, "Because you have seen Me, you have believed. Blessed are those who have not seen and yet have believed."*

John 20:29 NKJV

Lord, I love when You walk with me in the light of the day, but I am more grateful when You hold me through the darkest nights.
Amen.

## Go, God!

God is not at a loss when He moves to bring us back to Himself.
He can woo or whip. He can draw or drive. He can work rapidly
or slowly, as He pleases. In other words, He is free to be God!
And in His own way, at His own pace, He brings us back.

Tom Wells

Are you starting to notice the signs of God's existence all around you? Do you find that people you hardly know are dropping His name into ordinary conversations? Do you see His hand at work in the things you do with others?

God is making a comeback and He does so every time you see Him coming. He wants to come back into every aspect of your life so that He can guide you. He wants to share the path with you so you are never alone. He wants to talk with you about things that trouble you or overwhelm you. Actually, He never left or stepped back anyway. If God is making a comeback in your life it's because you invited Him to take a bigger place in your heart. You'll see Him more and more everywhere you go.

*The Lord God is like a sun and shield; the Lord gives us kindness and honor.*
*He does not hold back anything good from those whose lives are innocent.*
*Lord, All-Powerful, happy are the people who trust You!*

Psalm 84:11-12 NCV

Lord, I thank You for making a comeback in my life over
and over again. Every time I manage to step away from You,
I discover that it isn't long before I miss having You close to
me again. Thanks for always staying true to me.

Amen.

## A little bit broken

*God can do wonders with a broken heart; if we give Him all the pieces.*

Anonymous

Nothing shakes the central core of our lives like going through a heartbreak. Often that experience revolves around a spouse or a significant other, but sometimes we're heartbroken over the actions of our children or the loss of a longtime friend. A broken heart means that something very deep and important happened in the relationship, something that may go beyond words.

God understands a broken heart. As a parent, He certainly endured a multitude of heartbreaks from the prophets and disciples of old. He continues to be saddened over the actions of His children today, because He loves us. Love means that you want more for someone else. Love means that you want to sustain a long relationship that brings you both joy. Love means that you want to fulfill the things that are meaningful to your heart.

When your heart breaks for love in one form or another, go to the Creator of all love and ask for His help. He sees you and will comfort you. He understands what it feels like to have a hole in your heart.

*"He has sent Me to heal the brokenhearted, to proclaim liberty to the captives and recovery of sight to the blind, to set at liberty those who are oppressed."*

Luke 4:18 NKJV

Lord, please help me to recover from this difficult situation.
Help me to heal from my sense of loss and from my broken heart.
Amen.

## *Go-getters!*

A pure, simple, and steadfast spirit is not distracted by the number
of things to be done, because it performs them all to the honor of
God, and endeavors to be at rest from self-seeking.

Thomas à Kempis

Are you a "to-do" list maker? When you have a lot of things to accomplish on any given day you know you better make a list and check them off one by one. Certainly some plan of action and organization is a good thing, but like all things we have to be careful not to become slaves to our own lists. It's helpful sometimes to take a little inventory of what motivates us to take so much on in the first place.

Someone has said that we've become a culture of "human doings" instead of "human beings." The assumption is that we aren't really good at simply "being". We aren't comfortable when everything stops and we're at rest.

As you become more aware of the way God wants to work in your life, stop now and then to see what motivates you. Are you really doing everything to His glory, or are you driven by something else? Be sure God is always at the top of your list.

*In all the work you are doing, work the best you can.*
*Work as if you were doing it for the Lord, not for people.*

Colossians 3:23 NCV

Lord, sometimes I have so much to do, I can't imagine how it will all
get accomplished. Help me to be better at setting priorities and guide
my choices according to Your will and purpose for me.

Amen.

## God calling ... Are you there?

God did not direct His call to Isaiah – Isaiah overheard God saying, "... who will go for Us?" The call of God is not just for a select few but for everyone. Whether I hear God's call or not depends on the condition of my ears, and exactly what I hear depends upon my spiritual attitude.

Oswald Chambers

One of the delightful things about your awareness of God's presence in your everyday life is that you see even more clearly what His plan is for you. He's a master at unfolding things just at the right time. He knows exactly what you need to get there and He equips you even before He calls you to begin the task. After He calls, He continues to supply what you need.

If you're moving in a new direction in your life and you wonder whether you have what it takes to get the job done, pray. Fix your thoughts on God and ask His help in claiming a victory in your new situation. Ask Him to give you everything you need to make things work together for the good of others and for His glory. He picked you for a reason and He won't let you down.

God is calling you into greater and more beautiful things because He knows you're the right woman for the job!

*God's gifts and His call can never be withdrawn.*

Romans 11:29 NLT

Lord, help me to answer with a resounding "yes" when You call and then bless me with the ability to do the task at hand.

Amen.

# The question of who you are

*Let your only evaluation of worth derive from the awareness of God's love for you. All other measures leave one in a state of delusion.*

Anonymous

---

Sometimes we look up to people we think have accomplished much more than we have. We imagine that they must be very special in God's sight to have done so well. We look to them for inspiration and for leadership, or for ideas about how we might become more like them.

The problem is that when we look up to others, we lose two things. We lose our awareness of the gifts God has given to us, the things that make us unique and worthy in His eyes, and we lose that sense of knowing God has truly designed all that is good for us to accomplish as well. Taking note of what another woman does, or what she has of this world's material goods, isn't any kind of statement about your worth or your ability.

The important thing is to always know who you are, and whose you are. When you have that set in your mind, all things are possible for you.

*Do not be shaped by this world; instead be changed within by a new way of thinking. Then you will be able to decide what God wants for you.*

Romans 12:2 NCV

Lord, I admit that I'm often a bit envious of some of my friends. I imagine that they must have done something better than I have, or they must be smarter than I am to have accomplished so much. Please help me to focus on You and forgive me for those thoughts.

Amen.

## *Here's the skinny!*

What lies beyond us and what lies before us are
tiny matters compared to what lies within us.

Ralph Waldo Emerson

Do you want to know the secret of life? Here's the skinny on life. It's about recognizing who you are in Christ. It's about knowing that the One who holds all of your tomorrows knows you and loves you and is working with you to shape you into the best possible version of you. If what you recall from yesterday doesn't always make you proud, or it keeps you stuck in the past, let it go.

If what you want in the future is eating up every moment of today, let that go too. The secret of your life is all about you and your relationship with God. He's not only the One who created you in every way, but He's an interior designer as well. He works from the inside out to make you more beautiful.

He knows you and He's pleased with what you're becoming right now. Yesterday is gone, today is the day to celebrate being wonderful you!

*I know that everything God does will continue forever. People cannot add anything to what God has done, and they cannot take anything away from it.*

Ecclesiastes 3:14 NCV

Lord, help me when I get stuck in the sins of my past, wondering if
You can truly forgive me or if I've become better since then. I trust
in You and Your forgiveness and Your direction for my life today.

Amen.

## Little things mean a lot

*Small kindnesses, small courtesies, small considerations, habitually practiced in our social intercourse, give a greater charm to the character than the display of great talents and accomplishments.*

Mary Ann Kelty

When you look at the things that brighten your day, they aren't usually big things like planning a great vacation or celebrating a big event. They're more about the little things. You have coffee with a good friend and smile about the warm memory of your conversation. You get a hug unexpectedly from your child. These are little things, but they make a big difference in your life.

As you practice doing little things for others, all it takes is a momentary reflection on the joys you receive from giving and it makes it easy, even fun to do more. You can surprise someone with a small bouquet of flowers for no reason at all, or bake some cookies and share them with your neighbors. Each little kindness has a built-in reward. It makes you feel even better about yourself and it causes you to rejoice in all that God does in your life to make it good.

*Do not forget to do good to others, and share with them,*
*because such sacrifices please God.*

Hebrews 13:16 NCV

Lord, I love it when someone does some little gesture of kindness
for me. Help me to remember that and do more kind things
for others today.
Amen.

## A little quiet contemplation

The study of God's word for the purpose of discovering God's will is the secret discipline which has formed the greatest characters.

Henry David Thoreau

---

Sometimes we think about Bible study as a task. We think about going to our neighborhood Bible study or one at church as one more thing we have to do. Those studies are certainly good for us and often give us great insights into what God has in mind for us. Better yet, is to intentionally take time to spend with God all on your own, just the two of you, because you honor your relationship together.

God loves to spend time with you and He wants to guide you as you walk with Him each day. Sometimes He can offer the best advice right from His Word. His Holy Spirit can translate a passage for you in a way that causes its truth to shine like a light on your path. You can have an insight into where you should go next or what you should understand about something that has troubled you. All of this quiet time will help you become even more of what God wants you to be.

Study His Word and take the time to get to know the God of your heart in ways that will enrich your spirit and your life always.

*Your Word is like a lamp for my feet and a light for my path.*

Psalm 119:105 NCV

Lord, help me to be more disciplined in my study of Your Word.
Fill me with desire to spend more time with You, one on one.
Amen.

## *One good deed deserves another*

Loving one another with the charity of Christ, let the love you
have in your hearts be shown outwardly in your deeds so that,
compelled by such an example, the sisters may always grow
in the love of God and charity for one another.

St. Clare of Assisi

Wherever your sisters in Christ might be, they no doubt look to
you as an example. They love that you radiate God's grace and
goodness and that you do so much to help others.

Sometimes it's easy to forget just what others might see
when they look at you. They look to your kindness when they
need encouragement and to your sweet spirit when life has
become more than they can bear. There are those who may not
be aware that your kind heart and good deeds are an outcome
of your love for the Lord, but that doesn't matter. God uses your
delightful example to draw others closer to Himself. He knows
that you help to give Him a good name.

As you go about your work and your play today, keep in mind
that someone somewhere may just be seeing the light of Christ
as it shines through you. What a joyful thought that is!

*Therefore, as we have opportunity, let us do good to all people,*
*especially to those who belong to the family of believers.*

Galatians 6:10 NIV

Lord, let me be a "sister" to all the people I connect with today,
being willing to do whatever good I can for each of them.
Amen.

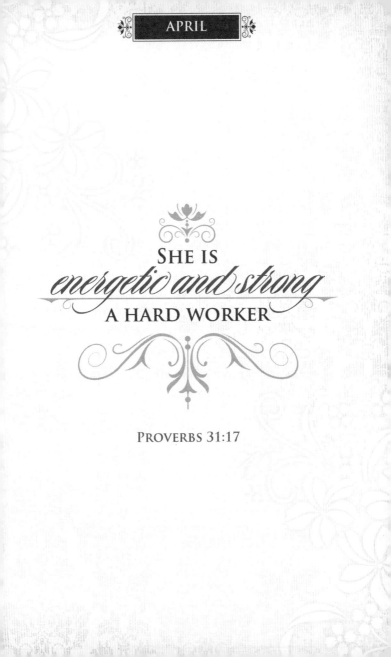

SHE IS
*energetic and strong*
A HARD WORKER

PROVERBS 31:17

# Come on, smile!

*There is no personal charm so great as the charm
of a cheerful temperament.*
Henry Van Dyke

---

There seems to be some truth in the idea of "smile and the world smiles with you." After all, most of us appreciate people who are in a good mood and are willing to share the upside of life.

The beauty industry spends billions of dollars each year trying to help us look younger, have more radiant skin, perfect hair, and anything else that will set our faces and our hearts aglow. We, in turn, reward them by stepping up to the counter and buying anything new that might give us just a bit more of whatever it is we think we're lacking.

The good news is that a smile enhances your face in a moment, doesn't cost a cent, and radiates your goodness and your charm in an instant. People are drawn to you and want to know more about you. Perhaps if you could bottle your smile, you'd make a fortune. Yet, God gave you that radiant face for free.

Share your smile today.

*A glad heart makes a happy face.*
Proverbs 15:13 NLT

Lord, thank You for making it so easy for me to telegraph
joy to others. Help me to keep my smile on all day long.
Amen.

# Turn that frown upside down

It is not fitting, when one is in God's service,
to have a gloomy face or a chilling look.

Francis of Assisi

Chances are you've had a gloomy day or two. You've probably even been concerned about letting anyone know you were feeling so blue. There's nothing wrong with needing the encouragement of others. Life presents matters that challenge us all the time. The good news is that when you can focus on it again, you probably recognize how many reasons you have to look on the bright side. You have been blessed with more smiles than frowns.

God knows your heart and He understands that you can't dismiss the things that bother you as though they aren't going on. He wants to comfort you when you need comfort. But, on the other hand, He hopes you can see how much He's blessed you. He hopes you can look around you and find more reasons than you can count to keep you smiling. Count your blessings one by one and your joy will overflow.

Give God the glory for every reason you have to smile today.

*A cheerful look brings joy to the heart.*

Proverbs 15:30 NLT

Lord, forgive me when I go around with a frown on my face.
Remind me that everything around me brightens a little
when I choose to smile.
Amen.

## Go, get 'em!

*Destiny is not a matter of chance; it is a matter of choice.*
*It is not a thing to be waited for; it is a thing to be achieved.*

William J. Bryan

When we look at successful people, we probably imagine that they are just luckier than we are, better at making connections or being in the right place at the right time. Chances are, they aren't luckier or more blessed or in any way slated for more favor, they probably are people who persevered. They probably didn't wait for destiny to ride in on a white horse. They went seeking destiny instead.

It's not easy for us to take a great leap of faith and try something we haven't tried or move in a direction that feels foreign. When we have to get out of our comfort zones, we aren't as sure of our steps.

God is! God still knows what the steps are that you have to take and He goes before you in your pursuits to help pave the way for you. Only you can choose the moment when you'll decide to act. Just be reassured that when you're ready to go out there, you won't go alone!

*A desire accomplished is sweet to the soul.*

Proverbs 13:19 NKJV

Lord, You know what I need to do and how I'll get there.
Help me to take the most direct route to the things You want
me to achieve by following You more closely.

Amen.

## *Excuse number 107*

People are always blaming their circumstances for what they are. The people who get on in this world are they who get up and look for the circumstances they want, and, if they can't find them, make them.

George Bernard Shaw

Hopefully, you're not a person who has a ready excuse for why your dreams have not yet come true. It's easy to make excuses. It's not so easy to accomplish the goals we set for ourselves. Sure, we can blame our upbringing. We can say that we just don't have enough money or the right education or the people behind us to support our dreams, but what then?

What happens to the dream? When you want to make a difference, and you want to change in ways that your circumstances haven't quite made possible, what can you do? You can stop making excuses and start making plans, even if they are much smaller steps. You can pray and seek direction and then do one thing, just one simple thing today that moves you closer to the goal. God knows you and wants you to succeed.

*The race is not to the swift or the battle to the strong, nor does food come to the wise or wealth to the brilliant or favor to the learned; but time and chance happen to them all.*

Ecclesiastes 9:11 NIV

Lord, I do pray for the right timing and the right circumstances to follow through with the goals we have set together. Help me to be awake to the possibilities and open to the direction You would take me, without hesitation or excuses.

Amen.

# The delight of a good friend

To ease another's heartache is to forget one's own.

Abraham Lincoln

❖❖❖❖❖❖

Have you ever had one unfortunate thing happen and then in what seems like no time at all, before you've even adjusted to the first thing, something else happens? Then, you start to wonder if you're becoming a bit like Job of the Bible and that God is somehow not happy with you.

The most difficult element in the above scenario is that it is all about you. When your focus is on you and what you need or what you're missing or what you want, you become obsessed with that and can be of little or no value to others.

Perhaps when you're suffering, the best thing you can do is go out and find someone else who is suffering and offer them comfort and love. Maybe if you focus your attention in the direction of someone else and help them to feel better, you'll start to feel better yourself. More than that, you'll discover that your sufferings are not insurmountable and perhaps that they aren't even comparable to what others are going through.

Look up and look out, and God will heal what's happening to you from within.

*"Do not let your hearts be troubled and do not be afraid."*

John 14:27 NIV

Lord, I do get absorbed sometimes in my own difficulties and I forget to reach out to others who have much greater needs than I do. Help me to trust everything about my life to You.

Amen.

*How will you handle today?*

Every tomorrow has two handles. We can take hold
of it by the handle of anxiety, or by the handle of faith.

Anonymous

Tomorrow has two handles: the handle of fear and the handle
of faith. You can take hold of it by either handle? Which one will
you choose today?

Fearless! Wouldn't it be great if you could step out into the
world with all confidence, boldness, and fearlessly go after the
things that are important to you? If you can remember that
you're not alone, that you have angels who protect you and a
loving Savior who walks with you, then you have some pretty
powerful friends and you can do anything.

You can go through the day filled with worry and wonder
and dreading each step. You can, but why would you? Grab
hold of the Lord's hand and in His strength that gets even more
powerful when you are weak, go and meet the day. Choose to
trust that faith will take you where you want to go and remember
that you have everything you need to get things done. You are
the daughter of a King, and not just any king, but the One who
reigns over all the earth.

Can you handle that?

*Jesus said, "My grace is all you need. My power works best in weakness."*

2 Corinthians 12:9 NLT

Lord, let Your power flow through me today so that I handle
everything with trust and joy.

Amen.

## It's worth the effort!

The greatest works are done by the ones.
The hundreds do not often do much – the companies never;
it is the units – the single individuals, that are the power and
the might. Individual effort is, after all, the grand thing.

Charles H. Spurgeon

Some days you may wonder why you even try! Why do you try to become a better woman, a more holy woman, a more deeply committed follower of Christ? After all, it doesn't appear that most of the world is working that hard at becoming better, so why should you be the only one who tries so hard?

If you ever think like this, stop! Stop and look at what you have and what is available to you because you are a daughter of God, beloved and beautiful. You have a place to go with every trouble you might encounter. You have others who believe in a similar way who offer you encouragement and support. You have more joy in knowing who holds the future and more joy in knowing that you are a very special part of that future.

God thought you were worth the effort when He sent His Son to die just for you. Every day, in some small way, share your gratitude with Him and keep making the effort to be wholly His.

*"You must love the Lord your God with all your heart,
all your soul, all your strength, and all your mind."*

Luke 10:27 NLT

Lord, I know You're worth the effort and that there is a lot for me
to learn. Help me to become the woman You know I can be.
Amen.

# The search for inner peace

First put yourself at peace, and then you may better help others be at peace. A peaceful and patient woman is of more profit to herself and to others, too, than a learned woman who has no peace.

Thomas à Kempis (adapted)

Being at peace isn't about your brilliance. You may handle a great deal of responsibility every day. You may be the reason a lot of people are happy they get up in the morning, because they want to be part of your life. You may seem to be totally in control of everything around you, but you can still forfeit peace in the process.

How do you put yourself at peace then? Perhaps you start by getting grounded, centered in Christ, and focused on the Word. Perhaps you take a walk and look out at the tall buildings, the landscape, and the sky above you and you ask God to be with you, to watch out for you and to give you His divine peace. Whatever you do, it's important to everything else you'll attempt today for you to be at peace with yourself. Once you are, you can take on everyone and everything around you with blessed assurance.

*God is not a God of disorder but of peace.*

1 Corinthians 14:33 NIV

Lord, I pray for peace in my heart today and ask You to be with me wherever I am, guiding me, and giving me Your blessed assurance.
Amen.

# What God wants from you

> It does not require great learning to be a Christian and be
> convinced of the truth of the Bible. It requires only an honest
> heart and a willingness to obey God.
>
> Albert Barnes

Sometimes you may wonder what God might want from you. After all, you're just one woman doing your best to live one day at a time, hoping to become more of God's image of you. Does God want your intellect? Yes, as far as it serves Him and the people around you. Does He want your strength and your steadfast efforts and your sense of humor? Yes! Yes! Yes!

But what He wants more than anything else is your heart. He wants to know that you are His body, mind, and spirit. He wants to know that you're willing to give Him first priority in your life, that you will seek Him above all other things.

You can excel at your job and at being a parent or being a good servant to those around you, but first and foremost, you must offer God your heart and then He'll help you with everything else that comes your way.

Keep seeking Him today.

> *What does the Lord your God require of you? He requires only*
> *that you fear the Lord your God, and live in a way that pleases Him,*
> *and love Him and serve Him with all your heart and soul.*
>
> Deuteronomy 10:12 NLT

Lord, please help me to follow You with an open and willing heart.
Amen.

# *Lighting more candles*

If you're not lighting any candles, don't complain about the dark.

Anonymous

Do you ever worry about what's going on in the world? Do you wonder why there is so much chaos and trouble, or why so many teenagers seem to have no direction, or why so many people are simply walking in the dark?

Can you make a list of things you've done in the last three days to turn up the light a little? Can you find the places where you've intentionally helped others overcome the darkness?

The job we have as Christian women is to always be willing to bring the light, going everywhere with a candle ready to shine. If it helps you, put a little candle in your purse today and remind yourself that there are places that are waiting for you to shine your light and offer your love, places that God has called you to go. Help Him any way that you can to overcome the darkness.

*Give freely to your neighbors and to the poor and needy in your land.*

Deuteronomy 15:11 NCV

Lord, help me be willing to light a candle anywhere that seems dark.
Bless the people around me with Your precious light.

Amen.

# Choose a great day!

It's a beautiful world to see, or it's dismal in every zone. The thing it must be in its gloom or its gleam depends on yourself alone.

*Anonymous*

Having a nice day isn't always about the circumstances around you. You could in fact have the exact situations happen to you on two different days and in one case, you'd come away thanking God for the day, and in the other, you'd come away wondering what you did to make heaven so moody. The variable in each of those days is you.

Most of the time, we choose what kind of day we want to have. If we decide before our feet hit the floor that we're letting God be in charge of the whole day, then we'll probably notice the things He does and offer thanks and praise for each moment. If we decide to go out there on our own, not giving the day to God, but simply getting through it the best way possible, we might find that the day itself seems gloomier.

Yes, you cannot choose every circumstance you'll come up against today, but you can choose your response to it.

*"Seek first His kingdom and His righteousness and all these things will be given to you as well."*

Matthew 6:33 NIV

Father, help me to seek You in all I do today
and to choose to have the best day possible.
Amen.

## Glass half full

The optimist says, the cup is half full. The pessimist says,
the cup is half empty. The child of God says, my cup runneth over.

Anonymous

Have you noticed that some people never seem to have a good thing going on in their lives? Every time you see them they are experiencing more drama, another setback, and nothing is ever going their way! Other people you know share their time and their smiles even when things aren't going well for them. They see that God is still working on their behalf and they trust that soon things will be all right again.

It's important to determine if you want to be a glass half full or a glass half empty kind of person. The fact is that everyone experiences both the good and the bad things of life. What makes a difference is where you put your focus, how you choose to see the difficulties and even the victories to help you discover rainbows. God is always with you. His love overflows for you and so whatever the circumstances may be at the moment, He is seeking the best ways for change to occur. Change the way you think and you'll discover that you are more blessed than you may realize right now. Your glass is full all the time.

*Always be full of joy in the Lord. I say it again – rejoice!
Let everyone see that you are considerate in all you do.*

Philippians 4:4-5 NLT

Lord, thank You for blessing my life today. Help me to
remember that You are always working things out for my good.
Amen.

## *A little more wisdom*

*When I was young, I used to admire intelligent people;*
*as I grow older, I admire kind people.*

Abraham Heschel

When you were growing up and working hard to educate yourself at school, you were probably rewarded for your efforts. You may have even received honors for your incredible skills in learning French or mathematics. You may have gotten trophies for being a great volleyball player or the best on the tennis courts. Culturally, we're good at giving out accolades to people who demonstrate brilliance in one way or another.

It's interesting that we don't as often recognize people for being incredibly kind. The Bible talks about how important it is for us to be kind and elevates kindness to a place of honor. Perhaps the difference is that kindness emanates from the heart and most other forms of intelligence come from the head or our athletic prowess. Your heart is the key to becoming more of what God hopes you will be as you move forward.

There is indeed great wisdom in being kind.

*Flee the evil desires of youth and pursue righteousness, faith, love*
*and peace, along with those who call on the Lord out of a pure heart.*

2 Timothy 2:22 NIV

Lord, thank You for teaching me to be loving and kind.
Help me to honor acts of kindness in myself and in others today.
Amen.

*Making this your best life*

*Wisdom is the power to see and the inclination to choose the best
and highest goal, together with the surest means of attaining it.*

J. I. Packer

Have you stopped to think about the role you play in your own life? In fact, you're the star, the number one headliner. No one else has the part you are meant to play and so you can do it to perfection. At least, that's how you were designed. God gave you everything you need to play the role of a lifetime and He is always near ready to encourage you, direct you, and put you closer to the flood lights. He sees your star quality.

When it comes to making a life, you want the best possible circumstances. You want to star in a successful, fulfilling, dynamic story. The Author of the universe has given you total creative license. You can change the script any way you want. You can take His advice, accept His coaching, and honor His discipline. When you do, you live passionately and well. You have an opportunity every day to make this life amazing! Be wise.

*Who, then, are those who fear the Lord? He will instruct them in the ways they
should choose. They will spend their days in prosperity.*

Psalm 25:12-13 NIV

Lord, help me to create the best possible life by making choices that please You and that bring me closer to being all that I can be for You.

Amen.

# It's good to have questions

The important thing is not to stop questioning.
Curiosity has its own reason for existing.

Albert Einstein

There's nothing wrong with being curious. In fact, it's a good thing. Asking questions is a good way to get needed information. Sometimes we don't ask enough questions and we come to regret that at a later date.

God gave you free will so that you could think for yourself and discover what's important to you. He wants you to ask Him questions too. The more you seek Him, the more information He will gladly give you. He doesn't want to overload you or overwhelm you, so He may not tell you some things until you ask.

When you ask Him how you can become even more of the daughter He wants you to be, He's going to answer. He's going to answer gently and with ideas for how you can share your love for Him with others. Since God is the only real Source of all things, you can ask Him anything!

*"Everyone who asks receives; the one who seeks finds;*
*and to the one who knocks, the door will be opened."*

Matthew 7:8 NIV

Lord, thank You for giving me the chance to ask questions.
I come to You as a curious little child, eager to know more of You.
Amen.

# *Love tips the scale*

Beware you be not swallowed up in books!
An ounce of love is worth a pound of knowledge.

John Wesley

———

When you think about it, would you rather have someone read a solid definition of what love is to you when you're feeling down, or would you rather have someone not say a word and put their arms around you? Expressions of love delivered at the right place and time will always outclass volumes of wisdom written on the topic.

There's a time for learning new things, reading great books, and writing thoughtful research papers on a topic. There's a time for sharing our philosophies and our hopes through discussion and debate. Greater than any of those things, is the ability and the willingness to express genuine heartfelt love for another person at a moment when nothing else would heal their wounds or help them feel confident about life again.

Offer your heart first, your hugs next, and your thoughts last. When people know that you love them, you can share anything with them.

*The whole law is made complete in this one command:*
*"Love your neighbor as you love yourself."*

Galatians 5:14 NCV

Lord, let me never forget to begin with love in any relationship
I have and let my actions speak louder than my words.
Amen.

## *You make me laugh!*

Laughter is the shortest distance between two people.

Victor Borge

---

You probably have friends that lift your spirits almost the moment you get in the same room with them. They make you laugh … in a good way. They remind you to lighten up a little and put down your load. They are good for you.

God knows we don't laugh enough. We are so focused on our worries and our schedules and our workloads or our children or something else, that we can't even imagine a moment of laughter. This may be an area where you actually have to practice developing and growing your laughing skills. That's right. You may have to allow yourself a little more fun.

God created you with a multi-level and multi-dimensional character. That means He gave you a wide range of emotions. If you've missed out a bit too often on the pleasures derived from sharing some laughter with good friends, then rethink your day and see where you can fit that in. It will do you a world of good.

*A cheerful heart is good medicine, but a broken spirit saps a person's strength.*

Proverbs 17:22 NLT

Lord, I confess that I forget to lighten up sometimes.
Help me to enjoy moments of laughter and
friendship with those around me.
Amen.

## Thinking your own thoughts

*Guard well your spare moments. They are like uncut diamonds.
Discard them and their value will never be known. Improve them and
they will become the brightest gems in a useful life.*

Ralph Waldo Emerson

When God declared that we should rest every seventh day, He knew what He was talking about. After all, most of us don't really know when to quit. We work around the clock and even on the weekends and wonder why we don't have time to think our own thoughts. We may not even be sure of what it means to breathe normally.

If you never have time to think, to rest, to put your ideas together either just in your head or in your journal, you're missing out. You're deprived of the opportunity to create your dreams in new ways, to shape your life differently, or simply to spend more quiet time with your Savior.

Today, if you can, take a deep breath and just relax for a few minutes. Give yourself some freedom to think lofty thoughts or to send your thoughts aloft to God so that you can share the moment. Rest is good for the body and for the mind.

*Oh, that I had the wings of a dove! I would fly away and be at rest.*

Psalm 55:6 NIV

Lord, I know that You declared a day of rest for my good.
Help me to take the time and use it in ways that profit my soul.
Amen.

## Avoiding the rumor mill

A little lie is like a little pregnancy –
it doesn't take long before everyone knows.

C. S. Lewis

Lies aren't always intentional or told to deceive someone in a negative way. Sometimes we imagine that we are protecting someone's feelings if we don't disclose the whole truth about a situation. Those half-truths or maybe they're half-lies that we tell, aren't really meant to hurt someone. But, those lies that truly deceive, often find a way of rising to the top and coming back to haunt us.

It may seem innocent enough sometimes to pass along an unsubstantiated rumor, but later when the real truth of the situation is discovered, you may regret what you've done. Instead of sharing the gossip, maybe you could take the time to pray for the person in question. Instead of asking someone else if the rumor is true, perhaps you could go to the person in question and offer to help in some way.

Good news gets around in its own time, but bad news travels like lightning. Try not to be one of those conducting that electricity.

*A troublemaker plants seeds of strife; gossip separates the best of friends.*

Proverbs 16:28 NLT

Lord, help me to step aside when gossip is going
around so that I don't have any reason to lie to my friends
or co-workers. Guide me into all truth.

Amen.

*How to have a fabulous day!*

Take the life that you have and give it your best,
Think positive, be happy, and let God do the rest.

Anonymous

---

Every morning you get a brand-new opportunity, a new chance to look life squarely in the face and give it your best. You get to choose whether to go after it with gusto or whether to drag yesterday with you into today. How can you have a fail-safe formula for a fabulous day?

Simple! You start with an enthusiastic hello to your Lord and Savior before your feet ever hit the floor. Then you thank Him for giving you another day to stretch your wings and try your best. After that, you seek His guidance for every thought and every action you will have for the day and then you rise and shine.

From there, you can let God do the rest. He's already got you covered on the important things and you've just given Him permission to walk with you through the day so the only thing your day can be … is fabulous!

*Be strong and immovable. Always work enthusiastically for the Lord,*
*for you know that nothing you do for the Lord is ever useless.*

1 Corinthians 15:58 NLT

Lord, thank You for giving me a chance to start another new day.
Help me to appreciate everything that happens
to me and give You the glory!
Amen.

*Wisdom for life*

Order your soul; reduce your wants; live in charity; associate in
Christian community; obey the laws; trust in Providence.

St. Augustine

———————

This advice from St. Augustine may not resonate with the culture
we live in today. After all, we're more about "getting" more things,
rather than "reducing" our wants. We're more about ordering our
finances and making sure we have big retirement nest eggs,
than we are about ordering our soul.

Setting a priority to trust in Providence though could turn
your life around in the way that you discover more of what it
means to live in charity and reduce your wants. It might just
cause you to desire to be even more of a giver than you are now.
When we associate in Christian community, it means we seek to
put Jesus at the center of all that we do as we relate to those
around us. It means that we want to shine as givers and that we
rely on God's grace and goodness.

What would it mean to you today, to just take this day and
focus on getting your life in order, starting with your soul? God
is with you.

*He satisfies the longing soul,*
*and fills the hungry soul with goodness.*

Psalm 107:9 NKJV

Lord, let me truly take the time to breathe
in Your love and direction and nurture my soul today.
Amen.

## *Can you see in the dark?*

All the darkness in the world cannot
extinguish the light of a single candle.
Francis of Assisi

Most of us appreciate it when the sun comes up. We love to do our favorite things in the light of day. We breathe in blue skies and sunshine and thank God above for creating such beauty in the world. We are women of light and we make a difference.

One of the differences we make is that we help other people to see better. We help them to understand the things of God so they can see in the dark and move into the light. We are beacons for those around us.

You know that your eyes adjust to the darkness when you have to walk through it, but as a source of the Light of the World, you are needed everywhere you go to illuminate the path. God put you right where you are because someone nearby needs your help so they can see Him better. Shine on!

*"I have come as light into the world so that whoever*
*believes in Me would not stay in darkness."*
John 12:46 NCV

Lord, bless me with a willingness to share
Your light wherever I may be today.
Amen.

# The absolute joy of Easter

God proved His love on the Cross. When Christ hung, and bled,
and died, it was God saying to the world, "I love you."

Billy Graham

———❖———

However you celebrate Easter, perhaps with flowers and brightly colored jelly beans, or with big family dinners and new shoes, you also celebrate the absolute gift of Easter. God's gift to us! God not only sent Jesus into the world as a tiny baby, fragile and needing the love of a human mother, but He kept His promise through His only Son, our Savior. He redeemed us and gave us a way to come back home when our earthly work is done.

The absolute, remarkable, beautiful joy of Easter is that we know our relationship with God is eternal. We are His sons and daughters forever and nothing can change that. It's spring in our hearts from now on and love will always bloom.

Celebrate Easter all year through and let love prevail in your heart forever!

*For God so loved the world that He gave His one and only Son, that whoever believes in Him shall not perish but have eternal life. For God did not send His Son into the world to condemn the world, but to save the world through Him.*

John 3:16-17 NIV

Lord, I praise You with all my heart, and mind,
and soul as I celebrate Your amazing gift of eternal life.
Amen.

### Take a break — from yourself!

The most effective remedy for self-love and
self-absorption is the habit of humble listening.

E. Herman

---

We can't help getting caught up in our own stories. After all, we play the starring role there and everything seems to be about us. The truth is that we can be overwhelmed with our own self-absorption and not even realize that we've neglected those around us. We probably don't really hear anything others have to say to us. We may give them a passing nod, but the fact is we don't see their needs as being as important as ours. The danger is that we can get stuck in the place of "me, me, me" for a time and get comfortable there.

God loves you and in some ways it really is "all about you." But some days you need to take a break from yourself and set your focus on those things that make a difference for others. You need to be able to listen from the heart to what God has to say to you. Let God be at the top of your list and when He is, He'll guide you into all the things that are good for you because He knows what you need all the time.

Take a day off from your own story, for your own good.

*People may be pure in their own eyes, but the LORD examines their motives.*

Proverbs 16:2 NLT

Lord, help me to get out of my own way, to not be so
involved with my needs that I neglect others who need me.
Amen.

# *Everyone has an amazing story!*

Helping others, that's the main thing. The only way for us to help ourselves is to help others and to listen to each other's stories.

Elie Wiesel

God has a story! His story is the tale of creation and how He made everything from nothing and how He brought all life together so that He would have people to love and people to love Him right back. It's an awesome story and we're each part of that.

Your family has a story and within that and apart from that, you have a story too. You are learning more about your story all the time, coming to understand just what God created you to be. The more you learn about yourself, the more you can carry out His plans and help others.

At some point, the story may end. God gave us His Word and a chance to actually read the story all the way to the end before it happens. He wants us to know Him and His love so well that we'll be prepared for the things that are ahead. He included us in His story.

It's a good day to listen to the tales being shared all around you.

*Everyone should be quick to listen, slow to speak and slow to become angry.*

James 1:19 NIV

Lord, help me to really listen to the stories others choose to share with me about their lives today and offer to help in any way I can.

Amen.

# Through the looking glass

*Contemplate the love of Christ, and you will love. Stand before that mirror, reflect Christ's character, and you will be changed into the same image from tenderness to tenderness.*

Henry Drummond

Mirrors are helpful. Sure sometimes we're not too pleased at the image we see looking back at us, but for the most part we appreciate having a chance to glance through the mirror and take a better look at who we are.

If your faith was a mirror, you might be able to see how you reflect the beliefs that you claim guide your life. You'd be able to see as in a prism the colors of your love and how it is reflected all around you. You'd be able to see how your beliefs impact your work each day and the life you live. It may be very revealing.

As you look in your faith mirror, remember that you're not looking for perfection. You're looking for glimmers of hope, moments of joy that bring a witness to all that you are and all you believe. Hopefully, what you see is a woman who has been enhanced by a lot of growth and change as you have become more of God's reflection through the years.

*For now we see only a reflection as in a mirror; then we shall see face to face. Now I know in part; then I shall know fully, even as I am fully known.*

1 Corinthians 13:12 NIV

Lord, help me to examine my beliefs as carefully
as I might examine the image of my face that I see in the mirror.
Help me to reflect Your love to others.

Amen.

# *This is your day!*

RESOLVED: To live with all my might, while I do live.

Jonathan Edwards

---

What if this was it, the last day of your life? What if you only had this one day to get it right, or to tell someone important to you how much you love them, or to let God know you love Him?

Since that last day is an unknown for most of us, it's a good idea to pour everything you've got into each day, making the most of it, learning as much as you can, celebrating life, and sharing God's goodness.

It's not likely that mopping the kitchen floor or dusting the piano would come to mind if you had only this day to live fully. Take today and live it as completely as you can … dance a little, love a little, pray a little, and give God the glory for giving you breath and life and possibility. Then, when this life is done, you can thank God for taking you back into His loving arms and offering you eternal salvation.

It's your day! You get to choose how you'll use those precious minutes and hours.

*Lord, make me to know my end, and what is the measure of my days,*
*that I may know how frail I am.*

Psalm 39:4 NKJV

Lord, I know I'm guilty of taking my days for granted.
I have squandered countless hours and have not taken
advantage of even enjoying my leisure time. Remind me
to be more careful of my time and to use each day well.

Amen.

# Will the real you please stand up?

We are living in a world today where lemonade is made from
artificial flavors and furniture polish is made from real lemons.

Alfred E. Newman

The world leaves you dizzy and confused. We used to put our
citrus into fruit salads and now we put it into furniture polish and
hair shampoo. We used to feel it was safe to send our children to
school and now we have to pray for their safety even in a country
that intends for every child to have a free education.

We used to know how to behave on a date or how to treat the
elderly and yet now, nobody seems to know the rules. Nobody
seems to recognize that things are really upside down and all
the marbles are rolling around in different places waiting for us
to go slip sliding through life.

It feels like that sometimes, but the fact is, you are not
confused. God did not give you a timid spirit or a confused one.
He guides you and gave you a spirit that will lead you into all
truth. You do know who you are and what is real, because the
love of Christ is within you.

*Your faith should not be in the wisdom of men but in the power of God.*

1 Corinthians 2:5 NKJV

Lord, though I don't claim to understand all that goes on around me,
I thank You for keeping me grounded in Your love and in my faith.

Amen.

# Becoming more beautiful each day

*O Lord, forgive what I have been,*
*sanctify what I am, and order what I shall be.*

Thomas Wilson

What you were yesterday is not quite the same as who you are today. Yesterday has passed and God has already forgiven you for those things that you asked Him to forgive. Today He sees you as perfectly beautiful. Today He loves who you are as His holy and precious daughter. He rejoices in what you are now and what you are becoming.

Forgiveness means you can let go of the heartbreaking things you've done in days gone by, the things you can hardly forgive in yourself. You can trust that God does not hold those things against you because you've already come to Him and asked Him to make the slate clean. He has done so and today, He sanctifies you and embraces you.

Tomorrow will still require God's help and guidance. All you have to know for sure is that He will be there, never leaving you lonely or alone for even a moment. He will walk each tomorrow with you. Trust Him with everything you are.

*Let all things be done decently and in order.*

1 Corinthians 14:40 NKJV

Lord, it's so hard for me to forgive myself sometimes that I have trouble knowing You truly do forgive me. Help me to believe that You've given me a clean slate and help me to make choices more worthy of You today.
Amen.

# Tomorrow comes with hope

*There is not a heart but has its moments of longing,*
*yearning for something better.*
Henry Ward Beecher

———————

Can you identify those subtle longings in your heart? Sometimes they seem to take a back seat in your life and you travel along without giving them much thought. Other times, they seem to catapult into the driver's seat, determined to take you with them wherever they go. You can't seem to do anything but go along for the ride.

God put some of the longings within you that fill your heart. You may feel restlessness and far from home, far from the place that will satisfy every desire you have forever. After all, while you're in the body, you're away from your real home.

Some of your longings come from a hope for better life circumstances, or better opportunities or prayers whispered on behalf of people you love. God hears the longings of your heart and the hopes you have for yourself and others. He is working to bring all things together for your good right now.

*It is sad not to get what you hoped for. But wishes that*
*come true are like eating fruit from the tree of life.*

Proverbs 13:12 NCV

Lord, there are some holes in my heart, some secret
longings that I share only with You. Please fulfill those desires
that are of You and let the others melt away.

Amen.

SHE
*opens her arms*
TO THE POOR AND
EXTENDS HER HANDS
TO THE NEEDY

PROVERBS 31:20

## Blossoms of love

Love makes the music of the blest above,
Heaven's harmony is universal love.

William Cowper

———————

You're a loving woman with a big heart and a ready embrace. You put others at ease in your presence and offer them encouragement and friendship. Your kindness knows no bounds. No? That's not you?

All of us are actually still learning about love. We're trying to understand how to love our spouses and our children. We're trying to manage the relationships of various members of our families and praying for satisfying outcomes. We're looking at ways to reach out to those around us in love as well.

We do it because we know how important it is for people to feel loved. God knew that the first time He looked at Adam's lonely face. He knew that somehow human beings got more out of life if they were loved. Of course, He knew that because He designed us to be lovers. He wants us to be lovers of each other, of life itself and of the planet. He wants love to blossom every place we plant our feet. Love is yours to give and receive today.

*Let us love one another, for love comes from God.*

1 John 4:7 NIV

Lord, thank You for all the blessings of love that have come into my life.
Help me to never outgrow my need for love.

Amen.

## *Love what you do!*

The Lord doesn't look so much at the greatness of our
works as the love with which they are done.

Teresa of Avila

Most of us like to rank people and things into some kind of order
that makes sense to us. For instance, we might think the pastor
at the church is more important to the congregation than the
choir director or the head of housekeeping. We might think that
the chef who creates the main course is more important than the
one who made the salad. Whatever it is, we imagine that some
people are important. If we do that, does it mean we think others
are not important?

Getting back to the jobs that we do and the work we do in
the world though, we have to remember one thing. It's not just
a matter of how important a job seems to be, for what really
matters is the attitude we hold toward what we do. When we do
our work, no matter what it is, for the Lord, then we do it with
great love and we do it as a calling on our lives. That love and that
calling are of high importance to God.

*Remember that the Lord will reward each one of us for the good we do.*

Ephesians 6:8 NLT

Lord, thank You for giving me the right work to do and the right heart
to do that work. Bless all those I work with today with great love.

Amen.

# *The courage to love*

A little courage helps more than a lot of knowledge,
A little human sympathy helps more than courage,
And the least amount of love of God, helps more than all.

C. S. Lewis (adapted)

---

It's great to gather all the facts about something and be able to prepare yourself for upcoming events. It helps to be aware of what might limit your ability to handle a given situation. That's all good, but at the end of the day, life takes courage because we face incredible odds to get through it. You have courageous choices to make about what you want to know and what you want to do.

It helps a lot to know that other people care about what you're going through, that they identify with your sorrow or your situation and want to offer you encouragement. Sometimes other people give us the kind of courage we need.

We know one thing for sure. We know that God faces every fear we have, every heartache, every illness, ever bit of chaos that crosses our paths. God gives us a place where we find our greatest strength and our sense of hope. When we give God a little love, He gives us a lot of support and courage.

*Be strong and take heart, all you who hope in the Lord.*

Psalm 31:24 NIV

Lord, thank You for being with me when I have tough decisions to
make, or sad news to endure. I know that with You by my side,
I can face most anything.

Amen.

# Becoming a heart and soul woman

*A soul enkindled with love is a gentle, meek,
humble, and patient soul.*

John of the Cross

―――・◦✕◦・―――

You may think it's not worth it to try to become even more gentle, meek and mild. After all, the world will simply run over you if you do and might not even notice you at all. Somewhere along the way, you understood the concept that the "squeaky wheel" gets the grease, that is the attention and so meek and mild doesn't really cut it.

So what does it mean to be meek in God's terms? Perhaps it means that even when someone is wrong, you have no need to point out their flaws, but instead, you pray for God's grace in their lives. Perhaps it means when you're frustrated with the kids, you don't send them to their rooms, but you stop everything else you're doing and simply give them attention and love.

You may have to define for yourself what it means to be a gentle, meek, and humble woman for God, but you can be sure He'll bless your efforts every time.

*"Take My yoke upon you. Let Me teach you, because I am humble and gentle,
and you will find rest for your souls."*

Matthew 11:29 NLT

Lord, help me to listen more closely to Your loving and
gentle Spirit. Teach me to be more like You in this way.

Amen.

# *The charity choice*

*Who shuts his hand has lost his gold, who opens it, has it twice told.*

George Herbert

—◦◦◦◦◦⊱◦✕◦⊰◦◦◦◦◦—

There are so many charitable organizations vying for your donations of goods and time and materials, you may feel overwhelmed. In fact, you may almost feel like not giving to any of them, because everyone seems to beg for help and you can't always take care of yourself and your own family.

God's intention for us is not to deprive our own families of basic needs so that we can look charitable to others. Our opportunity is always to open our hearts and our hands to those in need in ways that we can. After all, if God loves a cheerful giver, then it means He didn't have to pry our fingers open to get the donation out of our hands.

Giving is always a choice and charity is a beautiful thing. We each have to choose which organizations we feel can most benefit from our help. In any case, you hold the gold … the chance to pray for the connection between God and His people in need. In that way, you can always be a "cheerful" giver.

*Each of you should give what you have decided in your heart to give, not reluctantly or under compulsion, for God loves a cheerful giver.*

2 Corinthians 9:7 NIV

Lord, let me always have a humble heart and a desire
to give to others any way that I can.
Amen.

# *There's no one quite like a mama!*

A mother holds her children's hands for a while …
their hearts forever.
Anonymous

Safe to say, we each had a mother. What kind of mother we had varies greatly from the ones who never quite figured out what motherhood was about to those who were the great masters of mothering, nearly divine in their skill and tenderness. Probably your own mother was neither of those, and if you're a mother, you're somewhere in-between as well. The thing is that to someone out there, there's no one quite like mom to make a difference in the little things of life.

Mothers are usually the safe havens, the place where children know they can go when things are confusing or complicated. They are the people who somehow know how to fix everything with a chocolate chip cookie and a hug. They know that no matter what is going on, a little listening and a lot of love can make everything better.

Whatever day Mother's Day is officially celebrated, it's always good to recognize the woman who did her best to create a way for you to become who you are today. Ask God to bless the mothers in your life enormously today.

*Be devoted to one another in love.*

Romans 12:10 NIV

Lord, thank You for my own mother and bless all
mothers who gently love and nurture their children.
Amen.

## The gift of praise

Children are likely to live up to what you believe of them.

Lady Bird Johnson

---

Do you ever have trouble giving or receiving a compliment? Sometimes as parents we can forget how much it means to our children to receive some praise from us about the things they do. We set boundaries and expectations for them and often they rise to those expectations. Sometimes though, we simply acknowledge that they met the expectation with little fanfare and then propose a new standard of excellence.

If we had to work that way in our own jobs, we probably wouldn't love our work very long. We'd know that doing a good job would simply mean we'd be given even more of a load to endure and perhaps without further praise or compensation.

The idea here is to simply remember that we all thrive on adoration, even a little bit from those around us. We need to compliment each other, and we especially need to do that for children because that is how they grow best. That's how we grow best too.

*Be joyful in hope, patient in affliction, faithful in prayer.*

Romans 12:12 NIV

Lord, bless my children and the children around me.
Help me to remember to honestly and lovingly encourage
their hearts and minds with praise.
Amen.

## Growing and becoming more

*She is only advancing in life whose heart is getting softer, her blood warmer, her brain quicker, and her spirit entering into living peace.*

John Ruskin (adapted)

When you were a little girl, you probably dreamed about what you would be when you grew up. You may have tried to imagine what it would be like to be an actor, or a world traveler, or even a mom. You've been growing and becoming someone special every day since you were born.

You're not only special to your family, you're special to God. He looks forward to seeing you evolve into the person He already knows you can be. He applauds your efforts and encourages you to try again when you fail. He knows that you can stretch yourself further, bend a little more, reach a little higher, all without breaking, and all for a good reason, to get to be a little more like Him.

As you get older, you have opportunities for your heart to become tender and more authentic. You care for others and love them, growing sweeter and kinder in the process. God has entered each area of your life to bring you His beautiful Spirit of peace. May you continue to grow in Him always.

*When I was a child, I spoke and thought and reasoned as a child.*
*But when I grew up, I put away childish things.*

1 Corinthians 13:11 NLT

Lord, help me to grow to be more like You so that I warmly and lovingly reflect Your image to everyone around me.

Amen.

# God is everywhere...
# but He still needs mothers

*God could not be everywhere and therefore He made mothers.*

Jewish proverb

Since we know that God is Spirit and not in bodily form, we can refer to Him as our Father, but we can also refer to Him as our Mother, for it is truly the mothering side of God that nurtures and teaches us and cares about every detail of our lives. Surely, the best mothers anywhere emulate the God who made us in every possible way.

God knows what we need. He knows us better than we can ever possibly know ourselves because He's always been there with us, even before we were born in the womb of our own dear mother.

As you consider the woman you think of as one of the dearest mother's anywhere, and as you celebrate her life and her willingness to love her family, then reflect too on the heart of your own Father/Mother God, who loves you unconditionally and holds you close forever.

*"How often I wanted to gather your children together,*
*as a hen gathers her chicks under her wings!"*

Matthew 23:37 NKJV

Lord, thank You for all the times You have been willing to "mother" me and keep me under the shelter of Your wings.
Amen.

## So proud of you

Pride is one of the seven deadly sins; but it cannot be
the pride of a mother in her children, for that is a compound
of two cardinal virtues – faith and hope.

Charles Dickens

It's right to take pride in the things we do, because it means we work carefully, skillfully, always doing our best with the thing we're creating. Whether you're cleaning the house or cleaning out your files, you do it with care and with pride.

It's also good to be proud of others and the things they do. You cheer on your children when they excel at school, or your spouse when an award for excellence is received. You take pride in the work your committee at church does to help the homeless. That kind of pride gives you a sense of accomplishment and the welcome thought of having done a job well.

So as long as your sense of pride doesn't become a stumbling block, something that keeps you from helping others or sharing from your heart, then your motivations are good and God will fully bless you in your efforts. A sense of pride has to push your ego aside and walk hand in hand with humility.

*Serve the LORD your God with your whole being,*
*and obey the LORD's commands and laws.*

Deuteronomy 10:12-13 NCV

Lord, thank You for giving me an honest sense of pride in
my work and in those I love, but help me always to understand
that anything I do or can do comes from You.

Amen.

## *What we learn from mothers*

*You have omitted to mention the greatest
of my teachers – my mother.*
Winston Churchill

Moms may be different in their approach to parenting or in the tone they set in the household, but the best moms have some things in common. The best moms guide with love and teach you how to think things through and reason them out. They ask the right kinds of questions so you can discover for yourself whether your ideas are good ones or not. They give you the room to be yourself and to grow and to change, and help you when things fall apart.

They see all your potential and admire your efforts to try to achieve your goals. They pray for you and seek God's protection and mercy for all that you are and all that you do.

It's no wonder that we choose to honor our mothers because the good they started in us, is the good that we share with others today. The potential they saw in us is what keeps us striving to become more than we were. The faith they have in us continues forever. God bless all of our moms.

*I want to use the authority the Lord has given
me to strengthen you, not to tear you down.*
2 Corinthians 13:10 NLT

Lord, thank You for the moms everywhere who use their authority
lovingly and wisely over the children in their care.
Amen.

## Outside the law

Murphy's Law
1. Nothing is as easy as it looks.
2. Everything takes longer than you think.
3. Anything that can go wrong will go wrong.

Anonymous

You've probably had "one of those days." Maybe you've had lots of those days when you wondered if you were living under some kind of gray sky, some invisible umbrella of frustration, because no matter how hard you looked for the sunshine, everything seemed to break down.

It's not even comforting to note that things are more complicated than you expect. The visit at the cell phone store should have taken five minutes because you only had a quick question, but two hours later, you're still wondering why you don't have the answer, and then finding out that your son needs extra money for his graduation ceremony, and your dog needs to go to the Vet makes everything for the day feel just a bit overwhelming.

Murphy's Law happens to all of us, but God's law is that we can start again, ground our thoughts in Him and things will work together for our good tomorrow.

*We know that in all things God works for the good of those who love Him.*

Romans 8:28 NIV

Lord, please help me turn this day around
and usher in a brighter tomorrow.
Amen.

## *It's a jungle out there!*

The more I study nature, the more I am amazed at the Creator.

Louis Pasteur

———✦━┥╋╳═╋┝✦———

If you've ever been to the rain forest and hiked through the impressive vegetation with the big leafy green fronds of ferns that are taller than you are, and witnessed the amazing colors of a huge variety of humming birds and the incredible critters and creatures that inhabit the place, you probably gained a renewed sense of awe for our Creator. After all, with endless imagination, He created forms of life that inhabit the jungles and the oceans and the hot places and the cold places all over this planet and they all thrive.

God knew exactly what He was doing with each form of life. He knew what the environment would have to be for it to survive. When He put Adam and Eve in the garden, He provided all they would need to live well.

In the same way, God knows everything you need. He knows what you need in the environment of your heart to survive and to thrive. He knows what you need at home and at work. He's walked in the jungle, the mountainside and the seascape, and He walks with you every day.

*God saw everything that He had made, and indeed it was very good.*

Genesis 1:31 NKJV

Lord, thank You for being so imaginative, so detailed,
and so aware of all that every living thing needs to sustain life.
I trust You with my life always.
Amen.

# The earth is the Lord's

*We can almost smell the aroma of God's beauty in the fresh spring flowers. His breath surrounds us in the warm summer breezes.*

Gale Heide

When you're fortunate enough to step outside on a beautiful spring day and truly focus on God's handiwork, you can't help but feel blessed. God not only created a world that He knew could sustain life, but He did it in living color and in ways to excite our senses at every level. We get to truly breathe Him in and praise His name.

Today, take a few moments to recognize His work in nature wherever you are. See Him peeking through the tallest buildings with blue skies and sunshine. See Him in the gardens in your neighborhood or even in plant boxes on window sills. If you look for Him, you'll discover that He has put a measure of Himself anywhere you might be as a loving reminder of all that He wants you to enjoy.

Offer Him thanks and praise today for simply giving you a chance to take in the beauty of the landscape and the beauty of your environment right where you are.

*The earth is the LORD's, and everything in it. The world and all its people belong to Him. For He laid the earth's foundation on the seas and built it on the ocean depths.*

Psalm 24:1-2 NLT

Lord, sometimes I take flowers for granted,
and I forget that You created everything I see. I praise
You and thank You for Your incredible handiwork.
Amen.

## The decision to love

Do not waste your time bothering about whether you
love your neighbor; act as if you did … When you are behaving
as if you love someone, you will presently come to love them.

C. S. Lewis

It may not always feel to you that love is a choice. After all, some people make it very difficult to find reasons to want to be anywhere near them. The fact is that there's a difference between that genuine, heartfelt, emotional attachment you feel for the people in your intimate circle, and the kind of love that God expects you to share with your neighbor.

Genuine love comes from God. You can choose to offer God's love to your neighbor, to your difficult boss, or to a complete stranger. After all, God gave it to you to give away. He wants you to share His truth and His light with others. So, sharing that kind of love is a decision you can make every day.

Sometimes even the people you genuinely love, offend you and you have to call on God's love for them too. The understanding to have is that you always have love to give because you have God's love to share.

*"If you love only the people who love you, you will get no reward. Even the tax collectors do that. And if you are nice only to your friends, you are not better than other people. Even those who don't know God are nice to their friends."*

Matthew 5:46-47 NCV

Lord, help me to be willing to share Your love
with everyone I meet today.
Amen.

# Praying for each other's happiness

*There is no principle of the heart that is more acceptable
to God than a universal, ardent love for all mankind,
which seeks and prays for their happiness.*

William Law

———

We're pretty good at putting our requests in front of God when
we know someone has a problem. We pray for each other's health
and well-being and we pray for comfort when people mourn a
loss or are suffering. It may not occur to us as often to pray for
each other's happiness, pure and simple.

When you think about the people who are dear to you today,
say a prayer that this will be a day of God's favor for them, a day
when they will have a lot of things to smile about. Make it your
own personal campaign to set the Light of God's love around
them in such a way that they will feel His presence and rejoice.

When you pray for the happiness of others, you can't help
but feel happier yourself because you know that God is working
in their lives in a special way. Thank God as you pray for having
such a personal love for each of us that He truly cares about our
happiness and the things in life that make us smile.

*"Where two or three are gathered together in My name,
I am there in the midst of them."*

Matthew 18:20 NKJV

Lord, thank You for inspiring happy hearts in the people I love.
You are a merciful and gracious Father.
Amen.

# *It's always a good day to do the right thing!*

We must use time creatively … and forever realize that
the time is always ripe to do right.

Martin Luther King, Jr.

Time is elusive. One day melts into the next and by the end of
most days, we question what actually happened to the day
and what we accomplished. We're aware of time slipping away,
perhaps when we blow out another birthday candle, and we're
awed by how fast time goes. In fact, the older we get, the more
we're sure it speeds up. Those twenty-four hours in the day surely
go by more quickly than they did when we were kids waiting for
Christmas to come.

We have to be as intentional about time as we are about
other things. In God's view, He sees us as having a finite amount
of time to get His work done and to do as much good for as
many people as possible. We're His ambassadors.

As you step into a new day, be conscious of the moments and
how you are using your time. Be aware of the good you can do
in a matter of minutes when the opportunity presents itself. It's
part of your calling.

*"While it is daytime, we must continue doing the work of the One who sent Me."*

John 9:4 NCV

Lord, help me to be aware that my days are limited and that
I must do the good that I can do a little bit each day.

Amen.

# *Let hope carry you forward*

Optimism is the faith that leads to achievement.
Nothing can be done without hope and confidence.

Helen Keller

Have you ever tried to force yourself to work on something that you already perceived to be doomed to failure? You saw the writing on the wall and you suspected that no matter what you did, there was little hope of success. Chances are the project failed. Chances are you predicted accurately that it could not work because you had no confidence in it.

Maybe you've had the experience of something only you believed in, something others said would fail, but against all odds, you kept working at it and to everyone's amazement, it worked splendidly. What was the difference? The main difference was one of attitude. In one case you were optimistic and driven by that sense of possibility, you searched for every possible way to make it work.

When you have hope in something and believe in it fully, God sees the motivation of your heart and blesses your work. Move forward in hope today for the things you truly believe are possible.

*You are my hope, O Lord GOD; You are my trust from my youth.*

Psalm 71:5 NKJV

Lord, it's so easy to get discouraged when others don't believe
I'm on the right path, but help me to move forward any time
the path is one You are traveling with me.

Amen.

## Changing your perspective

*Patience and perseverance have a magical effect before which difficulties disappear and obstacles vanish.*

John Quincy Adams

---

Some days nothing goes as you planned. An appointment gets canceled at the last minute, the car suddenly springs an oil leak, the kids can't seem to get along and you're wondering if you should just go back to bed and start all over again.

In a way, you should. When the pressures of the day start mounting and the obstacles get higher and you're tired of running through the maze because you can't quite find your way out, then stop!

Imagine you're spending this lovely May day simply sitting by a little quiet stream, feeling the gentle breeze, and calmly getting grounded. As you do that, invite Jesus to come and sit with you in your serene space and share a few moments with you. Tell Him how your day has been up to now, and ask if He might help you patiently move forward.

You may notice things changing before you open your eyes. Prayer is a powerful thing.

*In my distress I cried out to the Lord; yes, I prayed to my God for help.*
*He heard me from His sanctuary; my cry to Him reached His ears.*

Psalm 18:6 NLT

Lord, help me to quiet myself when I get stressed and spend a few moments with You.

Amen.

## At the end of your rope?

Habits begin like threads in a spider's web, but end up like ropes.

Spanish proverb

---

Habits that are formed for a positive purpose can be a good thing, they're good habits. You may be in the habit of praying several times a day, perhaps almost spontaneously when you see another person in great need of prayer. You may be in the habit of taking a long walk when you have a lot on your mind so you can think things through.

Some habits don't secure your steps as much as they bind you to them in negative ways. Perhaps you're trying to lose weight or to stop smoking. You know it would be good for you to do so, but for some odd reason, you simply can't break the habit that binds you. What started out in your life so innocently, has somehow tied you down and you may be at the end of your rope.

Today is your day to try again. Today, you can park farther out in the lot so you have to get a walk in even if you weren't planning on it. Today, you can have one less cigarette than you had yesterday. You can start to change the thing that has you bound. Remember, you're already in alignment with the One who makes you victorious.

*"God blesses those who are poor and realize their need for Him,*
*for the Kingdom of Heaven is theirs."*

Matthew 5:3 NLT

Lord, please help me be victorious over those
habits that do not serve me well.
Amen.

## The big three

*Three grand essentials to happiness in this life are something to do,*
*something to love, and something to hope for.*

Joseph Addison

---

If we're lucky, there's a childlike innocence that sticks with us into adulthood. It doesn't quite give up magical thinking and boundless hope. It's the part that trusts and believes that all things are possible, especially all those good things that we believe God would want for us.

You might remember moments in childhood when you asked your mother, "What can I do?" You may have been bored or tired of trying to come up with ways to entertain yourself, but the fact then and now is that you always need things to do that fulfill you and give meaning to your days.

Few of us would argue that we also need love, either in a significant relationship of love, or simply to have an object of our affection, such as a love for reading books. Each day then brings us reason to hope and to seek God's favor to grant us His versions of these big three … the right things to do, the right person or things to love, and the right reasons to have hope.

Keep seeking His direction.

*Three things will last forever—faith, hope, and love*
*—and the greatest of these is love.*

1 Corinthians 13:13 NLT

Lord, bless my life with these essential gifts of grace,
mercy, and abundant joy.
Amen.

## The heart of happiness

Where your pleasure is, there is your treasure;
where your treasure, there your heart;
where your heart, there your happiness.

St. Augustine

---

We often witness the good things that happen to us as causing us to be "light-hearted." When we're light-hearted, we're happy and we see the world in a totally different perspective than when we're blue. If you think about it, it's not the world that changes so much, it's our thinking.

The things that bring you sustainable joy become your treasures, they become a moment in time that you long to return to over and over again. They are the experiences that help you believe in God's plans for the greater good in your life. Your thoughts help to generate the atmosphere of possibility, and cause you to bow your head in prayer.

Treasure the things that bring you great joy today and give God the glory for the pleasures and the treasures He has put before you. He is faithful to you wherever you are, whatever you might think.

*Hold fast what is good.*

1 Thessalonians 5:21 NKJV

Lord, help me see the good things you have
provided for my happiness today.
Amen.

# You're a beauty!

*There is no cosmetic for beauty like happiness.*

Countess of Blessington

---

Think about the women in your life that you would define as "beautiful!" Are they beautiful because they have fantastic figures or incredible eyes or other "movie-star" features? Or are they beautiful for other reasons?

Beauty may show up on the outside, but it radiates from within. When your heart is beautiful, everything about you strikes others as beautiful too. When you're happy, the people who connect to you walk away smiling and happy as well.

God made you a natural beauty. He did so by giving you a heart of gold, a radiant smile, a loving spirit and a sense of joy that lets others know you belong to Him. In His eyes, you become more beautiful each day.

*Happiness makes a person smile.*

Proverbs 15:13 NCV

Lord, thank You for giving me a happy face.
I pray that I will always radiate Your joy.
Amen.

## You don't have to take it!

*The happiness for which our souls ache is one
undisturbed by success or failure, one which will root deeply
inside us and give inward relaxation, peace, and contentment,
no matter what the surface problems may be.*

Billy Graham

A popular saying suggests you "fake it, till you make it." The idea is that when things aren't going well, you pretend they are okay, until they get better again. If you don't have enough financial stability, you pretend you do until you are more solvent. If you are in a poor relationship, you act as though it is okay, until it is.

There's a grain of truth in that idea, but the fact is that with God you don't have to fake it. You don't have to pretend to be all right, when your heart is breaking or your soul is hurting. You don't have to try to look happy in the midst of trouble.

What you can do, is draw on the strength from His Spirit, the strength that He has placed within you and that can never be depleted. You can tap into the Source of all that is good and even when the outward circumstances don't seem to measure up, the inward circumstances will carry you and bring you peace.

God bless you with inner contentment that is abundantly real.

*Wisdom is enshrined in an understanding heart.*

Proverbs 14:33 NLT

Lord, help me to be truly content even when things do not
appear to be going well. Help me rest my heart and mind in You.

Amen.

## The trying experience

*Heroes are not the ones who never fail,*
*but the ones who never give up.*

Anonymous

———

By now, we've all been there. Some days it feels like you're in an enclosed space playing bumper cars, because everywhere you turn there's another obstacle. By the time you get out of the car, you don't even know who won because no one actually seemed to get anywhere.

When the chaos stops, you could walk away. You could throw up your hands and declare that it just isn't worth it. The best take away from a trying experience though is to simply keep trying. Walking away turns out to not really be a choice, it just means you accepted defeat, even when victory was meant to be yours.

Today, be a hero in your own eyes. See the obstacles and temporary bumps on your road as ones that will most likely get smoother if you just keep going. So today, just bump and pray and go on your way! God knows exactly where you're meant to go.

*Roads with turns should be made straight,*
*and rough roads should be made smooth.*

Luke 3:5 NCV

Lord, thank You for being with me even when the path is bumpy.
Help me to keep trying and to follow Your lead.
Amen.

# What's on your t-shirt?

Remember your ultimate purpose, and when you set yourself to your day's work or approach any activity in the world, let "Holiness to the Lord" be written upon your hearts in all that you do.

Richard Baxter

———◦◦◦◦◦◦◦———

Maybe you plan ahead about the clothes you'll wear when you get up in the morning. You know what you have to do for the day and so you pick something to wear that is appropriate. Other times, you probably just get up and throw on the first pair of jeans and T-shirt you find in the closet. It doesn't matter so much because you're just doing errands today and cleaning the house.

What you wear might not matter so much to others. You probably have a bunch of T-shirts that display your favorite seasonal elements or your favorite brand logo. What you wear on the inside, though, makes a big difference to how your day will go. Remembering whose you are and intentionally designing your day to include the part of you that is "Holy to the Lord" can make a big difference. It might clothe you in wisdom and strength and the willingness to forgive. It might just be the most beautiful part of your wardrobe.

*"Blessed are the pure in heart, for they shall see God."*

Matthew 5:8 NKJV

Lord, help me to wear my joy in You wherever I may be today.

Amen.

## When life hurts

*The times have never hurt anyone. Those who are hurt are human beings; those by whom they are hurt are also human beings. So, change human beings and the times will be changed.*

St. Augustine

You've been hurt before. You may still bear the burdens of childhood hurts, memories that don't ever seem to wash away. You may have experienced more recent hurtful relationships, sometimes caused by your own actions and sometimes caused by the actions of others.

It may sound like an excuse to say that "we're only human!" After all, human beings make mistakes and are sometimes thoughtless and unable to even see the hurt they cause. We all give ourselves an out.

As women of worth though, we want to have an objective that doesn't give us simple excuses. We want to do our best to act in ways that spare others from the hurts of life, at least as much as that is possible through us. God knows we are fragile creatures and that we are easily hurt. He seeks to protect our hearts and minds and He hopes that we will always do the same for those around us.

Let go of past hurts and be champions of kindness today.

*Do what is right and good in the sight of the Lord.*

Deuteronomy 6:18 NKJV

Lord, forgive me when I offend or hurt those near me in any way and help me to seek to be truly kind to others today.

Amen.

## Your personal point of view

Perspective is everything when you are experiencing
the challenges of life.

Joni Eareckson Tada

❖❖❖

It's somewhat daunting to realize that most of the opinions we hold, the perspective we have, and the attitudes we put forth, are shaped by our history and environment. What that means is that somewhere along the way we make choices about the things we believe to be important or worthy or beautiful. We take up the cause of preserving a historic mansion because we believe it has value for a new generation. Someone else votes to take the house down because they feel it gets in the way of progress.

Your point of view is shaped by your beliefs and that's why it is so essential to your well-being to embrace all that God wants you to know as you live each day. The more you are aware of His Presence in your life, the more your views will be molded by holiness. God offers you a new way to see things and He works by encouraging your Spirit, loving you as you are, and shaping the way you think and see the world. Let Him guide your thoughts today.

*"My thoughts are not your thoughts, nor are your ways*
*My ways," says the LORD.*

Isaiah 55:8 NKJV

Lord, bless me with the kinds of thoughts that
please You and cause me to honor Your name.
Amen.

## *We need each other*

We are each of us angels with only one wing, and we can only fly
embracing each other.

Luciano De Crescenzo

It's great to be an independent thinker and a solitary contributor
to society … sometimes. It's great to be able to take care of
ourselves and no one would argue against that, but even when
we operate on our own the majority of the time, we still need
other people. We need encouragement. We need support and
love. We need to have great advisors and people who make us
laugh at ourselves. We need the people who are different than
we are, who bring us a new perspective and help us to stay more
honest in our approach to life. Yes, we truly need each other.

When you think about it, God designed us for community. He
created us so that we could be loved by Him and so we could love
Him back. He also wanted us to do that for each other. Honor the
people who are your angels today, who make it possible for you
to fly, even when it feels like you're flying solo.

Let God raise you up today.

*Put on your new nature, created to be like God – truly righteous and holy.*

Ephesians 4:24 NLT

Lord, thank You for the people in my life who are truly my angels.
Amen.

# Friends and family

*It really boils down to this: that all life is interrelated. We are all caught in an inescapable network of mutuality, tied into a single garment of destiny. Whatever affects one destiny, affects all indirectly.*

Martin Luther King, Jr.

---

If you haven't shared enthusiastic hugs and joy with your friends and family members in a while, today is a great day to start. These people are your connections, your network. They keep you grounded and support your ideas and life direction. They are the threads that help you stay bound to the good things God wants from you. Honor them!

In a world that gives us so many options for social networking, we can get lost keeping up with everyone "out there." If you notice that the only time you're able to chat with your friends is on Facebook, perhaps it's time to step away from the cyber relationship life, and give them a call. Let them hear your voice and know that you truly care about them.

You have great connections. Keep them close to you in as many real ways as you can. Talking over a great cup of coffee or tea is still a good thing!

*"I tell you that if two of you on earth agree about something and pray for it, it will be done for you by My Father in heaven."*

Matthew 18:19 NCV

Lord, bless my friends and family today and help us to take the time to truly connect with one another.

Amen.

# A matter of the heart

*Without humility of heart all the other virtues by which one runs toward God seem – and are – absolutely worthless.*

Angela of Foligno

What does it really mean to be humble? Does it mean that we have to be wall flowers and fade into the scenery, never making our presence known or felt? Does it mean that we acknowledge everyone else as superior to us and so we always let them take the lead? Does it mean we never wear a fancy dress or get our hair done in a new style that makes us happy? No! It doesn't mean any of these things.

Humility is not about acting as though you are not valuable. Humility is a matter of the heart, a sense that you understand how blessed you really are by the talents you have been given and the material things that make your life comfortable. It's about knowing when to step back and applaud the people around you and when to take a bow because something you did turned out well.

Whatever you do, part of its value is tied to your attitude about it. Your humble heart makes a big difference in everything you do.

*Good people, rejoice and be happy in the Lord.*
*Sing all you whose hearts are right.*

Psalm 32:11 NCV

Lord, help me to have a humble heart and to know when
to step back and applaud those around me.

Amen.

WHEN IT SNOWS
*she has no fear*
FOR HER HOUSEHOLD,
FOR ALL OF THEM
ARE CLOTHED
IN SCARLET

PROVERBS 31:21

## *Know what you believe*

> We know what happens to people who stay
> in the middle of the road. They get run over.
>
> Aneurin Bevan

---

Making choices sometimes means we have to take sides. We have to know enough about what we believe to take a stand. If we believe that red is the best color in the world, chances are good that we have a number of red outfits in our closets and probably some red dishes in the kitchen. We like people to know that we have a special love for red.

If you go to church every Sunday and think that having faith is a nice thing then that's a start in taking a stand about what you believe. If you share your testimony with others whenever the opportunity arises, that tells people where you stand as well. On the other hand, if you have a faith you never talk about or demonstrate in any public way, people might not know what your faith means to you.

When we choose to follow God, He wants to know where we stand. He wants us to be willing to come out wearing our red shirts, shiny faces and bright dispositions because we are willing to tell the world what we know.

> Then Joshua said, "You are your own witnesses
> that you have chosen to serve the Lord."
>
> Joshua 24:22 NCV

Lord, help me to always be willing to take a stand for
You and let others know what I believe.
Amen.

## Smile! it's good for you

A kind heart is a fountain of gladness,
making everything in its vicinity freshen into smiles.

Washington Irving

---

Have you ever sat by a fountain on a warm, sunny day? You listen to the water as it sends its refreshing and cooling spray of water all around you. You hear children laughing who try to put their hands in the spray, or see people enjoying a calm, quiet moment just for themselves.

Kindness is like that. Kindness is the thing that makes people smile because it often comes unexpectedly. It rushes from nowhere in the face of someone passing by, or in the brief words of encouragement from a total stranger. It stops you in your tracks as you seek to take it in and hold on to the moment. It's your moment of sitting peacefully by the fountain.

May your kindness fall on others like a warming spray of joy, always bringing a cooling sense of hope and peace and charity.

*A kind woman gets respect.*

Proverbs 11:16 NCV

Lord, help me be ready at any moment
to share a smile and a bit of kindness.

Amen.

# Getting to know God

God is continually drawing us to Himself in
everything we experience.

Gerard Hughes

When you look back at your life, can you find those God moments? You know, those moments where you recognized that God was in the midst of what was going on, or that you felt His presence, or you knew without a doubt that He would help you get through something. You've probably had a lot of those moments because all your life, God has been there. Whether you were able to notice Him or not, doesn't change the fact that He has always known you and has walked with you since your birth.

You're in the process while you visit planet Earth of getting to know God. You're becoming more aware of what He can do to shape your life and guide your thoughts and direction. You're learning more all the time about what it means to be His daughter.

God uses everything He can to get your attention because He doesn't want to miss one opportunity for you to get to know Him better.

*By His power we live and move and exist.*

Acts 17:28 NCV

Lord, thank You for knowing me so well. Help me to be aware
of all the ways that I can get to know more of You.

Amen.

# *Cleaning up the messes*

Once you become aware that the main business that you are here for is to know God, most of life's problems fall into place of their own accord.

J. I. Packer

—⊹⊱⊱⊰⊰⊹—

You probably have friends who stick with you through thick and thin. That means they are always there for you in the good times and the messy times. They know you so well that they love you and would do anything for you. They are the best friends you've ever had.

You became friends with those people though because you share a special relationship. Not only are they concerned for you, but they celebrate with you when things go well and they want to share important life moments with you. The same is true in your relationship with God. You are His friend and He is concerned for your well-being. He also celebrates your joys and the things that give you a glad heart.

Your relationship with Him matters so much that He wants to get to know you better and He wants you to know what He can do to help any messy parts of life feel better. He will never, ever give up on you because you are so valuable to Him. Keep your heart open to all that God has for you today.

*"Be still and know that I am God."*

Psalm 46:10 NKJV

Lord, thank You for being with me in the good times and in the more difficult ones. Help me always seek to build my relationship with You.

Amen.

## Knowing yourself

*Human beings must be known to be loved;*
*but divine beings must be loved to be known.*

Blaise Pascal

Becoming the real authentic you is about really knowing yourself. It means that you know where your boundaries are and what "pushes your buttons" when you feel a bit angry. You know what kind of music you like and what makes an evening feel like fun. You know your fears and your hopes and your dreams. You know your short-comings and the things you secretly hope no one will ever know about you.

As in other relationships, you can love and appreciate yourself more when you know yourself well. In the case of knowing and loving God, it's a bit different. God seeks to help you know Him. He reveals Himself to you over time so that you can grasp more of His divine nature as you mature. You have worked to know more about Him because you already love Him.

God knows everything about you, even those secrets you might like to hide. He knows you and He loves you. Keep letting Him into your life, into every area of your being, and you will come to know Him as a true and loving friend.

*Everyone who loves has been born of God and knows God.*

1 John 4:7 NIV

Lord, help me to invite You further into my life so that I might know more of You and build my relationship with You.
Amen.

## *How you figure things out*

It's just human nature to try and figure things out. So, when we're in
the midst of a situation, we usually try to reason our way through it.

Joyce Meyer

---

When things aren't going well, it can feel like you've simply got
the wrong pieces for your personal jigsaw puzzle. The fact is that
like a good jigsaw puzzle, you can't always see the whole picture
until you get enough of the pieces together.

If you take one piece at a time, using a sort of trial and error,
learn as you go method, you'll find some of the right pieces. If
you build a framework that looks right, then you may simply
have to trust that you'll be able to finish the work even when
doubt sets in. The more you keep working with it, the better
you'll get and ultimately, your effort will pay off. Your skill will
improve with practice.

The final picture will come together, but it means you had
to know from the start that it would. You had to know that
the beginning and the end would take you to the same place
because truth begets truth and love begets love.

Figuring things out is partly about the end result, but it's
mostly about the process and how you get there is important to
God. Take it one piece at a time today.

*Faith means being sure of the things we hope for and knowing
that something is real even if we do not see it.*

Hebrews 11:1 NCV

Lord, help me to trust You as I put all the pieces of my life together.
Amen.

## *Heavenly hopes*

God's retirement plan is out of this world.

Anonymous

---

We tend to give thoughts of heaven a passing nod, knowing we may well have to deal with it sometime, but probably not today. We may go for a long time before we think of it again, only to be reminded when someone dear to us passes on or we read of tragedies elsewhere on the planet.

We may pray that we'll have an eternal life and even imagine that it will be so, but we may not live each day as though we truly have the hope of heaven in our future.

As we become stronger women of faith, women who understand the work God is trying to get done on earth and the part we might play in that work, the more we might reflect on our future hope and the fact of our own mortality.

One reason to reflect on your heavenly home is to remember that no matter what is going on for you here on earth, this isn't all there is. This isn't the end of your existence, and perhaps it's just the beginning. You're God's heavenly daughter as well as His earthly daughter and you always have a place to call home. The fact is that you arrived on earth with a round trip ticket.

*Jesus said, "I go to prepare a place for you."*

John 14:2 NKJV

Lord, thank You for giving me reminders of heaven,
especially on those days when I'm a little too tied to the earth.

Amen.

# *Remembering where we are*

*The world brings only change, it is never constant but in its disappointments. The world is but a great inn, where we are to stay a night or two, and be gone; what madness is it to set our heart upon our inn, as to forget our home?*

Thomas Watson

Whether you imagine yourself creating the starring role in your own drama, or you see your visit to earth as a short stay at an enormous inn, the fact is that the experience is fleeting and like any ride at an amusement park, is over before you know it.

You may still remember when you thought you'd live forever, or when you thought you'd never get to be 18 or 21 or whatever magical age you hoped would tell the world you had arrived.

Somehow as you've gotten older, the whole cycle of things seems to be spinning faster and faster. You feel like each day melts into the one coming in and months go by without you even taking notice.

However brief your stay at this inn called Earth, it is always with the knowledge that it only gets better from here. The Great Innkeeper of heaven already has the light on for you and awaits you with warm hugs and joy. Even so, He wants you to enjoy your visit because He provided the inn of Earth with great joy.

*In the beginning God created the heavens and the earth.*

Genesis 1:1 NLT

Lord, create an awareness of heaven in me so that
I might live in joy all the days of my life.
Amen.

## The reason for hope

God often gives in one brief moment
that which He has for a long time denied.

Thomas à Kempis

Have you ever set your heart on something that you thought was probably out of your reach, yet you couldn't let go of the idea? You filed it away and pulled it out every now and then to see if it still made your heart sing and it did. In fact, the truth is, you kept the hope alive for a long time because God Himself put that hope within you. Only He knows the perfect timing for your hopes and dreams to come to fruition.

Hope is a beautiful thing when it causes us to have to wait, and even more so when the waiting is turned into deep longing. Hope keeps us seeking more for ourselves. It keeps us focused on something that is truly important to us. It gives us a reason for sweet joy.

Today, review for a moment those things that you have hoped for in the past that have now come together. Look at the timing of those things and give God thanks and praise that He brought them to you at just the right moment.

*Hope deferred makes the heart sick, but a dream fulfilled is a tree of life.*

Proverbs 13:12 NLT

Lord, thank You for knowing me so well and for giving
me wonderful reasons to always have hope in You.

Amen.

## Big love

The love of God is like the Amazon River
flowing down to water one daisy.

Anonymous

One of the great themes of television and movie shows over the years is one that depicts one helpless person, struggling against the world, waiting for help and then suddenly, out of nowhere, comes the hero, swooping in to save the day. In some ways, your relationship with God is a little like that. He's your hero!

God would come to save you even if you were the only one left on the planet that was worthy of His love. He watches over you in the midst of troubles, giving you peace and comfort. He is near you in every life situation for just one reason, because He loves you.

God would be there, and He is there! He's the refreshing spirit that comes in like a cool breeze when things seem hot and sticky. He's the rainbow after too many clouds on a given day. You're one of His favorite beings and He will never forget about you and the things you need.

*The Lord God arranged for a leafy plant to grow there, and soon it*
*spread its broad leaves over Jonah's head, shading him from the sun.*
*This eased his discomfort, and Jonah was very grateful for the plant.*

Jonah 4:6 NLT

Lord, thank You for taking care of me. I know that You are protecting
me and providing for me in every way. I praise Your name!
Amen.

*Living in love*

In His love He clothes us, enfolds us and embraces us; that tender
love completely surrounds us, never to leave us.

Julian of Norwich

---

Have you ever been disappointed by someone you love? Maybe
they weren't there for you when you hoped they would be.
Maybe they did something to create tension between you or to
hurt your feelings. Maybe they didn't even realize what they did
to offend you, but you felt it, deep in your heart.

People may offend you. Even someone who loves you very
much, might offend you, but God will never offend you. God will
love you because of you and in spite of you, always seeking the
best for you in His grace and mercy.

When Jesus said He would be with you always, He didn't
mean that He'd be there just when you paid attention to Him. He
didn't mean that He'd be with you from nine to five, with maybe
a little break for lunch. He meant He'd be there always, every day,
every moment of your life and that's why nothing about you
surprises Him. He knows you better than you know yourself.

Let Him know right now how glad you are that you are never
alone, that you always can trust He is by your side.

*Jesus said, "I am with you always, to the very end of the age."*

Matthew 28:20 NIV

Dear Lord, thank You that Your precious love surrounds me always.
Amen.

## *Understanding perfection*

God, who needs nothing, loves into existence wholly superfluous
creatures in order that He may love and perfect them.

C. S. Lewis

———

Isn't it wonderful to know that God knows you're not perfect? He knows you are still learning and growing and becoming the woman He meant for you to be. He knows your imperfections and He makes it His aim to love you into being more than you are today. When you strive to learn more of Him and what He would want for you, and when you observe His Spirit in others and respond to it, He is able to instruct you and give you opportunities to grow. You are His beloved and He is proud of you each time you take a step in His direction.

God knows that human beings are imperfect. He knows that we make a lot of mistakes and that we make a lot of foolish choices. He is not sitting by in some cosmic arena waiting to see how many bad decisions you'll make, or how many times you might turn your back from Him. He's cheering you on, extending grace and mercy to you in every possible way.

Bless the work God is doing in your life and offer applause and praise and shouts of joy for what you are doing together.

*As for God, His way is perfect: The Lord's word is flawless;*
*He shields all who take refuge in Him.*

Psalm 18:30 NIV

Thank You, Lord, for keeping watch over me and guiding
me to perfectly love You in my heart, soul, and mind.
Amen.

## That rock in your shoe

*If God sends us on stony paths, He will provide us with strong shoes.*
Alexander MacLaren

———————

Did you ever have a tiny pebble in your shoe? At first, you might have thought you could keep walking anyway, that the little stone would reposition itself so that it would all be comfortable again. However, it didn't take long for you to realize that the pebble was not going to go away. In fact, the farther you walked, the more you knew that it would nag you. Finally, there was no choice but to stop everything, take off your shoe and send the pebble back to earth where it belonged.

Sometimes you have days like that. You know that you're uncertain about your direction, but you keep walking anyway. Now and then, you get a nagging thought that perhaps you should just stop walking and take some time to pray. The notion lingers and the further you walk, the more you feel something just isn't right. It takes some nagging, perhaps like having a stone in your shoe, but you finally stop everything, open your heart to God, receive a sense of peace, rise, and go your way again. Somehow the walking seems much easier.

*"This stone has heard everything the Lord said to us. It will be a witness to testify against you if you go back on your word to God."*

Joshua 24:27 NLT

Lord, just as the stone witnessed to the people of Israel,
let me pay attention when a stone causes me to have
to stop and pray and connect once more to You.

Amen.

## Knowing where you belong

You are to think of yourself as only existing in this world
to do God's will. To think that you are your own is as absurd
as to think you are self-created. It is an obvious first principle
that you belong completely to God.

William Law

Do you belong to any clubs? Maybe you belong to a gym where you go to work out during the week. Maybe you belong to a bowling league or to a book club. Why did you join? Usually, we join a club, or a church, or an organization because we feel the need to "belong" somewhere. We want to connect to people who think like we do. We want to participate in life in a positive way.

Now and then, we forget that we belong to God. We joined Him the day we accepted Jesus Christ into our lives and hearts. We do not exist here on our own. We do not exist for our own benefit.

God designed us to be in fellowship with each other so that we could share what we have learned, offer assistance when we're needed and have a place to go when we feel alone. It's great to know where you belong.

*The secret things belong to the Lord our God, but those things*
*which are revealed belong to us and to our children forever.*

Deuteronomy 29:29 NKJV

Lord, thank You for giving me a place to belong in Your kingdom.
Help me to embrace others who share a love for You.
Amen.

## *Be people-centered, anyway!*

People are unreasonable, illogical, and self-centered.
Love them anyway.

Anonymous

---

You've probably been hurt many times in your life by the thoughtless gestures or attitudes of people who are dear to you, and perhaps even by strangers who don't know you at all. Human beings have a long way to go to reach perfection and in that regard we're all seeking to become better than we are today. We want to be a blessing to each other and strengthen each other in all things.

When you encounter people who cause you to struggle through your feelings, who injure your sensitivities or simply act in a way that you can't understand, it's good to remember that all of us behave in ways we'd hate to admit sometimes.

All of us fall far short of the glory of God. We are seeking to be better people, and with that in mind, we must seek to love others in spite of their acts and actions. After all, it is truly how God loves us.

*All have sinned and fall short of the glory of God, and all are justified freely by His grace through the redemption that came by Christ Jesus.*

Romans 3:23-24 NIV

Lord, thank You for declaring me not guilty, when I know I've been guilty many times of things that offend You and people I love. Help me to live up to Your standards.
Amen.

## *Hold that thought!*

Words must be weighed, not counted.

Anonymous

⋯⋯⋯⋯✕⋯⋯⋯⋯

No doubt you stay away from gossipy people who seem to always have a story to tell of someone else's troubles and heartbreaks. You're wise to do so because those same story tellers probably waste no time telling your stories too, whether they know them to be true or not.

It's curious how often we get taken in by those stories that may give us pause, and yet fail to pause and simply pray for the people in question. If someone was circulating a story about you that was only partially true, would you want them to share their version with someone else, or would it be better if they simply offered your situation up to the Lord, the only One who can really do something about it.

The next time someone chooses to tell you their stories about the hard luck of someone else, step back and suggest that the two of you say a prayer, and then move on, because you have far better things to do.

*Without wood a fire goes out; without a gossip a quarrel dies down. As charcoal to embers and as wood to fire, so is a quarrelsome person for kindling strife. The words of a gossip are like choice morsels; they go down to the inmost parts.*

Proverbs 26:20-22 NIV

Lord, help me to walk away from those who share gossip
and pray for all Your people in need.

Amen.

# Abounding in blessings

*Be on the lookout for mercies. The more we look for them, the more of them we see … Better to lose count while naming your blessings than to lose your blessings to counting your troubles.*

Anonymous

---

If your blessings don't seem to be piling up all around you like leaves on a breezy fall day, maybe it's because you've forgotten how to count them, or how to take note of them. After all, you could start with having a warm bed, getting a good night's sleep, enjoying your morning routine, and knowing that you have work that only you can do in front of you. Then you could remember that your heart functions perfectly and your eyes can see the road ahead of you, and by the time you do all that, you might realize that you are indeed, abounding in blessings.

It's easy to get caught up in the drama of the day, paying close attention to those things that aren't quite going your way. When you do, you can get stuck there like a butterfly in a net, knowing there are ways to get out, but uncertain how to do that.

If you're getting tired of counting all the things that are not quite up to par in your life, move over to the more positive side and start thanking God for each thing that has been perfectly given to you. You may be amazed at how wealthy you really are!

*May God be gracious to us and bless us and make His face shine on us.*

Psalm 67:1 NIV

Lord, thank You for Your infinite blessings, Your kindness, mercy and love. Help me to share those gifts with others today.

Amen.

# Becoming more grateful

See that you do not forget what you were before, lest you take for granted the grace and mercy you received from God and forget to express your gratitude each day.

Martin Luther

Part of the beauty of your desire to become a woman of even greater worth is that you are intentional about your efforts. You know that you were not totally what you meant to be before. You know you aren't there yet. But, you also know that with God's help, you'll be shaped and renewed and beautifully designed in the ways you were meant to be.

If you need to, put a "before" and "after" picture on your refrigerator, just like the women do who have successfully lost weight in their favorite program or those who have significantly changed a hair style. Remember who you were only so that you can give God the glory for who you are becoming. He didn't set any limits on His love for you and His willingness to create a more wonderful you. That means you have no limits to your praise and gratitude.

*We are brought down to the dust; our bodies cling to the ground.*
*Rise up and help us; rescue us because of Your unfailing love.*

Psalm 44:25-26 NIV

Lord, thank You for rescuing me and restoring me and helping
me to become more of the woman You want me to be.
I remember who I was and I long for who I am yet to be.
Amen.

## More tape, please!

When God measures the greatness of an individual,
He puts the tape measure around the heart not the head.

Anonymous

Imagine that God wants to measure all that you are by putting a tape measure around your heart. How much tape would He need? Chances are that you would feel it all depends on the day. After all, some days you feel warm and generous and loving to everyone. Other days, you want to hide away from the world and protect yourself from life's drama.

The wonderful thing is that the size of your heart doesn't depend so much on how you feel on any given day. It depends on how much of God's love you allow to go through you and out to the rest of the world. It depends on how much love you're willing to share. The size of your heart is a matter of love and you have a lot of love to bless those around you. No doubt, the more you discover about yourself as you lean in closer to God, the more you'll realize that your heart is bigger than you even imagined. God may indeed need a bigger tape measure.

*A good person produces good things from the treasury of a good heart.*

Matthew 12:35 NLT

Lord, bless me with a desire to have a bigger heart for
those around me, being willing to see any affliction and offer
my help however You lead me to do.

Amen.

## *Keep going!*

*If you are pleased with where you are, you have*
*stopped already. If you say, "It is enough," you are lost.*
*Keep on walking, moving forward, trying for the goal. Don't*
*try to stop on the way, or to go back, or to deviate from it.*

St. Augustine

It's good to be satisfied. God wants you to be content with what He gives you and what He does for you. He wants you to be at peace about yourself and all that you are meant to be. Most of us cannot live long enough to become all that God knows we can be, but we don't let that stop us. We keep turning over a new leaf, checking for new ideas and direction, and praying that He'll keep guiding us forward.

Celebrate where you are right now. Rejoice that God has brought you this far. Then turn another page, pray another prayer for guidance, and understand that you are still on your way to becoming all you can be. You're a daughter of a King and there are lots of things to learn about sharing in His kingdom. Ask Him what you need to work on this week.

*No longer will you need the sun to shine by day, nor the moon*
*to give its light by night, for the Lord your God will be your*
*everlasting light, and your God will be your glory.*

Isaiah 60:19 NLT

Lord, thank You for being an everlasting light in my life. Help me to always look to You when the world seems dark to me and help me to never stop wanting to grow more aware of You and Your love.
Amen.

## *Another reason for hope*

Nothing worth doing is completed in our lifetime;
therefore we must be saved by hope.

Reinhold Niebuhr

---

Take a moment and think about the hopes and dreams you had just five years ago. Are they the same now as they were then? Have you changed or received the blessings you wanted by now? Chances are that you have gotten answers to some of your prayers and you have seen some dreams come true. God is gracious and good and promises to look after us. You probably also have other dreams that have not yet begun to manifest, ones that you wonder about, or believe are too hard even for God to handle.

Dreams are a matter of hope. They are just ahead, over the hill and around the bend. We know they are there, but we're not far enough along to see them come into view. God wants you to have dreams and aspirations and hopes. He wants you to strive to do more and to be more and to live more generously and abundantly. He's drawing you closer, to the dreams He has prepared and He's giving you a lifetime to get there. Live in His hope each day.

*Continue in your faith, established and firm,
and do not move from the hope held out in the gospel.*

Colossians 1:23 NIV

Lord, help me be ever faithful to You and to the hopes in my heart.
I long to fulfill my dreams according to Your will and purpose.
Amen.

# *Never say never!*

*There are no hopeless situations; there are only people*
*who have grown hopeless about them.*

Clare Boothe Luce

No matter how optimistic you are, you may have given up on some of your dreams by now. You may have decided that it's just not meant to be for you to be a ballerina or an Olympic athlete. It's realistic at some point to let go of the fanciful dreams we might have harbored as teenagers and young women.

But where are you now? Are you living the dream you wanted for yourself in any way? Are you seeing God's gracious hand at work in your life each day? Are you tempted to give up hoping for things that just seem to never come together no matter how often you've prayed for a better result?

It may be tempting for you to throw in the towel and decide to simply give up, in fact, it may be the right thing to do. However, God has something better for you and He knows what joy will be yours when you get on the path He alone has designed. He knows your heart will blossom with the fragrance of new hope and joy. Let Him carry you back to the place of great hope today.

*For in this hope we were saved. But hope that is seen is no hope at all.*
*Who hopes for what they already have? But if we hope for what*
*we do not yet have, we wait for it patiently.*

Romans 8:24-25 NIV

Lord, I will continue to hope for the things that are dear to my heart
until You take those desires away. Help me to continue in hope.
Amen.

# *How can you help?*

Therefore, sisters, if you wish to lay good foundations, each of you must try to be the least of all, and the slave of God, and must seek a way and means to please and serve all your companions.

Teresa of Avila

Chances are when you read the story of Mary and Martha, you're pretty much on Martha's side. Martha was used to serving, but she didn't always like the idea that the responsibility seemed to all be on her shoulders. Why could Mary just sit there at Jesus' feet?

We have to take the time to sit at God's feet and really get to know what He wants from us. We have to immerse ourselves in His stories and His Spirit so that when we serve others we don't grow weary or bitter or angry. That's what Martha was missing. She didn't get a chance to sit quietly with her Savior and she was still hungry for Him.

You have that chance though. You can be of great service to those you love every time you take some time alone with the One who fills your soul to overflowing.

*Listen, O daughter, consider and incline your ear; forget your own people also,*
*and your father's house; so the King will greatly desire your beauty;*
*because He is your Lord, worship Him.*

Psalm 45:10-11 NKJV

Lord, let me honor You with the works of my hands
and with my heart my whole life through.
Amen.

*Laughing matters*

*Humor is the great thing, the saving thing.*
*The minute it crops up, all our irritations and resentments*
*slip away and a sunny spirit takes their place.*

Mark Twain

Jesus wept. He also laughed! We need to practice His presence with others by showing our sunnier selves, our playful spirits. After all, we've got more reasons to smile than anyone else, because we know the future is clear and bright.

Laughter is certainly good for your face and it's good for the soul. It reminds you that there are lots of things to sing about, cheer about, and enjoy. We were meant to enjoy all that we have been given because that pleases your heavenly Father. How would you feel if your children never found a reason to smile or laugh?

Today, stop to consider all the things that tickle your funny bone. If you don't find enough reasons to smile, check with some friends and find out what causes their lights to shine. After all, you were designed to walk in the sunshine.

*Sarah said, "God has brought me laughter,*
*and everyone who hears about this will laugh with me."*

Genesis 21:6 NIV

Lord, clearly You have a sense of humor since You built
an ability to laugh into each of our spirits. Remind me that
sometimes a smile is the best way to lighten the load.
Amen.

# Imagine that!

*I am enough of an artist to draw freely upon my imagination.*
*Imagination is more important than knowledge.*
*Knowledge is limited. Imagination encircles the world.*

Albert Einstein

You're like a diamond with so many sides and angles, you can glow in the dark. You have more talents than you have even discovered. Perhaps when you think of Albert Einstein, you don't think of him as an artist. You may see him as a scientist or an inventor or even a philosopher, but perhaps not an artist.

What about you? Do you define yourself by the work you do and then forget that you're a lot of other things too? You may be a teacher or a dancer or a skilled computer geek, but probably you're a mom, a friend, a volunteer, a choir member, a baker, a housecleaner, a cook, a counselor, and a whole host of other things. You're amazing!

You definitely have knowledge to speak on a good many subjects and you have talents and skills, but if you allow yourself to drift away through your imagination, you might discover the keys to doors you have not even opened yet. God knows they are there and He wants you to imagine being everything you can possibly be.

*"According to your faith let it be done to you."*
Matthew 9:29 NIV

Lord, help me to believe that there is much more that I can do, joys I have not yet discovered that You will guide me to find. Bless my faith.
Amen.

# I'm possible!

Until we reach for the impossible through fervent,
faith-filled prayers, we will never fulfill our created purpose!

David Smithers

---

You probably know people who always start with why something can't be done, before they ever really consider how to get it done. They have a default button that simply says, "no" about almost anything. For them, any obstacle takes away a possibility.

Not you though! You have a track record of answered prayers and some of those things seemed pretty impossible at the time. You make things possible each time you say "yes" to an idea, add a prayer to get the right direction, and bring a positive spirit to any situation.

Possibility thinkers don't limit themselves by what they see, or sometimes by the "facts" that are before them. They step out in faith, seeking the favor of the One who can make all things come together for good, and solutions they never imagined present themselves. With God, and with your prayers, all things are possible!

*We know that God causes everything to work together for the good*
*of those who love God and are called according to His purpose for them.*

Romans 8:28 NLT

Lord, I believe You called me to be a possibility thinker and to
believe that You will work out the details of things I do not yet see.
I believe in all that You have for me to accomplish.

Amen.

# *Be strong!*

No one can make you feel inferior without your consent.

Eleanor Roosevelt

———————————

Some people just seem to have it all together! They enter a room with a big smile and everyone turns to embrace them. They have an easy air of confidence and charm and the world gathers near. People like that might unintentionally make you feel inferior. You look at who they are or what they've accomplished and you imagine that you don't quite measure up.

Women have cycled in and around this dilemma since they were waiting to be picked for a dance at the school gym or hoping to be elected to the student council. When it always seems someone else might be better for the job than you would be, maybe you have forgotten how strong you are.

Your strength comes from God's Spirit of grace and truth. He pours that Spirit on you whenever you need His help. You are strong in Him at all times even when you don't think you are. Don't spend time giving your strength and power away to others that you assume are more qualified than you are. God has fully equipped you to do the work He has planned and no one else can do it better than you can. Stick to your strengths … in Him!

*"In quietness and trust is your strength."*

Isaiah 30:15 NIV

Lord, help me to escape those old ideas that hold me back
and keep me from being all that You would have me be.
Let me find my strength in You.
Amen.

## Cleaning up the interior!

*If better were within, better would come out.*

Thomas Fuller

Since we're all a work in progress, making an effort to be better people, it's probably safe to assume that we have days when thoughts emerge from our subconscious minds that surprise us. Sometimes they are foolish thoughts and sometimes they're even mean thoughts and we're not even sure where they may be coming from. The best we can do is to keep trying to sweep out the cobwebs of those thoughts and ideas that really don't reflect who we are, and clean up our interior design.

Of course, we can't really do that by ourselves. We need help. That's what God does. He sees where we need work and gets busy handing us a broom to clean up the places that are still a mess. Maybe those errant thoughts come to mind simply so you can recognize them for what they are, pray for cleansing and get on with your life.

Create in me a clean heart, O God!

*Create in me a clean heart, O God, and renew a steadfast spirit within me.*

Psalm 51:10 NKJV

Lord, I lean into You and lean on You to help me be the
best woman I can be for the sake of Your kingdom.
Purify my thoughts and help me to shine Your light today.

Amen.

## *Mountains out of mole hills*

Jealousy sees with opera glasses, making little things big;
dwarfs are changed into giants and suspicions into truths.

Cervantes

———————

Envy is an odd thing. It may even surprise you when it comes swooping into your thoughts. You may think that you're not really a jealous person, until your co-worker gets recognition for something you put twice the amount of work into, or your ideas get shared by your boss without any credit being given to you. It's hard not to have moments of jealousy.

God knows you and what you've done and so the fact is, you already have great recognition for your efforts. Trying too hard to be sure the rest of the world gets how wonderful you are, might not serve you as well.

Look at the things that cause you momentary stirrings of jealousy and give them all to God. He delights in you and knows everything about you. He wants you to have total faith and confidence in the woman He designed you to be.

*I almost lost my footing. My feet were slipping, and I was almost gone. For I envied
the proud when I saw them prosper despite their wickedness.*

Psalm 73:2-3 NLT

Lord, help me to keep away from envious thoughts.
I realize that I don't always understand when things don't
appear fair in this life, but I know that You are the ultimate
judge and You know what motivates my heart.
Amen.

## *Your favorite color*

Do you sometimes forget that you have something amazing to celebrate every single day? What if you simply woke up and thanked God for the very fact that you were awake? What if you thanked Him for your fuzzy slippers and your hot coffee? Your list would be unending.

God has designed a world for you that is full of character and color. That means nothing about it is commonplace or boring. Everything about it is worth giving Him the praise and the glory.

You may have favorite colors, like daffodil yellow or rose red, and as simple as those things seem, they bring you delight. God wants you to delight in His handiwork all the time. Look around you today and see if you can begin to count all the colors you see that make your life radiant and joyful. Thank God for giving you a bold, bright, beautiful world to discover and enjoy.

*God said, "I give you every seed-bearing plant on
the face of the whole earth and every tree that has fruit
with seed in it. They will be yours for food."*

Genesis 1:29 NIV

Lord, thank You for feeding me all the richness of life from the
abundance of Your creation. I marvel at all You have done.
Amen.

SHE IS
CLOTHED WITH
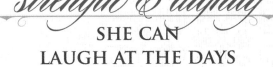
SHE CAN
LAUGH AT THE DAYS
TO COME

PROVERBS 31:25

## *Let your joy overflow*

The great enduring realities are love and service. Joy is the
holy fire that keeps our purpose warm, and our intelligence
aglow. Resolve to keep happy, and your joy and you shall
form an invincible host against difficulty.

Helen Keller

---

Maintaining a joyful attitude may seem like an insignificant
goal, but if you've tried to do so even for the space of one whole
day, you recognize the challenge it presents. God wants you to
experience abundance and joy so that it washes over you like
a cool rain on a hot day with a kind of peace that quiets every
negative thought within you.

Having a joyful spirit is not necessarily about your present
circumstances, but it is about your sense of knowing that you
always have a future and a hope. Hope gives way to joy no
matter what you're going through.

As you love and serve others, you'll recognize how much
giving adds to the joy that flows through your heart and soul.
It's in that perfect place that you connect with your Savior, the
Source of all your joy.

*Light shines on those who do right; joy belongs to those who are honest.*
*Rejoice in the Lord, you who do right. Praise His holy name.*

Psalm 97:11-12 NCV

Lord, thank You for being the Author of joy and of all
things that bring meaning and value to my life.
Help me to love others with that kind of joy.

Amen.

## *Remarkable you!*

*Let us preach You, dear Jesus, without preaching … not by words but by our example … by the casting force, the sympathetic influence of what we do, the evident fullness of the love our hearts bear to You. Amen.*

Mother Teresa

You're a woman with an incredible heart. You shine for God in just the right ways and share your love with those who might not see His divine presence otherwise. You help them to understand that God is near.

Sure, you may not believe you're quite that fabulous every day of the week and you probably have moments when you're less willing or able to be a quiet beacon of joy for the Lord, but you do it more than you realize. You influence those around you simply be being a kind and warm person.

Today, remember wherever you are that it's okay to be remarkable, to be an outstanding woman for God. You're blessed to be a blessing.

*"I will bless those who bless you, and I will place a curse on those who harm you. And all the people on earth will be blessed through you."*

Genesis 12:3 NCV

Lord, thank You for blessing my life with so many wonderful things to appreciate and delightful moments to share. Help me to always be willing to show Your love to others.

Amen.

## *That's so tempting!*

Whatever good is to be attained, struggle is necessary.
So do not fear temptations, but rejoice in them, for they
lead to achievement. God helps and protects you.

St. Barsanuphius

The more life presents its challenges to you, the harder it is to step away from those easy solutions that come through to tempt you. Our enemy knows when we're down and when we're most vulnerable. He delights in our plight and tries to get us further off track. Sometimes we let him in without even realizing it.

God knows we need Him to be close to us and so His words come through loud and clear each time we pray, "Lead us not into temptation, but deliver us from the evil one" (Matthew 6:13). Temptation isn't unusual, it sits out in the open on almost any street corner and beckons you. When you feel drawn in its direction, stop everything and ask God to take your hand and walk with you until you're safe again.

God is willing to guide you so that temptation does not destroy the things you've worked so hard to achieve. He will guide you and protect you.

*"Watch and pray, lest you enter into temptation.*
*The spirit indeed is willing, but the flesh is weak."*

Matthew 26:41 NKJV

Lord, I am weaker than I even like to admit. Please help me
to avoid those temptations that would only hold me back
and keep me from being all that I can be for You.
Amen.

# Celebrate wonderful you!

*If doing a good act in public will excite others to do more good,*
*then … "Let your Light shine to all …" Miss no opportunity to do good.*

John Wesley

Do you ever stop to simply celebrate the fact that you were born and that your life makes a difference to the people around you? You are somebody's special friend, beloved family member, or generous partner. You are someone whom others have come to count on and you make their days go by more joyfully.

God designed you in a unique way. He didn't get out cookie cutters and create you just like everyone else, molded from His template as simply a reflection of those around you. No! He designed you from head to toe to be His own special creation, His own bit of light in the world. When He looks at you, great joy fills His Spirit because He knows that you do not miss any opportunity to do good things for those close to you.

Wherever you go today, pay special attention to the chances you have to beam your smile, radiate your love, and delight those near you in a special way. It's always your day to shine!

*"You should be a light for other people. Live so that they will see the good things*
*you do and will praise your Father in heaven."*

Matthew 5:16 NCV

Lord, thank You for shining Your amazing light directly into my heart.
Help me to share the blessing of Your joy and love with others.

Amen.

## Living in harmony

*Tune me, O Lord, into one harmony with Thee, one full responsive vibrant chord; unto Thy praise, all love and melody, tune me, O Lord.*

Christina Rossetti

Sometimes you have to take your car in for a tune-up. It looks good on the outside and it still runs okay, but it's not running at its peak performance. It simply gets a little out of sync with what it normally delivers.

You are the same way. You still look good on the outside and you're still operating okay in the day to day world, but you're not really in tune, not really running at your peak performance level. That could mean that you're simply in need of a little extra time in prayer and Bible reading. It could mean that you need to quiet the world and reconnect with God's Spirit.

When you're feeling a bit out of tune, a bit frazzled and not quite capable of finding the harmony of life again, then make an appointment with yourself and with the One who loves you more than anything, for a personal tune-up. It could make all the difference.

*Live in harmony with one another.*

Romans 12:16 NIV

Lord, please help me get up to speed with what
You want me to be. I am not feeling like I'm especially in
tune now and I know I need Your help.
Amen.

## How about a picnic?

There is not one blade of grass, and there is no color in this world that
is not intended to make us rejoice.

John Calvin

Perhaps we need the rainy, gloomier days to remind us how inspired we are by the sunny and glorious ones. God has blessed the landscape wherever we live with infinite beauty, intricate design and incredible color. He didn't hold back one thing when it came to using His full imagination or His great creative ability. The outcome of His creativity is the blessing of the world we see and get to celebrate being part of every day.

If your imagination is suffering, then maybe it's time to stop everything, pack a lunch and go on a picnic. Find a spot somewhere to simply take in the beauty of all that you can see and then give thanks to your heavenly Father for making it all possible.

When you have had your fill of it all, then remember as you leave that place, that God has made all things possible for you too. He created you and everything you need to become the woman He wants you to be. Praise His name!

*The Lord is good. His unfailing love continues forever,*
*and His faithfulness continues to each generation.*

Psalm 100:5 NLT

Lord, You are indeed the Creator of all that is beautiful
in the world and in my life. Let me always remember to take
time to rest quietly in the garden with You.

Amen.

## *Thinking things through*

Watch your thoughts; they become words.
Watch your words; they become actions.
Watch your actions; they become habits.
Watch your habits; they become character.
Watch your character; for it becomes your destiny!

Anonymous

What do you listen to the most? Do you hear God's voice as He seeks to guide your life, as you read His Word, or sit with Him in prayer? Or do you let in the voices of the world until they become so loud that you are surrounded by chaos and noise?

The things you think about most will be the things that drive you to take an action and it is your actions that need guidance every day. We seek God's favor so that all we do will please Him and create opportunities for those around us to be blessed.

When your thoughts are out of line, that is, not in line with God's intention for your life, you need to come back to Him and seek Him once again. Let His words come into your heart and mind and your actions will bring you the fruit of goodness and joy. Listen for His voice and look for the things that bring you to your knees in praise today.

*Lord, listen to my prayer; let my cry for help come to You.*
*Do not hide from me in my time of trouble.*

Psalm 102:1-2 NCV

Lord, I hear the noise of the world way too much. Please help me be quiet enough to hear Your words of love and encouragement today.
Amen.

## *Let the good times roll*

Know that joy is rarer, more difficult, and more beautiful than sadness.
Once you make this all-important discovery, you must embrace joy as
a moral obligation.

André Gide

You probably never really considered the idea of embracing joy as a "moral obligation." After all, joy doesn't seem like something you can control or feel morally obligated about because it just happens to you, doesn't it?

Like other things in life, joy doesn't just happen. You create it and give it room to be in your presence. You find joy in little things, as in a conversation with a friend, or in your daughter's sweet smile. You sense the gift and the blessing of those things and it changes everything about your day. Joy then, is about the attitudes you hold toward life in general, toward the people around you, and toward all the possibilities that can be yours.

If you haven't actually made being a joyful person a life priority, you might want to examine why not. Try to embrace joy wherever you find it and carry it in your heart and mind. It will color the world for you in a brand-new way. Let the good times roll!

*Happiness makes a person smile, but sadness can break a person's spirit.*

Proverbs 15:13 NCV

Lord, You have blessed me with a happy heart.
Thank You for reminding me today what a gift that truly is.
Amen.

# Giving yourself a break

*Above all things, never think that you're not good*
*enough yourself. A person should never think that. My belief is*
*that in life people will take you at your own reckoning.*
Anthony Trollope

You know you do a lot of things right, and you do a lot of good things for the people who are dear to you. You're probably good at giving encouragement and praise to those around you. Also at recognizing that we all make mistakes and that we should forgive ourselves and move on. You're probably good at understanding the best ways to see things until it comes to you. Why?

Most of us are harder on ourselves than we are on anyone else. We need to give ourselves a break. We need to forgive our impulsive decisions and our unwise choices. When we do that, we give God room to help repair what we've done and move us forward again.

With each new day, you have a choice. You can keep choosing to put yourself up for ridicule, or you can quiet those voices by declaring that God is helping you even now to become a fabulous woman of great worth.

*There you will remember your conduct and all the actions by which you have*
*defiled yourselves, and you will loathe yourselves for all the evil you have done.*
Ezekiel 20:43 NIV

Lord, the Old Testament prophet was so right when he warned people that they wouldn't like themselves when they acted badly. Thank You for sending Jesus to help people like me to act better.
Amen.

*Friends matter*

*My friends have made the story of my life. In a thousand ways they have turned my limitations into beautiful privileges, and enabled me to walk serene and happy in the shadow cast by my deprivation.*

Helen Keller

Can you even imagine what your life would be like without the people who have become close to you, whom you cherish as your special friends? God knows we need each other to thrive. It is our friends who make life more bearable when trouble persists, and more enjoyable when happiness abounds.

Celebrate your friends and your relationships and remind yourself that being the right kind of friend to them makes a great difference in their lives. God has scattered beautiful stories of friendship all throughout the Scriptures to give us examples of what it truly means to connect heart to heart with others.

On the days when you feel limited by your own abilities or disabilities, remember that you are not alone, for you have terrific friends, and you have the friendship of the One who loves you more than anyone else can. God has called you His friend!

*A friend loves at all times.*

Proverbs 17:17 NIV

Lord, thank You for blessing my life so fully with friends
who mean the world to me. Thank You for them all.

Amen.

## Strike up the band

*Music is for the soul what wind is for the ship,*
*blowing her onwards in the direction in which she is steered.*

William Booth

Some days are simply for humming along. You can feel the music in your spirit as you start the day, and it keeps you in tune and delivers harmony to everything you do. You've got the music in you.

God equipped you with every possible form of joy and your appreciation for listening to music, playing an instrument, or simply being able to hum along to a good tune, is His gift to you.

Whatever is going on in your life today, you may not exactly feel like you're ready to strike up the band, but you can always soothe your soul by singing hymns of praise and clearing your head with the sweet, soft sounds of music. Sing to God and give Him a chance to hear your beautiful voice of praise.

*Sing a new song to Him; play well and joyfully.*

Psalm 33:3 NCV

Lord, I'm not sure I have the best singing voice, but perhaps
by the time it reaches Your ears, it sounds glorious.
I sing to You my loving praises.
Amen.

## *Keep on dancing*

*Dancing is the loftiest, the most moving, the most beautiful of the arts, because it is no mere translation or abstraction from life; it is life itself.*

Havelock Ellis

If you're starting to feel like you have two left feet and somehow missed your dance lessons, think again. You don't have to be a talented dancer, knowing the proper form and every nuance of the next step in order to become immersed in the dance itself. The important thing is to join in and become part of the music and let your spirit rejoice in the melody.

Maybe you haven't actually thought of your life as a dance, but whether you fancy yourself a waltz or a foxtrot, you are moving with a rhythm that is honored by your Father in heaven. He wants you to share in the music of all that He created and He wants to bring joy to your life.

If you've forgotten that among all the other things you are, you're meant to be a woman of joy, then dust off your dance shoes and let the music begin.

*They should praise Him with dancing. They should sing praises to Him with tambourines and harps.*

Psalm 149:3 NCV

Lord, thank You for inviting me into the dance.
Let me follow Your lead every day of my life.
Amen.

## On busy bee wings

*It is not the mere touching of the flower by the bee that gathers honey, but her abiding for a time on the flower that draws out the sweet.*

Thomas Brooks

We've become so used to a disposable, instant gratification kind of world that pausing even for a moment has fallen into ill favor. We struggle with finding quiet time or chastise ourselves when we choose to relax. After all, we're supposed to be continually productive, constantly doing things, or so our culture might suggest.

If we look at the bee example, though, we come to realize that good things happen when we rest as well. When we sleep, we're able to renew ourselves and be refreshed to meet a new day. The honeybee sits quietly on the flower, knowing that its process is as important as the outcome.

Sit quietly with your sweet Savior today, and you will find all the goodness a day can bring.

*Bless the Lord, all His works, in all places of His dominion.*
*Bless the Lord, O my soul!*

Psalm 103:22 NKJV

Lord, I want to relax with You and gather strength from You.
Help me to create more opportunities to rest beneath Your wings.
Amen.

# Worthy woman

*The quality of a person's life is in direct proportion to their commitment to excellence, regardless of their chosen field of endeavor.*

Vincent T. Lombardi

You probably have people you admire. They may be people in the limelight in some way, faith leaders or celebrities. If you really think about it, what is it about them that catches your attention? What makes you want to emulate them in your own way?

One of the things that makes you a worthy and wonderful woman in the sight of God is that you don't give up. You keep trying to improve yourself, trying to find ways to foster excellence. You're committed to this goal and that makes a difference. Other people can see how hard you try, and your efforts make them proud of you and make them want to try harder as well.

Whatever your goal is, whatever your focus is in your life right now, you'll get there if you persist in the effort. You know the value of hard work and you're not afraid of that. You know where you want to go so stand up and be counted among those to be admired in the world. You are a woman of worth!

*We encouraged you, we urged you, and we insisted that you live good lives for God, who calls you to His glorious kingdom.*

1 Thessalonians 2:12 NCV

Lord, I am making an effort to become more of what
You designed me to be. I'm grateful that You think so highly of me,
and that You are as proud of me as any Father could be.
Amen.

# Stronger than you think

*She can who thinks she can, and she can't who thinks she can't.*
*This is an inexorable, indisputable law.*

Henry Ford (adapted)

Do you like to try new things? You may like to try something new if you have a sense that you can do it pretty well. You may not be as eager if you simply imagine that there's no way you could ever accomplish the task. Though we have inherent abilities and aptitudes, a large measure of our success in any part of life has to do with how we perceive it. We tend to get the results we believed we would.

God often has challenged our thinking and one way He does that is to remind us that if we believe something, then we will receive it. That sounds simple enough, but if your self-talk is always at the place of impossibility, then chances are you haven't believed enough to receive something important to you.

If you think you can win, the odds are, you will. If you think that nothing but defeat lies in front of you, that result will find its way to you. What do you want? Ask God for it, believe it, and receive it. He's on your side!

*"O, you of little faith, why did you doubt?"*

Matthew 14:31 NKJV

Lord, help me to be more of a "can-do" woman. Help me to believe that if You called me to do something, no matter how difficult it might look, with Your strength I can do it. Thank You, Lord!

Amen.

# Busy, busy, busy!

*O Lord! You know how busy I must be this day;*
*if I forget You, do not forget me!*

Sir Jacob Astley

If you're like most women, you've got about six too many things on your to-do list for today. You feel overwhelmed before you even walk out the door, tired before the day even truly begins.

No doubt, everything on your list is important. You've already prioritized it and delegated what you could, so what's wrong with just bucking up and moving like a freight train to get the work done. Nothing! There's nothing wrong with anything you have to do as long as you don't try to accomplish it alone. If you remember to stop, pray, and invite Christ into your day, you'll find it goes much more smoothly. You'll find that you have the strength to get it all done.

The busier you are, the more you need to make it a point to pray first. If you think the one thing you can take off the list is prayer, your list will seem never-ending. God wants you to accomplish great things, but He wants to help you do it.

*I find rest in God; only He can save me. He is my rock and my salvation.*
*He is my defender; I will not be defeated.*

Psalm 62:1-2 NCV

Lord, thank You for reminding me how much You long to
be part of the things I do. I pray that You will be with me
every step of the way as I go about my day.
Amen.

## Paying attention to your business!

We should have much more peace if we would not busy
ourselves with the sayings and doings of others.

Thomas à Kempis

Every now and then you get distracted. You aren't distracted by
your work load or your household chores this time, but you're
distracted by a bit of local gossip, some hearsay about a family
member or an old friend. You don't want to get caught up in it,
but before you know it, you become part of the drama, part of
the fuel that keeps gossip's fires burning.

Though it's never pleasant to be admonished to "mind your
own business," the fact is that it is good advice. If we keep focused
on our own business, which usually has some necessary repairs
needed anyway, we can change things for the better. When we
focus on other people's business, there is little good that can be
accomplished.

Today, stay totally focused on you and the business at hand.
You'll be glad you did. After all, participating in gossip is never
really a wise course of action.

*Keep your heart with all diligence, for out of it spring the issues of life. Put away
from you a deceitful mouth, and put perverse lips far from you. Let your eyes look
straight ahead, and your eyelids look right before you.*

Proverbs 4:23-25 NKJV

Lord, thank You for making me Your business.
Thank You for reminding me where to put my focus and
my priorities. I've got plenty to handle all on my own.

Amen.

# Where does the time go?

Don't waste time, it's all we have.

Anonymous

It's Monday again, oh wait, it's Saturday! No, it's the middle of the week, the middle of the year and it's almost Christmas! Time flies by! Some days we hardly notice where it went, and we barely can recount what we did with it.

Though God lives in an infinite universe that has no time, you do not. You are driven by time, by schedules, by appointments and by memories of days gone by. You live a lot of your life in the past and perhaps in the future, taking very little stock of what goes on today.

God wants to remind you that today is important, and today is all there really is. You have only the reflection of yesterday, and you have only the hope of tomorrow. Today is the key. Today is the place where you can have an effect on things of life, make changes, learn something new, become more than you were yesterday.

Don't let another day go by that you don't have a strong understanding of what you did with your time. Time is a gift and it needs to be opened with great care.

*A thousand years in Your sight are like yesterday when it is past,*
*and like a watch in the night.*

Psalm 90:4 NKJV

Lord, help me to always be aware that time is passing
and that today is the best day of my life.

Amen.

### *Learning curves*

*A man must be big enough to admit his mistakes, smart enough to profit from them, and strong enough to correct them.*

John C. Maxwell

---

Does your face ever turn slightly pink as you think about an embarrassing moment or some foolish thing you did in the past? You may not have intended to make a fool of yourself, but sometimes things take an unexpected turn. No matter what the situation was, you probably learned an unforgettable lesson.

First you learned that you never want to go through that experience again. Also, you may have learned that you're pretty good at handling a situation that totally goes haywire. You may have simply learned that life goes on and you're not particularly damaged by those crazy moments.

Sometimes though, you have to take a risk, and it might even be a risk that would make you look foolish if it didn't work out. Consider the risk Jesus took by coming to earth, or the risk Mary took at being His mother, or the one Moses took when he lead the children of Israel into the desert.

Yes, sometimes it's okay to be a little foolish, at least if the risk you're taking feels like an inspiration from your heavenly Father.

*Wise choices will watch over you. Understanding will keep you safe.*

Proverbs 2:11 NLT

Lord, please be with me when I make foolish choices and help me move on quickly. Be with me too, when I need to step out in faith and take a greater risk for You.

Amen.

## A good hostess

A kind heart is a fountain of gladness,
making everything in its vicinity freshen into smiles.

Washington Irving

Do you love having company? Is it fun for you to entertain your friends for game night? Being a good hostess can be a lot of fun for people who love to do those things, but if that's not really your style or your idea of a good time, it may be something you dread when your turn comes around to host the Bible study.

God wants us to be kind and to be good hosts for those who are coming into our homes, or sometimes those who step into our sphere of influence even for a moment, on an airplane ride or a walk in the park. Your kindness doesn't ever have to end, even if you're not planning cookies and tea.

As members of a greater family, a network of people who need each other, God only asks us to be neighborly and thoughtful. He asks us to exhibit His love wherever we are. If it's not your personal taste to have to act as a good host, then pray to the One who is the Host of heaven and ask His help. Who knows, you might have more fun than you expect.

*Practice hospitality.*

Romans 12:13 NIV

Lord, I like having company sometimes and when I'm in that frame of mind, I'm pretty good at being a host. Help me though with those times that I simply don't feel like inviting others in. Help me welcome anyone You send my way.

Amen.

*Designing your life*

Anyone who stops learning is old, whether twenty or eighty.
Anyone who keeps learning stays young.
The greatest thing in life is to keep your mind young.

Henry Ford

Sometimes we get in the habit of simply continuing on our way without thinking that it is good to discover something new. We don't engage people in conversation so we can learn more about them. We don't keep a word list so we can challenge our ability to verbalize things more accurately. We don't spend time trying to memorize key Bible verses.

If you want to be an active participant in the design of your life, it's important to keep learning things. Maybe you just need to challenge yourself to look into a topic you don't know much about, or adopt the attitude of a scientist and experiment more or investigate details on a subject you don't know well. Maybe you could learn a new language.

The point is that you want to challenge your thinking skills and be willing to learn new things at every stage of life. God designed you with a capacity to be brilliant on a lot of subjects and He loves it when you take Him up on that challenge.

*I believe in Your commands; now teach me good judgment and knowledge.*

Psalm 119:66 NLT

Lord, help me be willing to investigate new things, to learn more about books or art, or Your Word. Grant that my mind will always be open to the things You want me to know.

Amen.

## *It's okay to start again*

The greatest amount of wasted time is the time not getting started.

Dawson Trotman

It's never our intention to get obsessed about time, whether we use it wisely every minute or let a few precious hours evaporate in favor of simply "vegging out." Our concern here is about the time we waste with our old nemesis, procrastination.

The things you put off, usually things you don't really like to consider, like dieting, or exercising or not smoking, are all things that won't change with just your willingness to think about them. The only way they'll change is when you do something about them.

If God is calling you to do more praying, or to get more involved with His Word, all the good intentions in the world won't give God the result He's hoping for from you. Today, make it your goal to not waste another precious minute of your life until you act on the thing that needs to be done. Keep your Bible open and let it help you grow in desire to become more faithful to the things that can truly make a difference in your life.

*We want each of you to show this same diligence to the very end, so that what you hope for may be fully realized. We do not want you to become lazy, but to imitate those who through faith and patience inherit what has been promised.*

Hebrews 6:11-12 NIV

Lord, forgive me for putting off the things I know will make
a difference in my life. Help me to be willing to get started
now and not waste another moment.
Amen.

## JULY 23

# *Tomorrow is another day!*

*Oh, how precious is time, and how it pains me to see it slide away,
while I do so little to any good purpose.*

David Brainerd

---

Do you ever wish you could just simplify life? Maybe you are tired of a schedule that is so full you barely have time to breathe, much less one that gives you no time to think. Maybe you are always the chauffeur, getting everyone in the family to their next appointment, or practice. All you really long for is the chance to sit back and put your feet up and have a few moments where no one needs anything from you.

Tomorrow is another day, but if it's going to be the same kind of day that today was, and if it's going to be one that gives you no time to stop and sample the simple things of life, then maybe you need to change things right now. Maybe you need to simplify your activities and give God thanks and praise for the little things that make your life feel good. You know you could count your blessings easily if you just focused on them.

Be happy today! Be grateful for each little blessing, each kind word, each joyful moment and give God the glory. No doubt, you'll wonder why you didn't do it sooner.

*Abide with us, for it is toward evening, and the day is far spent.*

Luke 24:29 NKJV

Lord, remind me to make better use of my days so that by evening,
I'm not the one who feels far spent. Help me to appreciate the many
beautiful gifts You've given me to enjoy each day.

Amen.

# *God is crazy about you!*

He who counts the stars and calls them by their names,
is in no danger of forgetting His own children.
He knows your case as thoroughly as if you were the only
creature He ever made, or the only saint He ever loved!

Charles H. Spurgeon

Imagine that you're looking at a brilliant night sky and you decide that you're going to give names to some of your favorite stars. It's a fun activity for a while, but before long you run out of names because there are so many stars, and you know there are billions more than you can even see from where you are.

Imagine that God, who created those stars, knows them by name and helps them to shine even more brilliantly. That is the God who knows your name. That is the One who created you and loves you beyond measure. You are His star in so many ways and He can't get enough of being near you. He never forgets about you and never leaves you alone.

Today, remind yourself that God has called you by name and that He sees you right where you are. He lovingly thinks of you and applauds your efforts to become even more cherished. He will always see you as unique and incredibly brilliant. Give Him thanks and praise!

*He determines the number of the stars and calls them each by name.*

Psalm 147:4 NIV

Lord, thank You for making me the person I am and for seeing me as brilliant and strong. Help me to live up to the name You have given me.
Amen.

*The practice of hope*

Practice hope. As hopefulness becomes a habit,
you can achieve a permanently happy spirit.

Norman Vincent Peale

---

Oh, sure, no one feels positive and hopeful all of the time. Obstacles to happiness arise out of nowhere, losses have to be dealt with, and change has to be managed, but you can work every day to make being a hopeful woman your best intention. You can make it a habit to look for the good side of life first and move more quickly away from the things that don't work well for you.

It's a matter of practice. When you want to become better at knitting, you practice. When you want to become better at making pie crust, you practice. The same thing is true of experiencing more hope in your life. If you want to make it the default mode of your thinking, you have to practice. You'll surprise yourself at how quickly things will improve with effort.

It's not simply a matter of practice though. It's a matter of trusting God's providence, His love for you, and His mercy and grace over your life. The more you understand of those things, the more hope you will feel. Practice that kind of trust and hope will fill your soul.

*I am worn out waiting for Your rescue, but I have put my hope in Your word.*

Psalm 119:81 NLT

Lord, help me to trust You in every area of my life and, with practice,
help me to become an ambassador of hope.

Amen.

## *Getting better all the time*

It's what each of us sows, and how, that gives to us character and pres-
tige. Seeds of kindness, goodwill, and human understanding, planted
in fertile soil, spring up into deathless friendships, big deeds of worth,
and a memory that will not soon fade out. We are all sowers of seeds –
and let us never forget it!

George Matthew Adams

———

We understand the imagery of seedlings breaking victoriously
through the ground, asserting themselves in the new form they
possess of leggy stems and leaves. They are on their way to
becoming beautiful flowers or delightful fruits. They grow better
over time until they reach their full potential.

You are like a beautiful plant growing stronger, enriching the
lives of those around you and discovering your potential, and
you are a planter of seeds, the one who brings kindness and
hope to others. Every good deed is a seed of possibility that you
sow into the life of someone else.

Wherever you go today, be conscious of planting new seeds
of possibility. Be the catalyst that helps someone else make an
important breakthrough. Recognize and compliment someone
who has managed to grow and change in positive ways. God
loves to see you be a blessing to others.

*Light shines on the righteous and joy on the upright in heart.*

Psalm 97:11 NIV

Lord, help me to bless the lives of those around me. Let me not miss
any opportunity to share a moment of kindness any time I can.

Amen.

## There's no one quite like you!

*I know a man who, when he saw a woman of striking beauty, praised*
*the Creator for her. The sight of her lit within him the love of God.*

John Climacus

Have you ever been awed by someone's natural beauty, or been humbled by a vista of God's handiwork? Sometimes beauty stops you in your tracks and causes you to breathe it in, capture it as a future memory, and create an impression that stays with you forever.

Your spiritual beauty has that impact on others. Oh, you might not think that your beauty compares to women you know, but that doesn't mean it isn't real and that it doesn't captivate those who know you. Your beauty comes from within and your face only highlights the glow you can't hide of God's handiwork. God has placed a portion of Himself within you and those who are around you love to bask in that light, lingering for as long as possible, even when they don't know why.

There's no one quite like you!

*Among the gods there is none like You, O Lord; nor are there*
*any works like Your works. All nations whom You have made shall come*
*and worship before You, O Lord, and shall glorify Your name. For You are great,*
*and do wondrous things; You alone are God.*

Psalm 86:8-10 NKJV

Lord, I may not be a natural beauty as some would define it, but I know
that something beautiful lives within me and brings joy to my heart
and soul. Thanks for being the most beautiful part of my life.
Amen.

# *Just keep believing*

Nothing binds me to my Lord like a strong
belief in His changeless love.

Charles H. Spurgeon

Sometimes even things you thought you could totally depend on disappear from view. Maybe you thought your spouse of twenty years would always be there, and you were blindsided when he asked for a divorce. Maybe you thought your job would simply last until you were ready to quit, but you were downsized with no advance notice.

We live in a world that changes quickly and is largely disposable. Nothing is built to last forever. Nothing is meant to be here a century from now, much less thousands of years from now. When you think about it, this much too disposable world makes you even more grateful that the God of this universe is faithful, that He does not change.

If you need something to rely on today, something that will still be there with each sunrise, then seek God. He is the same today and tomorrow, and He'll be with you every day of your life.

*God is not a man, so He does not lie. He is not human, so He does not change His mind. Has He ever spoken and failed to act? Has He ever promised and not carried it through?*

Numbers 23:19 NLT

Lord, I praise You and thank You for Your steadfast love and mercy.
I am grateful that You are not fickle and changeable, but that
You remain true to who You are forever.

Amen.

## *Talk tenderly to yourself*

The day that each person willingly accepts himself or herself
for who he or she is and acknowledges the uniqueness
of God's framing process marks the beginning of a journey
to seeing the handiwork of God in each life.

Ravi Zacharias

Did you ever try to be like someone else? Maybe you worked hard to be as accomplished an athlete as your brother, or you did your best to be as brilliant as your father was when he was in school.

The fact is that God does not want you to be anyone else. You're a unique design and you can only become all He wants you to be by being your best self. God loves you just as you are and wants you to recognize your full potential. Don't worry about whether you can compete with others because when it comes to you, there's no competition. God is pleased with the person you are and the one you're striving to become.

If it helps, step in front of the mirror before you leave home and talk tenderly to yourself. Give yourself encouragement and remind yourself to be the best possible you.

*God created man in His own image; in the image of God He created him;*
*male and female He created them.*

Genesis 1:27 NKJV

Lord, I have always tried to be more like someone I admire. Help me to honor the good things about others and about myself, and then to do all I can to walk with You and share more of who I truly am.

Amen.

# A golden touch

God's fingers can touch nothing but to mold it into loveliness.
George MacDonald

---

Do you remember the children's story of a king named Midas? Midas was given a gift that turned out to be a curse. Everything he touched would turn to gold. At first, he thought it was an amazing thing, until he realized that he truly could not touch anything, either his food or his daughter, without that thing becoming gold as well. After a while, Midas only wanted to lose his magic touch. He didn't want that gift.

The good news is that God has a "Midas" touch in the sense that everything He touches turns into something beautiful. When He touches a life, it changes and it becomes more valuable and perfect. God can shape and mold anyone into a thing of beauty with a heart of gold. God touched your life a long time ago and He has been shaping and molding you ever since. He is helping you to become a masterpiece of love and joy, a woman with a light that will shine for the world to see.

Praise God for His incredible touch of love and grace and mercy. His touch will always bring you joy.

*This is what the LORD says, who saved you, who formed you in your mother's body: "I, the LORD, made everything, stretching out the skies by Myself and spreading out the earth all alone."*

Isaiah 44:24 NCV

Lord, thank You for shaping me into someone who can be more beautiful in Your sight. You have touched my heart and soul forever.
Amen.

## On the tip of your tongue

Wisdom is knowing when to speak your mind
and when to mind your speech.

Anonymous

---

It's good to stand up for what you believe in and to speak truth as you feel guided to do so. It's good to share your faith with others and to do your best to live in a way that pleases God. It's also good to know when to hold your tongue, even if you're right.

Sometimes you can be on the right track, but not be at the right time and so signals get crossed and people are hurt. Like a runaway freight train, your words can cause a lot of damage.

One of the gifts of God is His timing. He knows the perfect time for you to share your heart with someone else, even to share His love with someone else. He knows when the other person will be ready to hear and when you'll be able to speak with a loving spirit.

Pray for wisdom when something is on the tip of your tongue and be sure that the timing is right for you to share your heart and mind.

*Keep your tongue from evil, and your lips from speaking deceit.*

Psalm 34:13 NKJV

Lord, help me remember that things have to be said and done according to Your plans for each of us. Help me to stay quiet when it's not the right time for me to speak up.

Amen.

## SHE SPEAKS

## AND FAITHFUL INSTRUCTION
## IS ON HER TONGUE

PROVERBS 31:26

## Make today count!

Today is the tomorrow you worried about.
Today is tomorrow's yesterday. Make it count!

Anonymous

Even though today is all we really have, most of us are such vivid story tellers, we continue the tales of yesterday or the ones we imagine will come into the future. We spent a great deal of time and energy on a potential problem for no good reason, and chances are, we missed some really good things we might have enjoyed about the day that we lost with the stories in our heads.

As women, it's part of our nature to worry about things. Where does God say to us, pray and then worry? Where does He tell us that if we only did a little more or tried a little harder to change our current situations, we'd accomplish it all on our own? Nowhere! He tells us, He'll help us if we just surrender those worries to Him. He reminds us that He is in the midst of everything we have to deal with and that we're never alone.

If you're going to worry, stop right now and turn your worries into prayers. You'll find that it's much more productive because you'll be instantly reminded that God is with you right where you are. Live today and pray for tomorrow.

*Worry weighs a person down; an encouraging word cheers a person up.*

Proverbs 12:25 NLT

Lord, thank You for being with me all the time. Help me to resist my temptations to worry about things from yesterday or those that are somewhere down the road. Be with me always.
Amen.

*Wait for sunny weather*

We must wait for God, long, meekly, in the wind and wet,
in the thunder and lightning, in the cold and the dark. Wait,
and He will come. He never comes to those who do not wait.

F. W. Faber

Ah, the waiting game! Generally, we aren't good at waiting. We've gotten so used to living in an instant gratification world that we think everything should boot up for us like a computer. We should be able to press a button and be the next one in line at the bank. We should be able to attach wings to our automobiles and get out of those nasty traffic jams. We simply do not like waiting.

Yet, God is patient with us. He waits steadfastly and faithfully for us. He doesn't get easily frustrated or angry. He knows us so well. He knows that in time we'll understand that waiting is a gift. Waiting brings clarity of purpose and commitment. It brings greater joy when the thing you've waited for comes to fruition. It brings an opportunity for heartfelt and intentional prayer.

Wait with joy and thanksgiving today.

*Since the world began, no ear has heard and no eye has seen a God like you,
who works for those who wait for Him!*

Isaiah 64:4 NLT

Lord, I know that I'm not very good at waiting for You to answer
prayers or simply waiting for the little events in my life. Please help
me find the treasure that waiting can bring.

Amen.

# *With God, there's a way!*

God is able to make a way out of no way and transform dark yesterdays into bright tomorrows. This is the hope for becoming better women. This is our mandate for seeking to make a better world.

Martin Luther King, Jr. (adapted)

Did you ever get stuck somewhere? Maybe you got lost on some country road and had to find your way back. Getting stuck is like walking in the dark. You can't see the way out and you can't even imagine what steps to take next. Sometimes you simply have to wait for direction or for God's timing. Sometimes you have to redirect your prayers and your thoughts.

Whatever you do, remember this: God keeps the light on all the time. He will not leave you in the dark, because with any temptation, or any sense of being stuck, or any path of darkness, He has a plan. He will guide you in the way that you should go.

Bleak moments feel like they'll go on forever. Try to imagine a candle glowing in the dark. Step aside from all that troubles you and imagine that tiny candle, alone in a big dark room, yet sending out a beam that is unmistakable. This is the light that is always present and never goes out. This is the light that transforms our dark days and gives us the hope of tomorrow.

*If from there you seek the LORD your God, you will find Him if you seek Him with all your heart and with all your soul.*

Deuteronomy 4:29 NIV

Lord, I get lost more often than I care to admit and sometimes feel stuck with my life or my work. Please shine Your light on me today.
Amen.

## *Trust and follow through*

There must be a beginning to any great matter, but the continuing to
the end until it be thoroughly finished yields the true glory.

Francis Drake

———⊰⊱———

It's usually fun to begin a new project. You enthusiastically dive
in to determine the best course of action, the steps needed to
get the job done, and you hold a picture in your mind of what
the finished product will be. Your work is exciting and everything
is humming along nicely and then it happens.

Halfway through, you bump into obstacles, you lose some
enthusiasm, you haven't gotten the momentum you were
hoping for, and it almost seems like too much work to keep
going. What do you do?

Remind yourself of the things that caused you to embrace
that project or that person right from the start. Remind yourself
of the goal and the purpose for putting time and energy into it.
Then ask God to help re-light the fire in your heart and give you
back the passion to get the job done.

You'll be glad you did!

*Their hearts are like an oven; they approach him with intrigue.*
*Their passion smolders all night; in the morning it blazes like a flaming fire.*

Hosea 7:6 NIV

Father, I do get lost along the way sometimes and
begin to doubt my efforts and question why I got involved
in something to begin with. Help me to keep trusting in You
to get to the finish line through Your grace and mercy.

Amen.

# *Effort is a beautiful thing!*

Be of good cheer. Do not think of today's failures, but of the success that may come tomorrow. You have set yourselves a difficult task, but you will succeed if you persevere; and you will find joy in overcoming obstacles. Remember, no effort that we make to attain something beautiful is ever lost.

Helen Keller

God is delighted when you keep taking steps to fulfill your dreams and to seek more of your calling. All of that takes a lot of energy and sometimes more effort than you ever thought would be needed.

Effort is what brings the reward. When you've tried and failed you know that the decision to keep moving is often the moment a breakthrough will come. If you have a tendency to look back at where you've been, or to recall all the things that you believe did not go according to your plans, it's time to turn around.

Look ahead and know that the One who loves you more than anything already goes before you, opening doors and finding new opportunities for you to succeed. He simply asks you to make the effort.

*May the Lord our God show us His approval and make our efforts successful.*
*Yes, make our efforts successful!*

Psalm 90:17 NLT

Lord, it isn't easy to keep trying when things just
don't seem to shape up in the right direction.
Please guide my steps and bless my efforts today.
Amen.

# What it means to be pious

Earth has nothing more tender than a
woman's heart when it is the abode of piety.

Martin Luther

Piety may well be an outdated word. After all, it's hard to actually imagine people who are truly pious. You might recognize someone who exhibits sweetly humble behavior, but it isn't something you think about very often.

As you become more aware of your value in the sight of God though, you can't help but be humbled by His love and mercy. You can't help but wonder with some sense of awe why the Creator of the whole universe sent His only Son to redeem you.

Having a humble and pious heart is one indication that you're drawing closer to understanding what it really means for God to love you. As you reflect on His love and that of others around you, offer God your love in return with humble gratitude.

*The LORD detests the sacrifice of the wicked,*
*but He delights in the prayers of the upright.*

Proverbs 15:8 NLT

Lord, thank You for giving me such a feeling of being
cherished by You. Please accept my humble adoration
for all You've done to help me in this world.

Amen.

# Home is where your heart is

*Make two homes for yourself, my daughter. One actual home and another spiritual home which you carry with you always.*

Catherine of Siena

---

Most of us treasure thoughts of home because it is the one place where we feel safe and free to be ourselves on every level. It's the place where we can express our joys and sorrows and the place where we receive and give love to others. In fact, if we're very fortunate, we spend a lot of time making sure that our homes are pleasant and nurturing places.

That same sense of love and peace that you feel when you think of your home is the same feeling God wants you to have as you picture your spiritual home. Your spiritual home is also a place where you are safe to be exactly who you are, in fact it is the place where your truth can be shared and it's a place you share with your friends of faith here on earth. You can express your heart and your feelings and your love in that home at any time at all. If home is where your heart is, then your spiritual home captures your heart as well.

*"A time is coming and has now come when the true worshipers will worship the Father in the Spirit and in truth, for they are the kind of worshipers the Father seeks."*

John 4:23 NIV

Lord, I guess it's true that there's no place like home,
and as much as I love my home and my family here on earth,
I cherish the idea of knowing that I already have a home there
with You too. Thank You for taking such good care of me.
Amen.

## Pleasing God

*Look to your heart and not only to your actions; to your ends,
and thoughts, and inward manner and degree.*

Richard Baxter (adapted)

When we think of becoming more than we are now, we focus on those things that will improve our skills or our minds or our physical appearance. We think of those places that we've neglected simply because we haven't wanted to deal with them.

God knows we're only human and though He isn't after us to try to make us perfect, He is pleased when we make the effort to change in ways that are good for our hearts and minds. He wants us to carry less weight of the world on our shoulders and more joy for the gifts He has bestowed upon us. He wants us to have great stories of "aha" moments when we realized a truth that we simply couldn't grasp before.

As we become stronger and more loving, more real and more joyful, we'll live more fully the life God intended. Let all your thoughts lead you closer to Him today.

*Do not conform to the pattern of this world, but be transformed by the renewing
of your mind. Then you will be able to test and approve what God's will is –
His good, pleasing and perfect will.*

Romans 12:2 NIV

Lord, I know that sometimes my own thoughts defeat me
and hold me back. Help me to look to You to clarify my
thoughts and my actions so that my heart responds in joy.
Amen.

## Finding that connection

*A blessed thing it is for any man or woman to have a friend,*
*one human soul whom we can trust utterly, who knows the best*
*and worst of us, and who loves us in spite of all our faults.*

Charles Kingsley

Probably one of our biggest complaints comes when we express our dismay that no one seems to "get" who we are. After all, we're not that complicated, or so we reason. We're not trying to make anything difficult for anyone else and yet, we stand back still feeling somewhat invisible, somewhat lost in a great big world.

God keeps you moving in different arenas until you find those connections that make you feel strong and at peace. Perhaps that kind of connection happens for you at church, or when you spend time at the gym. The fact is that the people closest to you at home may not be the ones who truly understand who you are. Keep searching for those places where you can be your best self and ultimately find your place in the world, for that is the space where you will feel contented and whole.

Pray that God will bless you with others who understand your heart and mind.

*It is the spirit in a person, the breath of the Almighty,*
*that gives them understanding.*

Job 32:8 NIV

Lord, I guess it's often confused me that the people in my family are not necessarily the ones who know me best. Thank You for bringing people into my life who celebrate the person that I am.

Amen.

## *Embrace love*

*Faith makes all things possible ... love makes all things easy.*
Dwight L. Moody

You don't live in a polite world. Sadly, you live in a noisy, often violent, usually rude, even irritating world. Yet in the midst of that world, you strive to find your way, to seek the best place to offer what you have and who you are to make the world a better place. The struggle that exists in the world is between those motivated by love and those who have so missed love's cornerstone that they don't know how to recognize it, much less, embrace it. Love doesn't hang its hat on rudeness and arrogance. Love seeks the heart that lives in hope.

If your heart is not feeling especially at peace today, or if too much of the world's noise is pushing its way into your life, then turn around. Take a deep breath, exhale those things that bring you discomfort, and look to the only Source of love in this universe to sustain you. Love will help you be more of the person you want to be today, someone who brings the blessing of joy to others.

*Let love be your highest goal! But you should also desire the special abilities the Spirit gives.*

1 Corinthians 14:1 NLT

Lord, help me to be a loving woman all the time, even in the midst of the clamor and the grip of fear that possesses so many. Help me to live in such a way that others can see You.
Amen.

## *Love's endless and ageless praise*

As long as you can admire and love, then one is young forever.

Pablo Casals

We can't stay young forever, but we can keep our hearts and minds young eternally. We can keep trusting and believing in the good things. We can keep expecting more of ourselves so that we are virtually new every day.

The beauty of love and praise is that they don't depend on the number of years we spend on earth. They don't become more magical as we get older or less desirable somewhere along the way. We always need to give and to receive love. We always want to have young hearts born of praise.

Today, as you pass by that mirror, smile at the woman you see there and give her a hearty round of applause. Send her some love and thank God for her in every way. You can be sure that when God sees you, everything about you is beautiful!

*Make every effort to add to your faith goodness; and to goodness, knowledge; and to knowledge, self-control; and to self-control, perseverance; and to perseverance, godliness; and to godliness, mutual affection; and to mutual affection, love. For if you possess these qualities in increasing measure, they will keep you from being ineffective and unproductive in your knowledge of our Lord Jesus Christ.*

2 Peter 1:5-8 NIV

Lord, sometimes I wonder if I have much left to give
or to discover. I've lived long enough to appreciate all that I am
and all that I've been. Help me to remember that with You, I can
always strive for something even more beautiful in my life.

Amen.

## A priority of prayer

*Is prayer your steering wheel or your spare tire?*

Corrie ten Boom

⤜⤜⤜✦⤛⤛⤛

Who takes the lead in your life? Is it you? Is it God? Leadership is a good thing, but there's a beautiful line between leading and following and it's good to know what that is.

When it comes to your prayer life, there's only one way to approach it, and that's with a humble heart. You have to take your hands off the steering wheel and let God drive. You have to sit quietly in the passenger seat until He shows you where you're going. You can't ask directions on how to get somewhere and then get in the driver's seat – you're sure to get lost.

Your prayers are an opportunity for you to put God in charge and give Him a chance to take you wherever He believes you will most be able to thrive. Think about it. If you can choose to go where God would lead you, or stumble along on your own, which would you prefer?

When you pray, pray with the awareness that God wants you to get to your destination and He may even know a better route than you do.

*Guide me in Your truth and teach me, for You are God my Savior, and my hope is in You all day long.*

Psalm 25:5 NIV

Lord, I know that I often pray and then proceed like I didn't.
In other words, I simply get right back in the driver's seat.
Help me to pull over and let You drive from now on.
Amen.

## Becoming a woman of prayer

*Love to pray. Feel often during the day the need for prayer,
and take trouble to pray. Prayer enlarges the heart until it is
capable of containing God's gift of Himself. Ask and seek
and your heart will grow big enough to receive Him.*

Mother Teresa

You already have a big heart. You share it with the people you love without hesitation. You deliver on your promises and give of yourself easily. In fact, you stretch yourself too thin sometimes, but it's just the way you are. You try to rise to whatever occasion or need is before you, and your friends and family appreciate that about you.

When it comes to things of God, you have a big heart too and when you need a few moments just for yourself, a few moments to simply sit with your Savior, you find it brings you a kind of joy that can't happen any other way. Your heart does expand to take in the love He has to offer and once you're filled to the brim, you go out and start over again to share all that you have with others.

You're a woman of prayer and that helps you become an even greater woman of worth, filled up and over with the love of God. Praise God for His generous gift of love for you.

*The peace of God, which transcends all understanding,
will guard your hearts and your minds in Christ Jesus.*

Philippians 4:7 NIV

Lord, please bless me today with that sweet peace that passes all understanding, the kind I only get when I spend time with You.
Amen.

# *Being present*

Happy moments, praise God. Difficult moments, seek God.
Quiet moments, worship God. Painful moments,
trust God. Every moment, thank God.

Anonymous

———◦◦◦———

This is it! Today! This is the moment, the twenty-four hours, the bit of time and space you have to call your own and it's all you have! Only fading memories take you back to yesterday, and only hopes and dreams can carry you into tomorrow.

Your choice, then, is to give this moment everything you've got. You have to be intentional about all you do today. Live it with all the grace and mercy and brilliance that you can muster, because only this moment exists. Invite God into your day as you rise with the sun. Let Him rejoice with you. Allow Him to share an awareness that you need to be strong, or bring a little light to guide you, or a soft word to warm your heart.

Be present in this moment and it will fade into something beautiful, something with no sorrow or regret, but a moment well-lived.

*God can see what is in people's hearts. And He knows what is in the mind of the Spirit, because the Spirit speaks to God for His people. We know that in everything God works for the good of those who love Him.*

Romans 8:27-28 NCV

Lord, I am guilty of trying too hard to figure out the future and therefore miss what is happening right now. Please be with me today and help me stay grounded in every moment.

Amen.

## Matters of the moment

*In matters of principle, stand like a rock;*
*in matters of taste, swim with the current.*

Thomas Jefferson

If you were threatened by a thief who wanted to steal the things of the heart that matter to you, what would you do? What would you say if the thief tried to steal your faith or your belief in the goodness of people? What would you do to defend the principles you hold dear so that no one could take them from you?

We don't usually think of anyone stealing our principles and yet in some measure, you're being asked to give up a little bit of what you think nearly every day. You're being asked to make compromises that are uncomfortable, or to get behind ideas that don't really sit well with you. Your boss gives you a directive and you do it because you believe you must to protect your position in the company.

Your principles and beliefs do matter and only you can stand up for them. Part of your calling as a woman of worth is to stand up for the things you hold precious.

God wants your heart to be anchored and immovable, so that He can always hold you in His hand.

*Be strong and take heart, all you who hope in the Lord.*

Psalm 31:24 NIV

Lord, please hold me closely and help me to guard those things that motivate my lifestyle and my thoughts, especially when they are ideas You've given me. Help me to be strong in You.

Amen.

## *Good, better, best*

Do not let the good things in life rob you of the best things.

Buster Rothman

Since you were a little girl, you've been taught that it's important to always do your best, no matter what the task. You learned early on that setting goals helps you achieve the things in life that bring you joy. This part of your education was good for you, but sometimes, as women, we become so absorbed in that aspect of life that drives us to do our best that we lose sight of things that are also just good for us.

God wants you to recognize that what is good is meant to bring you joy, but it can change. When it does, you may discover that what was good was simply a stepping stone to something even better. Maybe you need to bask in the love and care of other people, not demanding more of yourself, but just resting and listening. Perhaps you need to push yourself to go after a dream or you need to let go of some of your history. Whatever you need, if you reach out for what is good, God will help you discover what is best right now!

*"Seek first His kingdom and His righteousness,*
*and all these things will be given to you as well."*

Matthew 6:33 NIV

Lord, I know that I am not always certain of those things You might consider to be best for me. Help me to be very aware of listening to Your voice in all the choices I make today.

Amen.

# *Problem solving*

*Don't duck the most difficult problems. That just ensures that
the hardest part will be left when you're most tired.
Get the big one done – it's downhill from then on.*

Norman Vincent Peale

Do you ever get stuck on some issue you're trying to resolve?
You've already prayed about it and looked at it from a lot of
angles, but no mountains have moved in spite of your faith and
nothing has changed. When change doesn't come after a while,
it seems easier to put the problem aside and simply go on to
other things.

After you've let a difficulty hang over you like a sphere of
impending doom, you have only one choice: Face it and deal
with it right now. The fact is that the problem won't fix itself, so
you must dive into the mess and figure out what steps you can
take to clean things up.

God is used to sticky problems. He's guided you through
difficult choices in the past and delivered you. He's helped you
grow and you've become a better person, building your strength
and your faith as you worked out the hard things.

*Let us then approach God's throne of grace with confidence, so that we may
receive mercy and find grace to help us in our time of need.*

Hebrews 4:16 NIV

Lord, I am good at resolving most things that come my way,
but sometimes I get stuck on things that I simply do not
want to face. Help me stand strong in You.
Amen.

## Ode to procrastination

———

It's natural to put things off, especially those things that aren't much fun. If you're considering whether to clean the bath tub or go shopping, there's probably no contest. The bath tub isn't really that bad! If you're faced with doing a report for work or reading a good novel, only the deadline will drive your decision. You have a lot of options and sometimes the best choice is to leave something undone for the time being.

How do you prioritize your life? If you're good at making lists, but never follow them, maybe it's time to ask yourself why you bother with list making. Perhaps it's time to make very short lists so you have only one or two items to complete.

If your spirit is starving because you've procrastinated about prayer or Bible reading, ask God to help you with that. When you have a skinny spirit, you also starve your motivation. It's time to move on!

*Good sense will protect you; understanding will guard you.*

Proverbs 2:11 NCV

Lord, I know that I put off things that are actually good for me to do. Bring to mind the important things I need to deal with today and give me the courage to complete them.

Amen.

## Making progress

*We all want progress, but if you're on the wrong road, progress means doing an about-turn and walking back to the right road; in that case, the man who turns back soonest is the most progressive.*

C. S. Lewis

It's a good thing there's no sin in starting over, because most of us have had to reinvent, re-create and revive ourselves many times. We've made progress, met obstacles, turned around and started again. Actually, the experience of making progress is deceptive. Sometimes it seems like we're moving forward and then we discover we're on the wrong road. We have to always be aware of the path and look for the signposts that point us in the right direction if we truly want to make effective changes.

We may wish that getting older would make us wiser. Perhaps wisdom comes in knowing much more quickly when we've gotten off track, or when we're simply in a rut. Progress means being intentional about what we do, keeping God in the loop of our plans, and listening for His guidance. We have to be mindful of what we're doing all the time.

Keep walking and when you have to turn around, don't regret the turning, trust that God is guiding you back to the right road.

*Remember the Lord in all you do, and He will give you success.*

Proverbs 3:6 NCV

Lord, thank You for keeping me on the straight path.
I know I can get sidetracked pretty easily and I always
want Your help in making true progress in my life.

Amen

# Barometers

*We must not trust every word of others or feelings within ourselves,*
*but cautiously and patiently try the matter, to see whether it is of God.*

Thomas à Kempis

Feelings are fleeting. They come and go and whimsically change with the temperature or how hungry you are. Feelings are good things, but they can't be relied upon when you're trying to determine the best course of action. How you feel may certainly play a role in the choices you make, but if those choices are going to contribute in a positive way to your life, then you need to go beyond those feelings. You need to go directly to the One who inspires your heart, but fills your mind with truth.

It's not easy to be patient. It can even feel like a waste of time. Yet, if you can wait for God to help you with direction, you may not have to undo a mistake or revise a plan that wasn't well thought out. God is steadfast and He acts with the kind of love that makes a difference in every choice you have in front of you. Wait for Him to help you, no matter where your barometer is set or how the winds may blow. He is there for you!

*Good sense will protect you; understanding will guard you.*

Proverbs 2:11 NCV

Lord, thank You for always being the One I can count on to keep me grounded and to provide the wisdom I need to make good decisions. Help me to follow through on those things that help me become more of the woman You want me to be.

Amen.

## *Seek to know more of God*

*The main thing in this world is not being sure what God's will is,
but seeking it sincerely, and following what we do understand of it.
The only possible answer to the destiny of men is to seek
without respite to fulfill God's purpose.*

Paul Tournier

It may sound somewhat old-fashioned or even clichéd to imagine that you really strive to seek God's will and purpose. At least, it sounds like "church-speak."

It's time to re-set your intention. As you get to know more of what God wants for you, you'll be impressed by how big His plans really are and how wide His opportunities for you to succeed can stretch. He has a net that is so big, even you cannot fulfill all the things He would choose for you in a lifetime.

Your destiny is framed by choices and the ones you make with greater understanding of God's will and purpose will be the ones that change the world. God loves you, but His mission for you is life changing and He's anxious to help you define your purpose. Seek Him first.

*"You did not choose Me, but I chose you and appointed you that you
should go and bear fruit, and that your fruit should remain,
that whatever you ask the Father in My name He may give you."*

John 15:16 NKJV

Lord, I know that I often wonder about Your purpose for me,
but I'm not always sure how to figure out if I'm on the right track.
Help me to discover the truth of my life through You.

Amen.

*Respecting who you are*

Strength of character comes out of the decisions we make,
temptations we face, and the conflicts of life.

Wayman Mitchell

Women spend a lot of time evaluating and assessing the world around them. We continually seek to understand what is expected of us and how we fit into our culture. We seek to know about ourselves and what it is that makes us unique.

While we go through this discovery process, our unique design is giving way to our character, the person we really are, the one we see in the mirror when we're willing to stand there in truth. As we mature, we broaden our concept of what it means to be a woman of good character and of good faith. We develop a sense of self-worth and are grateful to receive the respect of others.

The hardest part of the process is recognizing that we are each responsible for the outcome. God will guide us, others will help us see the world in new ways, but how we present ourselves, what we choose to do or how we will act is all up to us, our responsibility. That sense of responsibility operates on a system known as character. May your character always serve as your able and steady guide.

*We also have joy with our troubles, because we know that these troubles produce patience. And patience produces character, and character produces hope.*

Romans 5:3-4 NCV

Lord, help me to be a woman of good character. Help me to honor others and to honor myself as well because of Your great love for me.
Amen.

## *That leap of faith!*

We gain strength, and courage, and confidence by
each experience in which we really stop to look fear in the face ...
we must do that which we think we cannot.

Eleanor Roosevelt

There's only one fabulous you! You're a heavenly design and a woman of great worth. God loves you simply because you're genuinely you. Sometimes He'll guide you to do things that are out of your comfort zone. He'll send you on a mission or direct your path in ways you never dreamed would happen.

Each time you answer with a willing heart to take His direction, you experience more of the abundance that this life has to offer. You become more of what He knew you could be. When you leave the door open for new ideas, new choices, even those you might face with a little fear and trembling, you are rewarded by an even greater understanding of God's faithfulness.

God is a Creator and so His imagination knows no end. Each time you tap into your own imaginative spirit, you can share in that sweet joy of taking a leap of faith. You instantly become more than you ever dreamed you could be.

*Keep their words always in your heart. Tie them around your neck.*
*When you walk, their counsel will lead you. When you sleep, they will protect you.*

Proverbs 6:21-22 NLT

Lord, I know I play it pretty safe most of the time.
Help me to be willing to move beyond my reach
and try some new things as You direct me.
Amen.

## Ready, set, grow!

One can never consent to creep when one feels an impulse to soar!

Helen Keller

Perhaps you can't remember when you were just a little tot learning to walk toward the outstretched arms of your mother. You probably tried and fell down, and tried again and fell down, but each time you got closer to her arms. Each time you laughed at the joy of your own accomplishment. Eventually you learned to run and you've probably been running ever since.

Today, take a little inventory of the things that motivate your heart. Are you running toward the things that will help you achieve your goals or are you running from the things that you simply want to leave behind? Once you know what you want to do and where you want to go, then there's nothing left for you to do but say your prayers, set your goals and move forward.

If you can see the goal you want to achieve, just like when you tried to get into the outstretched arms of your mother, you'll find great joy in the victory ahead. It's time to keep going and growing!

*The righteous will flourish like a palm tree, they will grow like a cedar of Lebanon.*

Psalm 92:12 NIV

Lord, I am not always even aware of my direction, but today,
let me take the steps that give me the faith and freedom to fly.

Amen.

## Creating an image

Much of our difficulty as seeking Christians stems from our unwilling-
ness to take God as He is and adjust our lives accordingly. We insist
upon trying to modify Him and bring Him nearer to our own image.

A. W. Tozer

Do you have a picture of God that you hold in your mind? Is it a
comfortable image where you give Him the same attributes you
might give to your grandfather or a kindly uncle? Do you imagine
an all-powerful God that you can scarcely grasp, but you know is
awe-inspiring? You probably create God in an image that is both
joyful and fearful, because God is Spirit and not easily defined.

Seekers of God strive to become more of what they imagine
He would want them to be, not so much in appearance, but in
action. Jesus often reminded us that we should strive to be more
like Him because He gave us examples of how to live an earthly
life based on what He knew of His Father in heaven.

As you seek to discover more of God, imagine the picture of
yourself that you want Him to see. His image is known to others
through you. Help them see Jesus in you today.

*Can you compare God to anything? Can you compare*
*Him to an image of anything?*

Isaiah 40:18 NCV

Lord, I know I don't always understand the image I hold of You,
even when I trust You. I want to be more like You and share
the love You have for me with others.

Amen.

# With a song in your heart

God respects me when I work, but He loves me when I sing.

Tagore

Most of us like to sing even if we don't have a great voice. We'll sing in the shower sometimes, or when we're alone in the car. We'll sing to our favorite songs on the radio, because music stirs up our souls like nothing else can.

The beauty of singing, even our singing, is that it goes right up to heaven in the form of praise. Being able to sing to God, over the act of working in other ways for Him is that we can sing with abandon and align our hearts directly to those angelic heavenly choirs.

Whatever you do today, see if you can do it with a song in your heart. You don't have to create a brass band or a marching parade, but the more you simply exist in that space of joy and praise, the more God's Spirit will spill out of you and into the lives of others.

Part of your purpose here on earth is to discover the important work that God would have you do in ways that serve Him and the divine order of things. Another part is to simply live in such a way that your heart sings with unending joy.

*Light shines on the righteous and joy on the upright in heart.*

Psalm 97:11 NIV

Lord, grant that I might know Your joy today and share it everywhere I happen to be. Let me lift up my voice in thanks and praise for all You are and all You do for me.

Amen.

# *Losing our sense of values*

We have a real problem in this country when it
comes to values. We have become the kind of societies
that civilized countries used to send missionaries to.

William Bennett

---

Culturally, we're upside down. We've forgotten who we are.
We've lost touch with the values and the sense of morality that
puts others before ourselves and honors each person on the
planet as a creation of God. We focus on what we need today
and forget about what we can do to inspire tomorrow.

If we want to become more than we are – offering God our
hearts and minds – then that is a step toward creating a more
informed and more compassionate culture. The steps you take to
become an even greater woman of worth will make a difference.

Whatever you're doing today, remember that your actions,
your words, and the skills you offer the world can make things
right again. God is counting on you to hold up the light of His
love.

*Now, my daughter, don't be afraid. I will do for you all you ask. All the people of my
town know that you are a woman of noble character.*

Ruth 3:11 NIV

Lord, I am often perplexed by the loss I feel over the shredding of our
moral fiber. Please help me to do what I can to hold the virtues of
goodness and kindness up for others to see.

Amen.

## Neither lonely nor alone

Our language has wisely sensed the two sides of being alone. It has created the word "loneliness" to express the pain of being alone. And it has created the word "solitude" to express the glory of being alone.

Paul Tillich

Being alone means you can take the time to read a book, get your nails done or simply think your own thoughts without interruption. It leaves you feeling refreshed and renewed.

When you're alone too long, though, aloneness turns into loneliness. Loneliness is not so much fun. It's the thing that causes you to be drawn into yourself, doing your best to protect yourself, whether you're alone in your room or walking down a busy city street. When you disconnect from others, you feel really alone. Human beings were made for community and fellowship and too much time alone can bring pain.

When you feel lonely, remember that God cares about you and He is truly near. In fact, He's a mere prayer away. Seek His help and His comfort when being alone becomes the pain of loneliness. God does not want you to be lonely or alone. He is always with you.

*The law never made anything perfect. But now we have confidence in a better hope, through which we draw near to God.*

Hebrews 7:19 NLT

Lord, I do pass through phases of loneliness. I'm always busy, always in the midst of others, but somehow my heart feels alone. Please guide me into true fellowship with those around me.

Amen.

## The flame of the spirit

Spirit-filled souls are ablaze for God. They love with a love that glows. They serve with a faith that kindles. They serve with a devotion that consumes. They hate sin with fierceness that burns. They rejoice with a joy that radiates. Love is perfected in the fire of God.

Samuel Chadwick

Do you remember when you first fell in love with the Lord? When you realized He was near and ready to answer your prayers and hear the joys and sorrows of your heart, you were passionate about Him. You longed to read the Word and to become immersed in the messages you received through your reading and prayer. It was a glorious time in your life and you grew quickly.

Do you still feel that passion? It's good to get comfortable with your relationship with God, because a loving relationship should be comfortable, yet nothing should stop you from sharing your passion and your heart for all that He does for you. Nothing should douse the flame of awe that you feel for Him.

As you go about your day, imagine that flame inside of you longing to know more of Him and share your love with Him again. God is always passionate about you.

*When my spirit grows faint within me, it is You who watch over my way.*

Psalm 142:3 NIV

Lord, I have lost some of the fervor I had when we first began. It's not that I take You for granted, I've just lost my focus. Help me to come back to You in great joy.

Amen.

# *Becoming stronger every day*

The devil does not sleep, nor is the flesh yet dead;
you must never cease your preparation for battle, because
on the right and on the left are enemies who never rest.

Thomas à Kempis

You probably don't spend much time polishing your armor and getting your home fortified against the enemies of the world, but that doesn't make those enemies any less real. The greatest enemy of a believer is the one who attempts to deceive you into thinking you don't need God's help anymore, that you can do it all on your own and that you're in control.

How do you arm yourself? How do you protect yourself from the one who is always preparing for your downfall, looking for your weaknesses and the places where you're most vulnerable?

You have clear options: You can wake each morning with a definite intention of prayer and pray for your home, your family and those you know. You can seek God in His Word and stand on His promises to be near you and to deliver you from evil.

God is your armor, but you must stay near Him to be protected. Don't leave home without Him.

*Put on the full armor of God, so that you can
take your stand against the devil's schemes.*

Ephesians 6:11 NIV

Lord, please be with me today, protecting me emotionally, physically and spiritually. Be with my family and the people I love and the people that you love. I ask this in Jesus' name.

Amen.

## *Learning to think more clearly*

In every day of trouble I'll raise my thoughts on high,
I'll think of that bright temple and crowns above the sky.

Sojourner Truth

You may not realize that you could benefit from "thinking" lessons, but you might be surprised. After all, your head is full of stories and only a tiny portion of those stories is true. Most of them are shadowy memories, or hazy perceptions, things you carry around with you even though you don't fully know why.

It's important to be clear about the thoughts you allow to run through your mind because they have a way of festering into worries and causing difficulty. As you plan your day, imagine what it would be like to have a totally clear head, and a mind that is ready to be filled by God's guidance. There's no residue of yesterday, no tension about tomorrow; you're only thinking about what you have to do right now.

Teach yourself to sweep away the cobwebs of things that no longer serve a good purpose and therefore don't need to take up room in your head. Move on to the things that give you joy and satisfaction with life.

*Do not deceive yourselves. If any of you think you are wise by the standards of this age, you should become "fools" so that you may become wise.*

1 Corinthians 3:18 NIV

Lord, I do keep a bit of clutter in my head. Help me
to clean out the things that I don't need to carry around
and to be perfectly mindful of You.

Amen.

## SHE WATCHES OVER THE AFFAIRS OF HER

*household*

## AND DOES NOT EAT THE BREAD OF IDLENESS

PROVERBS 31:27

# It's always about choice

We can't choose our relatives, but we can choose our thoughts,
which influence us much more.

Anonymous

From the beginning, God gave His children the freedom to choose. We could choose to watch out for the planet, we could choose to love, we could even choose His presence in our lives. He designed us with great minds and hearts. He knew that, given the opportunity, we would learn to choose well.

We have learned. We have learned that making good choices isn't always easy; in fact, it can be complicated. We know there's always a gift in choosing, even when we don't choose well, because each choice helps us to be wiser the next time.

We've learned that life is beautiful and that we are each working to understand it better so that we can become more of who we desire to be. God knew we'd fall down and need a Savior, and He knew we'd rise again to make Him proud. Today, remember that your choices are important and that God is with you every time you ask for wisdom in the choices you make.

*Today I have given you the choice between life and death, between blessings and curses. I call on heaven and earth to witness the choice you make.*

Deuteronomy 30:19 NLT

Lord, thank You so much for giving me choices. I have not always been wise in the direction I've taken, especially when I neglect to invite You into my decisions. Help me to always take my choices to You.
Amen.

## *What we learn from the world*

We travel to learn; and I have never been in any country where they did not do something better than we do it, think some thoughts better than we think, catch some inspiration from heights above our own.

Maria Mitchell

Even if you haven't had the opportunity or the inclination to travel to other countries, you can learn remarkable things from other cultures via books and the Internet. God designed all of us and placed us in the cultures that nurture us and teach us how we fit into the world.

When John 3:16 says that God so loved the world, He gave His only Son, it truly reminds us that we are all brothers and sisters in some way. We can choose to learn from each other, gleaning the best of what we have to offer, and sharing the best of what we can give. Beyond that, we can learn to love each other without condition, because God Himself wants us to do so. He loves us so that we can love all others.

Today, wherever you are, send a blessing to someone far away, even to strangers in another land, because God already knows them and He honors our prayers for each other.

*"Whoever does the will of My Father in heaven is My brother and sister and mother."*
Matthew 12:50 NKJV

Lord, thank You for the times I've been able to travel and discover more of Your wisdom in creating us as we are. Help me to remember Your people in need, even the people I don't personally know, in my prayers.
Amen.

## *Do you need to change?*

Everyone thinks of changing humanity
and nobody thinks of changing himself.

Leo Tolstoy

---

Ah, there it is! It's not about them after all. It's about you! Sometimes the hardest thing to acknowledge is that perhaps when change is needed, it isn't up to the other person; it is up to you! Sometimes God is calling you to think new thoughts and to seek a new perspective. Sometimes He wants you to know that you might be in a rut and that your thinking needs to take you to a new awareness and new opportunities to serve Him.

God gave you an incredible mind and heart and He knows that you have the ability to change. He knows this about you because at one point in your life, He fed you with sweet milk and honey to help you know He was there. Today, He feeds you with gourmet delights because He knows you can digest more of what He has to offer. Let Him help you change your life in any way that suits Him best. Life will get better almost immediately!

*If anyone is in Christ, the new creation has come: the old has gone, the new is here!*

2 Corinthians 5:17 NIV

Lord, I am not as quick to suggest that I need to change some of my own quirks as I am to think others need to take on that task. I realize, though, that You always seek my best. Help me to desire everything that will cause me to make changes for my own good.

Amen.

*Words of wisdom*

Just as at sea those who are carried away from the direction
of the harbor bring themselves back on course by a clear sign,
on seeing a tall beacon light or some mountain peak coming into
view, so Scripture may guide those adrift on the sea of the life
back into the harbor of the divine will.

Gregory of Nyssa

Remember when you were just a little girl and your mother had
simple sayings that she often quoted and were helpful to you as
you grew up? Maybe she would say things like "an apple a day
keeps the doctor away!" when she wanted you to eat more fruit.

The book of Proverbs is somewhat like those folksy adages.
It is full of practical wisdom that, practiced with diligence, can
become a natural part of your life. If you remember that a "friend
loves at all times," it can help you clear up a difficult situation with
a friend. If you remember "the one who gets wisdom loves life;
the one who cherishes understanding will soon prosper," then
you have tools to guide you toward greater wisdom. Consider the
Proverbs to be like text messages from God. Let those messages
take root in your heart, now and forever.

*Pay attention and turn your ear to the sayings of the wise;*
*apply your heart to what I teach.*

Proverbs 22:17 NIV

Lord, I am so grateful for the bits of wisdom I learned in my
family and even more so for the blessings of the book of Proverbs.
Help me to take to heart those things that keep me close to You.

Amen.

# The angst of waiting

*If you spend your whole life waiting for the storm,*
*you'll never enjoy the sunshine.*

Horace

---

Stormy days come into all of our lives. Sometimes we're prepared for them and we pass through them rather quickly. At other times we are surprised by them and have to rely on inner strength and faith to get past the threat they impose.

However, sometimes we don't actually face a real storm; we just imagine that a storm is coming and so we get up every day wondering whether this will be the day that lightning strikes and the wind blows. We simply can't trust that God has more for us than a bad storm.

What if you changed your view right now? If you imagined only good coming your way, you might find that storm clouds seldom gather anywhere near you. God wants everything to happen for your good because you mean so much to Him. He has prepared and planned for sunny days because He loves to see you radiate with happiness. Step away from impending thoughts of gloom, and let the sun shine in your life.

*We know that God causes everything to work together for the good of those who*
*love God and are called according to His purpose for them.*

Romans 8:28 NLT

Lord, I know that I let my worries get out of hand and often
anticipate things that never happen. Please help me to live more
in the present and find joy in the moments I'm living today.

Amen.

## Hoping against hope

If it were not for hopes, the heart would break.

Thomas Fuller

When we have hope in our hearts, it brings an infusion of things like faith and joy, optimism and possibility. Hope gives us the chance to breathe and to anticipate good things. We often face events and situations with uncertainty and are given the gift of hope to help us through them.

Hope manifests in a number of ways. You hope that your children will grow up strong and healthy and responsible. To that end, you do your best to nurture, protect and guide them. You hope that your career will flourish and when you hope for that, you work to make it even more possible. Sometimes, then, hope becomes an action that helps us achieve the goals we have in our hearts.

When you hope in the Lord, you simply have to nestle in by His side, lay your concerns at His feet and trust that He is there for you. He gives you every reason for hope, because He is the One who sees your heart and knows your desires. Rest in His hope and in His love today.

*It is sad not to get what you hope for. But wishes that come true are like eating fruit from the tree of life.*

Proverbs 13:12 NCV

Lord, I do have great hope for my friends, my family and also for my life. I thank You for being the greatest source of hope for me and for the people I love.

Amen.

# Putting out the welcome mat

The service we render to others is really the
rent we pay for our room on this earth.
Wilfred Grenfell

People who volunteer to serve others usually do so with more
than their hands and their resources. They put out the welcome
mat to bring joy and hope into the lives of those in need. When
we serve others from the heart, no matter what kind of service it
is, then every aspect of that experience is fulfilling.

As we grow more faithful as the woman God wants each of us
to be, we become more aware of others. We realize that as much
as we love to be the recipients of good things, we also love to
provide good things that bless other people's lives.

God gave His Son for us so that we might receive all that
is good from His hand. God put out the welcome mat so that
each of us can come home again. Let's do the same thing for
each other, giving all we can to make life more beautiful for the
people around us.

*Now we can serve God, not in the old way of obeying the letter of the law,*
*but in the new way of living in the Spirit.*

Romans 7:6 NLT

Lord, I don't go out and do volunteer work as much as I might,
but I do try to volunteer my time in little ways to those around me.
Bless those moments and help me to grow in my desire to give
more of myself and more of You to those who need me.
Amen.

## *Tough and tender*

*Give me a stout heart to bear my own burdens. Give me a willing heart to bear the burdens of others. Give me a believing heart to cast all burdens upon Thee, O Lord.*

John Baillie

---

Burdens are weights no matter what form they take in our lives. We might have personal burdens like debt or anxiety over our children. We might have heartache or loss or confusion and lack of direction. We might simply find ourselves weighed down by a sadness of spirit or fear or doubt.

Since it is difficult to take on the burdens of others when we're weighed down ourselves, the place to start is with God. We know that only God can lift our burdens and that it takes tremendous faith and trust to let the weight of the world wash away.

God will bless you as you pray for others, supporting them in their need, and He will bless you each time you come to Him and simply ask Him to carry your burdens. He does not want you to take on the world alone. He is always with you. Seek His comfort and strength today.

*"Come to Me, all you who are weary and burdened, and I will give you rest."*

Matthew 11:28 NIV

Lord, I think I'm pretty good at shouldering my troubles, and sometimes at being a good support for others, but I'm not always good at coming to You when I need help. Remind me how ready You are to help me for any need I may have.

Amen.

## *Teachers and mentors*

*The mediocre teacher tells. The good teacher explains. The superior teacher demonstrates. The great teacher inspires.*

William Arthur Ward

---

Do you recall a person in your life who encouraged you when you were young? Perhaps it was a teacher or a family member who recognized your love for art or your ability as an athlete They somehow kept that dream alive for you so that you had greater courage to pursue the dream later on.

God puts people in our lives at precisely the right moment to do just that, to encourage our hearts when we're considering a new direction. The best teachers in your life are the ones who guide you to a greater understanding of yourself, strengthening your potential to succeed in the things that matter.

Today, you may have a spiritual mentor or a friend who seems to know you better than anyone else. You may have a sibling or a co-worker who simply won't let you stop trying to become all that you can be. Know that those people are in your life by God's design, because He has called you into being an incredible woman of great worth for Him.

*Show them the way in which they must walk and the work they must do.*

Exodus 18:20 NKJV

Lord, thank You for the precious people who have done so much to
help me move with courage toward the best direction for my life.
Help me to be that kind of person for others.

Amen.

## *Prayer partners*

There is nothing that makes us love
others so much as praying for them.

William Law (adapted)

---

We know that God blesses our individual prayer time, but we also know that it can make a difference when we join with others to pray. You know that God is already in your midst, because He promised in His Word to be where two or more gather to pray. You know that He hears you and has prepared your heart for the time you are spending together. Sometimes with the strength of just two people in agreement in prayer, miracles happen.

As often as possible, practice praying with others. You become close in heart, mind and spirit and your friendships blossom. You become more aware of each other's needs and concerns and have a more genuine faithful connection. As you pray together and for others, your heart grows bigger, able to take in the very aspect of God's Spirit and filling you with even greater love for others.

God sent His followers out two by two for a reason. Consider whether He is calling you to join with a prayer partner near you.

*Jesus says, "For where two or three gather in My name, there am I with them."*

Matthew 18:20 NIV

Lord, thank You for the people in my inner circle who pray for me.
Help me to be more intentional about praying with at least one other
person on a regular basis. Thank You for always being there to hear the
concerns of our hearts.

Amen.

## Character matters

Out of our beliefs are born deeds; out of our deeds
we form habits; out of our habits grows our character;
and on our character we build our destiny.

Henry Hancock

---

You're a woman of incredible character. That means you pay attention to those around you, offering a helping hand as needed and speaking words of encouragement. You know that it's important to own your actions, asking forgiveness for those things that may happen along the way, and seeking always to understand others before needing to be understood.

You live up to your word. You speak from the heart and when you make a promise, you keep it, no matter what the cost. Your integrity in all areas of your life makes a difference and others depend on your generous and loving spirit.

Character is not something you inherit, nor do you fashion it overnight. It's something you build and understand more fully over time. You're a woman who sets the bar for those in your midst because you offer them a new standard of what it means to be a person of great character. Continue to grow and to walk on that path.

*Until the time came to fulfill his dreams, the LORD tested Joseph's character.*

Psalm 105:19 NLT

Lord, I strive to be a woman that You and others can depend on, no matter what the situation might be. Help me to own my mistakes and my successes with a kind and loving heart.

Amen.

## *Think twice*

*Not every affection which seems good is to be immediately followed. Sometimes it is expedient to use restraint even in good desires and wishes, lest through importunity you fall into distraction of mind, lest through want of discipline you become a stumbling block.*

Thomas à Kempis

You probably do a lot of things without thinking twice. You have a routine and follow it pretty much all the time. You like your coffee a certain way, fix your hair in the same style and keep tabs on your finances. These are things that are second nature to you, and not ones you have to spend a lot of time considering.

Sometimes, though, things come your way that you weren't expecting, or that required a lot more focus and attention. You have to think twice before deciding on your course of action.

It's okay to have "another think coming" because most of the time having a clear head and considering all the sides of any option will give you peace and a positive outcome. Think and think again when you need to. It will serve you well.

*The instructions of the LORD are perfect, reviving the soul.*
*The decrees of the LORD are trustworthy, making wise the simple.*

Psalm 19:7 NLT

Lord, thank You for giving me a lot of chances to think about things to gain the best perspective. Bless my thoughts and help me to be wise in my choices.

Amen.

## Where the wind blows

Not all those who wander are lost.

J. R. R. Tolkien

---

Do you like to wander around a bit with no particular purpose, just giving yourself the freedom to have no agenda at all? Maybe you want to go through a section of the bookstore you've never paid much attention to simply to see if you discover something intriguing. Perhaps you want to go on a hike and walk the trail, just to see if you can do it.

Sometimes you have to go where the wind takes you. You have to be willing to set your sails and go along for the ride. When you do, you may surprise yourself at what you learn. It's good to allow yourself flexibility and freedom to think new thoughts, to wander aimlessly or to explore new options.

Perhaps you could even explore the idea of wandering through your Bible, reading a passage here and there, wherever the Spirit leads you, to see if you discover something new. If you get lost in the pages, or in the moment, that will be okay, for it will serve you well. Go ahead and wander a bit.

*Do not be conformed to this world, but be transformed*
*by the renewing of your mind, that you may prove what*
*is that good and acceptable and perfect will of God.*

Romans 12:2 NKJV

Lord, I'm always so organized and scheduled that I don't often take detours. Let me wander closer to You through nature, through your Word, and discover what else You have for me.

Amen.

## *Laws of change*

Change is the law. And those who look only
to the past or present are certain to miss the future.

John F. Kennedy

God set the earth in motion and it's been changing and growing ever since. He gave it a framework and a structure that could sustain change and even flourish with change, and He did the same thing for you.

You might not always like change, or even value it if you aren't prepared for it, but you too can thrive and flourish in times of change. You have been designed to be beautifully resilient and strong. You're adaptable and capable and that means no matter what may happen, you can manage it.

God works all things together for good and He can even change difficult things or unwelcome outcomes so that they bring growth and new opportunity. He does not bring change into your life for the sake of change, but for your sake, so that you can become everything you were meant to be.

*All that is in the world – the lust of the flesh, the lust of the eyes, and the pride of life – is not of the Father but is of the world. And the world is passing away, and the lust of it; but he who does the will of God abides forever.*

1 John 2:16-17 NKJV

Lord, sometimes I resist change even when I know
it's good for me, even when I know the end result will be
more fulfilling. Help me to accept the changes that come into
my life, as guidance and love from You.

Amen.

## Prism of love

*Love is swift, sincere, pious, joyful, generous, strong, patient, faithful, prudent, long-suffering, courageous, and never seeking its own; for wherever a person seeks his own, there he falls from love.*

Thomas à Kempis

Love defies definition because it takes so many forms. Romantic love may come upon us like an unexpected lightning bolt that lights us up for the rest of our lives. Or, it can grow slowly, building over time, becoming real and supportive and genuine in special ways.

Love in any of its forms is much like a prism, multi-faceted, beautiful in the light of the sun, and colorful. Whether you love your spouse, your friends or your children, you recognize that love reflects the joys of your heart and sustains your spirit. However, that doesn't always make it easy to embrace love.

Sometimes love requires us to get out of our own way, put our egos aside and really work to make it become that unending, unconditional opportunity that God would have us know. Love humbles and exalts us and any earthly connection to love we may have is a mere glimmer of the steadfast love God has for us. Celebrate love and surround yourself with its infinite possibilities.

*Pursue love, and desire spiritual gifts, but especially that you may prophesy.*

1 Corinthians 14:1 NKJV

Lord, I thank You for the abundance of love that is part of my life. I'm awed at the blessings love brings to me each day.

Amen.

## Risk and reward

Christians are supposed not merely to endure change,
nor even to profit by it, but to cause it.

Harry Emerson Fosdick

---

It's one thing to take on a leadership role when you are part of something that is well-established or join a group that already has set all the rules. It's something else when you're carving out new territory and expanding passed the tried and true. Imagine what it must have been like for Abraham to leave his home and all that he knew was to go to a place that God would show him. Imagine how he dealt with questions like "Where are we going?" or "Are we there yet?"

You may feel a calling on your life and know that God is leading you somewhere special, but you're not always sure where you're going or when you'll get there. The good news is that as long as you let God lead, you'll get to the destination.

Once you arrive, your fantastic leadership skills will come together and you will be ready to take on a whole new order of things. Trust God to lead you there – He's the one with the map!

*"Take the bag of gold from that servant and give it to the servant who has ten bags of gold."*

Matthew 25:28 NCV

Lord, I know that You have a plan for my life, and oftentimes
I hear You asking me to step out in faith and take the lead.
Help me to keep following Your voice so that I can arrive at the
destination You have in mind for the good of others.

Amen.

## Stand tall

Passion drives perfection.

Rick Warren

———✦———

You probably have a lot of interests. Perhaps you like the theatere or taking in shows on Broadway. Maybe you like gardening or flower arranging. Hobbies and interests occupy your time in positive ways and add to your sense of joy.

Your beliefs are something else, though. Your beliefs come with a built-in passion that is unshakable. You know that being a good parent or doing a good job at work are important to you, so you work hard to do your best. You know that your faith means everything to you and so you keep building on your knowledge of Scripture and remain committed to your life of prayer.

You believe that God has a plan for you, and that belief makes a difference in how you conduct the day-to-day events of life. You believe in your goal to become more of a woman of worth in His eyes and so each day you take steps to make that happen. Give God the glory for all you are and all you believe.

*It is with your heart that you believe and are justified,*
*and it is with your mouth that you profess your faith and are saved.*

Romans 10:10 NIV

Lord, I do want to make You proud of me. I want to be willing to
step in and shine a light whenever the right moment presents itself.
I want to believe with my whole heart in all that You have done for me.

Amen.

# SEPTEMBER 18

## *Balance beams*

*The two hardest things to handle in life are failure and success.*

Anonymous

Have you ever watched a skillful gymnast on a balance beam? She might appear to leap across the beam without any awareness that it is just a five-inch wide piece of wood beneath her feet. She flips and turns with ease and everything looks flawless, until one misstep happens, one tiny bit of weight on the foot becomes too much and she sways, trying not to fall.

Success and failure are part of the balance beam we each tread and sometimes we enjoy a fabulous recovery and go for gold. At other times something we never even anticipated trips us up and we begin to fall. We know that God's scales are a bit more heavenly than a balance beam. He gives us a wide berth to explore, to stumble, to change direction and still come out a winner.

Most of the time, He's interested in our walk, how we get from one place to another. He already knows the final destination greets us with victory, so success is assured and failure only momentary. Try to balance your life so that your walk is steady and strong each day.

*Hold on to what is good.*

1 Thessalonians 5:21 NLT

Lord, thank You for keeping me balanced. I know I get off the track pretty easily and so I ask You to hold me up when I'm taking a risk. Be with me in all I do today.

Amen.

## Learning new things

An ounce of will-power is worth a pound of learning!

Nicholas Murray Butler

---

Even though you may have grown up hearing the adage "Where there's a will, there's a way," you may not always be sure of its truth. The thing is that nothing is accomplished without a strong desire. You can research something you're interested in, look at it from every angle, and finally talk yourself out of pursuing it because you imagine why it won't work. If you had simply given it a try, it may have been successful.

It's good to do research and make yourself knowledgeable about choices you're considering. After all, you learned a long time ago that it's a good thing to do your homework. However, if you don't have the willpower to really tackle something you may never know if you could have done it. If you read every article you can get your hands on about how to write a novel, but you never sit down to write, you'll never be on a best-seller list.

What's driving you today? Willpower or "won't power"?

*A desire accomplished is sweet to the soul.*

Proverbs 13:19 NKJV

Lord, help me to take a chance on things I really want to do.
Whatever I know about the facts won't truly help me know if I
could have accomplished my desire by simply going and doing it.

Amen.

## *Zipping past your comfort zones*

Never forget that only dead fish swim with the stream.

Malcolm Muggeridge

———————

When we're young, we spend a lot of time trying to figure out how to fit in with the crowd so that we seem like everyone else. Eventually, we learn the beauty of simply being ourselves and defining our own terms for addressing the world. That learning process often takes us outside of our comfort zones. After all, if we don't like to place attention on ourselves, it's easier to simply fade into the crowd.

Jesus gave us some wonderful examples of what it means to be the person God called you to be. He was always His best self, whether He was talking to kings or fishermen. He may have experienced uncomfortable moments, but He knew so well what He needed to accomplish that He just blew past those things and got the job done.

You have a calling too. You may find that you are put in places or conversations or situations that are simply out of your arena of comfort. That doesn't mean you're not supposed to be there. It simply means that God knows you can deal with it for His glory. There's nothing wrong with going against the tide now and then.

*Do not love the world or anything in the world.*

1 John 2:15 NIV

Lord, You know me so well and You know when I'm struggling with a certain situation or feel like I'm simply in unchartered waters. Please help me to act with faith that You are right there with me.

Amen.

## The fruit of faith

*Obedience is the fruit of faith; patience, the bloom on the fruit.*

Christina Rossetti

As a concept, we get the idea of obedience. After all, we want to obey God in all that we do so that He'll be proud of us and be able to draw closer to us. In practice though, it's not as easy as it sounds.

Obedience would dictate that you might rise every morning and pray without ceasing through the day. It might dictate that you would make wise decisions, always taking each one to God before you act. It might even suggest that you would put God first in everything you do. No doubt you want to do those things, and often you succeed at doing them.

Obedience might go so far as to remind you when you succumb to temptation, overspending or overeating, or not doing what is best for your body, mind and soul. It's good to be obedient and it truly is one of the gifts of faith, but it's a good thing that one has to walk with patience, or we might not experience the full bloom of joy meant for our souls. Be patient with yourself, seeking to be obedient to God's call, and giving yourself the freedom to grow a bit more each day.

*It is those who obey the law who will be declared righteous.*

Romans 2:13 NIV

Lord, I know that I have high expectations for myself. I should be willing and able to obey You at all times, but I know I don't. Please forgive me when I behave in ways that are disappointing to us both.

Amen.

## Thoughtful and thankful

*We have short memories in magnifying God's grace. Every blessing that God confers upon us perishes through our carelessness, if we are not prompt and active in giving thanks.*

John Calvin

If we challenged ourselves to write down our ten top disasters and our ten top blessings as fast as possible, it might be interesting to see which list we would start first and how quickly we'd name the items on that list. Most of us have had blessing after blessing fill our lives. We've had a warm bed to sleep in, good friends to cheer us on and reasonable health. It's important to remember that we always have reasons to be thankful to God for our daily lives.

If you started your list with the disasters, keep going, but then create the blessing list and compare the two. Chances are you'll see the awesome goodness your heavenly Father has toward you. God always seeks your good.

Set your blessings before you today and give God the thanks for each one of them.

*Always be joyful. Never stop praying. Be thankful in all circumstances, for this is God's will for you who belong to Christ Jesus.*

1 Thessalonians 5:16-18 NLT

Lord, I know I have many things to be grateful about in my life. You have known me and blessed me in more ways than I can count. Help me to draw on those things when difficult times arise.

Amen.

## Thrifty and brave

Difficulties and obstacles are God's challenges to faith. When hindrances confront us in the path of duty, we are to recognize them as vessels for faith to fill with the fullness and all-sufficiency of Jesus.

A. B. Simpson

The main reason you don't see a lot of people taking great leaps of faith is that they are afraid to walk away from their comfort zones. They are uncertain about the steps needed to run and jump, much less leap and fly. A leap of faith takes you past today and asks you to trust God with everything you have for tomorrow.

We don't know what tomorrow will bring and so we make plans and project into the future, trusting it will be there, trusting God has a plan for our lives. Why then is it so difficult to simply get off the ground when we want to try something new?

Your desire for safety is a good thing, but your desire to become more of the woman you were designed to be is an even better thing. Trust God for those things that take you into uncertainty and cause you to have to wrap yourself in courage. He'll be there for you, just like He is in every other area of your life.

*Be of good courage, and He shall strengthen your heart,*
*all you who hope in the LORD.*

Psalm 31:24 NKJV

Lord, I am a bit timid about taking new steps and trying new ventures.
Please help me to trust You always for each new effort I make.
Amen.

## Moving on again

Taking a new step, uttering a new word, is what people fear most.

Fyodor Dostoevsky

———✦———

If you've ever studied another language, you may remember the first time you tried to speak it aloud and how funny the sounds seemed to you. Even though you knew the phrases and the right words, the language itself was still uncomfortable when you shared it with others. Over time, you learned to overcome your fear of speaking in a tongue that was not your own.

As women, we spend a good share of life overcoming the uncertain fears that present themselves to us. To any of those unknowns, we add fear and hesitation and sometimes sorrow and regret, because we don't always believe in ourselves or in God's ability to walk with us. God is with you always and He delivers you from fear. You were not designed with a spirit of timidity, but a spirit of strength and grace. Rely on Him and on that spirit in all you do.

*The Lord is my light and the one who saves me. So why should I fear anyone?*
*The Lord protects my life.*

Psalm 27:1 NCV

Lord, I've tried a lot of things in my life, attempting to
be bold in my own way. Sometimes I've succeeded and sometimes
I've failed miserably. Though I have a fear of trying new things,
I have an even greater fear of disappointing You. Help me to
take on those things You call me to do, in great trust.
Amen.

## Talking to God

Pray and let God worry.

Martin Luther

You may have heard the adage that it's a good idea not to "borrow trouble." Worry is a form of borrowing trouble because we make up a story in our heads that something is wrong, or someone is going down a path that is out of our control and we need to worry about them. Given the chance, we can find a basketful of things to worry about every hour of our lives.

God doesn't want you to lug around your basket of worries. He doesn't want you to spend your waking hours wondering what else you might have done, or how you could have changed things so that there would be a different result. He doesn't want you to blame yourself for each thing that doesn't go quite right.

The thing God wants is your trust and your faith, and your understanding that He will never leave you. He knows what you need before you even ask. He knows the things that weigh you down and make you weep. He knows everything about you. That's why you can find the courage and the joy to move forward, because God knows what you need even more than you do. He will not abandon you and He doesn't need your worries. He only needs your love and your prayer.

*You are all around me – in front and in back – and have put Your hand on me.*

Psalm 139:5 NCV

Lord, please help me to feel Your presence today
and trust You with my life and the lives of those I love.

Amen.

## *Trusting God*

*Oh, how great peace and happiness would he possess who should cut off all vain anxiety and place all his confidence in God.*

Thomas à Kempis

If someone were to ask, "Do you trust God in your life?" you would probably say, "Yes!" You would probably assume even to yourself that you squarely put your trust in God for everything. The problem is that the theory seems to work well, but reality can cause you to face uncertainty and make you question your level of trust.

If you find yourself having moments of doubt, wondering if God really will come through for you, then welcome to being human. As women, we are often more comfortable with questions than we are with answers. We can know the right things to say and do and still wonder if we are making the right choice.

Come to peace with yourself, and you and God will work things out together. He wants you to know His favor and His peace that passes all understanding. You can trust Him for that.

*Commit your way to the Lord; trust in Him and He will do this: He will make your righteous reward shine like the dawn, your vindication like the noonday sun.*

Psalm 37:5-6 NIV

Lord, I do trust You for my life, but I also recognize that at times I simply walk off without You, worrying about everything in front of me and wondering what I'm doing. Help me to stop and pray when I've lost my way and my sense of peace.

Amen.

## *Remarkable you!*

God has created me to do Him some definite service;
He has committed some work to me which He has not
committed to another. I have my mission – I never
may know it in this life, but I shall be told it in the next.

John Henry Newman

---

The reason the world loves a hero is that heroes always have a strong sense of mission and they don't let anything stop them from meeting their destiny. There's a hero inside you. There's a woman of incredible courage who knows who she is, where she wants to go and even how to get there. That woman may not wear a cape and fly through the air, but she wears a smile and is so protected by the armor of faith that nothing can really stop her. She is ready to go wherever God would send her, because she has everything she needs to get the job done.

Today, stop at the mirror and look at a hero. See the woman that God sees when He looks at you, the one who is capable, strong, and so full of His grace and mercy that nothing can change her direction. You are that woman in every way and God is with you. The world will stand aside for you as long as you walk in His Spirit everywhere you go.

*Take delight in the Lord, and He will give you the desires of your heart.*

Psalm 37:4 NIV

Lord, help me to keep moving in the direction You have planned for me so that I may serve others with compassion, strength and love.
Amen.

## Fear factors

*I am not moved by what I see. I am not moved by what I feel.*
*I am moved only by what I believe.*

Smith Wigglesworth

---

What prevents you from moving forward in your life? What keeps you stuck in an old pattern that you know does not serve you well? What prevents you from making new choices?

When we're young, we listen to those who parent us and nurture our lives. We need to for our own protection since we're still too innocent to take on the world by ourselves. Sometimes, though, even as adults we allow ourselves to stay back in that childlike place that keeps us secure, but doesn't let us grow and move to a new level of opportunity and success.

What moves you? It's a good day to see how your beliefs affect your life and encourage your steps. Ask God to help you see the truth of your actions, moving you to a new level of faith, acceptance and courage. You have everything you need to move forward, because you believe in God and He believes in you.

*Ensure Your servant's well-being; do not let the arrogant oppress me.*

Psalm 119:122 NIV

Lord, I know that I have often allowed my feelings to rule
my actions. I have let moments of uncertainty or disappointment
rule in my heart. Help me to believe much in You so that
I can move bravely and swiftly forward.

Amen.

# *What's inside?*

Christian love, either towards God or towards man,
is an affair of the will.

C. S. Lewis

What's inside your heart and mind will make all the difference to the things that happen inside your life. What happens inside your life also makes a difference in the things you attempt to do in those areas that are outside your personal life, aspects of Christian love in service to others. If you are filled with love , then it is easy to let that love flow out to others. If you feel deprived and malnourished in your spirit, then you will not be able to serve God and those around you with joy.

What can you do, then, to guard and protect your heart and mind, and be aware of what flows from you on the inside? Go to the fountain of God's love, the Source of all that you are and rest there until you feel His peace flow through you. Offer Him your life and surrender your will so that He can infuse you with new power – His power.

If you will let God guard you and guide you, you will have the power of His strength and His love to share with others. Loving God and loving others is an affair of the heart.

*Above all else, guard your heart, for everything you do flows from it.*

Proverbs 4:23 NIV

Lord, I want to serve others well and I know that I need Your direction and Your grace and mercy to do so. Help me to have the will and the desire to serve You more fervently today.

Amen.

## Don't stop now!

*The person who really wants to do something finds a way;*
*the other finds an excuse.*

Anonymous

Since you're three-quarters of the way through the year, it might be a good idea to take a little inventory on those things you wanted to accomplish. You remember that list of New Year's resolutions you made back in January? Yes, that list! Go back and take a look and see how you're doing. If you've accomplished all the things on your list, then bravo for you! If not, check in with yourself to see why not.

Did you lose those five pounds? No? Why not? Did you simply not put the effort into doing it, or did you give yourself an out because you couldn't find the time to exercise? Did you start that prayer journal? Yes? You started it, but by the middle of February, did you let it go more often than not?

As human beings, we're really in touch with the things we need to do that will make our lives better. God has equipped us to accomplish great things. Today, kick those excuses to the curb and give yourself a chance to try again. It's not too late and there's no reason to stop now!

*The desire of the righteous ends only in good.*

Proverbs 11:23 NIV

Lord, I know I have tossed a bunch of excuses around for the things
I still have not accomplished this year. Please help me to stay true to
myself and to You and start again to get things done.

Amen.

# HER CHILDREN ARISE AND

*call her blessed*

# HER HUSBAND PRAISES HER

PROVERBS 31:28

## A little preparation

It's easier to prepare and prevent, than to repair and repent.

Anonymous

We're pretty good at preparing for the things we know are on our to-do list. If we have a meeting to attend, we plan ahead about what we might contribute. If we have a child's birthday to celebrate, we think of all the things we can do to make the day more fun. We like to feel prepared for the important things in our lives.

Sometimes, though, we forget to prepare our hearts. We forget to sit with God and seek His guidance for the day. We don't always know what's ahead or how to prepare for those unknowns, but God does and if we stay close to Him, He can help us. Don't let your spirit get dry and disconnected from the Source of your love and your life.

Prepare the way for God to help you, not because He will ever leave you, but so you are more able to feel His presence when you need Him. It's always a good day to prepare your heart for Him.

*Prepare the way of the LORD;*
*make straight in the desert a highway for our God.*

Isaiah 40:3 NKJV

Lord, thank You for sticking by me even when I have failed
to wait for You. Help me to stand close to You so that nothing
can ever come between us.

Amen.

## *Pumpkin-patch dreams*

*The mundane tasks of everyday life can lull you to apathy and push God to the back of your mind. Refuse to become self-sufficient in life. You need God every day, whether you're facing a storm or not.*

Paul Chappell

Excitement reigns when you are beginning something that brings joy to your heart. You anticipate getting that much closer to fulfilling your dreams. However, if the task you have to begin is the one of cleaning out the attic or sorting through boxes in the basement, it's less thrilling.

One good thing is to find the joy you might derive from the activity. Maybe it's simply that you would be able to cross that item off your to-do list. The sooner you begin, the sooner you'll see the beauty of your accomplishment. Maybe you'll run across a sweet memory packed in a box in the attic. Maybe you'll discover you don't owe as much as you thought on your taxes. You won't really know until you tackle the job.

In everyday things and in big things, like the dreams you carry in your heart, you have one choice: begin! Get started! When you do, you'll find reasons to smile.

*Consider what a great forest is set on fire by a small spark.*

James 3:5 NIV

Lord, whether my dreams sit out there like pumpkins in the patch, or my work feels full of weeds, I know I have to get things moving if I want them to be completed. Help me to do what must be done with joy today.

Amen.

## People you know

*You never met a mere mortal. Remember the people you see are eternal; if you knew what they'd become you'd fall down and worship.*

C. S. Lewis

Here's something you might try today. Look for the divine in each person you meet, the place where their spirit and yours and God's might intersect. C. S. Lewis recognized that as children of God, as spirits wrapped in a body, we are each eternal, each carrying an aspect of heaven within our framework.

If we were to seek out the best in each other, noticing that aspect that is a bit more divine than human, we might give God the praise and thank Him for each other more readily.

You are a woman after God's own heart, growing and changing and becoming more of what He has in mind for you. You are His light on earth and even after you're back home with Him, you'll shine that eternal light forever.

When you observe the divine in those around you, you'll notice something wonderful: Your light and theirs will become as one because you have the same Father, the same source for all that you are. Help others to shine with you today.

*You, however, are not in the realm of the flesh but are in the realm of the Spirit, if indeed the Spirit of God lives in you.*

Romans 8:9 NIV

Lord, thank You for putting Your spirit within us so that we can feel Your presence, not only in ourselves, but in each other. Bless those who shine Your light today.

Amen.

## Latitude and attitude

*Any fact facing us is not as important as our attitude toward it,*
*for that determines our success or failure.*

Norman Vincent Peale

You are growing and changing all the time. You've been doing so since you were born, and if you're willing to do so, you'll keep becoming more of what you were designed to be with each passing day. That's the plan, and God is in it with you with a lifetime guarantee. He wants you to be your best self forever.

Your attitude about aging, growing and changing makes all the difference in your personal life. Your attitude about the events you may face in the future impacts you too. You can choose to see God's hand at work in your life at every opportunity or you can choose to blame yourself or others when things don't go well.

Success in any venture is not always about the outcome, but is often about the process, the journey, the attitudes you display on your way there. Remember, God sees you already as a success story. He gives you room each day to see His hand in everything that happens to you and to give Him thanks and praise.

*The LORD looks deep inside people and searches through their thoughts.*

Proverbs 20:27 NCV

Lord, I know that I don't simply default to joy when things are not
going my way. I tend to look for reasons why something didn't
turn out well, and most of the time I find a way to blame myself.
Today, give me an attitude of possibility and joy, no matter what I do.
Amen.

## Discovering what it's worth!

*For anything worth having one must pay the price; and the price is always work, patience, love, and self-sacrifice.*

John Burroughs

---

By now, you have enough life experience to know that most of the things that bring you a sense of accomplishment and fulfillment take work. The work is most satisfying when you do it with an attitude of joy and love, and when you are willing to be patient in the process. The work may also require that you be willing to alter your course if a better option presents itself, or that you be willing to receive help along the way if necessary.

When your business is about discovering the value of something, or finding true worth and fulfillment, then you must be willing to sacrifice, to strive, and to overcome the obstacles to make those things happen. How?

One way is to start toward your goals with a plan, and the first item in your plan should be prayer. God should always be your first step, no matter what you are trying to achieve. He is the Creator and therefore the Source of all that brings true value to the things you do.

*Rejoice always, pray continually, give thanks in all circumstances;*
*for this is God's will for you in Christ Jesus.*

1 Thessalonians 5:16-18 NIV

Lord, remind me that You are near and help me always to come to You as I seek to discover more of life's true worth and value. Please be patient with me as I strive to know You better.

Amen.

## Remember when

*The past should be a springboard, not a hammock.*

Edmund Burke

---

Sometimes we simply want to rest on our laurels. After all, we've worked hard at living and we deserve a break. You need to build breaks into your daily life and you need time to rest, but don't get stuck in the hammock. Rest a little, dream a little, and then get back out there because you have a lot to accomplish.

The beauty of remembering things you've accomplished is that you can recall the moments of anticipation before a project started, the amazing amount of work it took to get everything done, and that rewarding feeling of having met your goals. Those memories serve you well and become the springboard for future projects and dreams.

It's great to reward yourself for the good things you've achieved, to rest in quiet gratitude with the One who helped you get there. Then move on again, leaving that sweet memory behind so that you can create brand-new memories to enjoy. God has so many wonderful things in store for you.

*Be careful never to forget what you yourself have seen.*
*Do not let these memories escape from your mind as long as you live!*

Deuteronomy 4:9 NLT

Lord, I am grateful for each thing that I've managed to get done,
especially those things that reflect my love for You. Help me to rest
briefly in that joy and then to move on and serve You even more fully.
Amen.

# *Good or bad*

Let nothing good or bad upset the balance of your life.

Thomas à Kempis

---

We have a tendency as women to set things down in absolutes, making them good or bad, or black or white. When we do that, we start to draw lines around our problems and put them into little boxes that simply don't give us enough room to open another door. When you've put yourself into enough little boxes, it doesn't take long before they begin to overwhelm you and life gets out of balance. You feel stuck and imagine that all the doors have closed.

God wants you to get beyond those early judgments that make things good or bad and see them with new eyes. See each event in your life as an opportunity to discover more of who you are and as a chance to strengthen your character or your attitude about something.

Only God knows what is good. The rest of us simply try to imagine what the concept of goodness might be. We strive for that sense of goodness, giving ourselves continual freedom to learn more of what God wants and to discover what it truly means to live a balanced life in Him.

*Whatever is good and perfect is a gift coming down to us from God.*

James 1:17 NLT

Lord, help me not to judge myself or others, thinking too quickly that I know what is good or bad. Help me to see through Your eyes each thing that happens in my life.

Amen.

## OCTOBER 8

*Gaining perspective*

Let us not look back in anger or forward in fear,
but around in awareness.

James Thurber

---

How often do you feel truly connected to the things around you? Most of the time we live at such a swirling pace, we don't even feel we have time to think our own thoughts, much less assess what is happening as we walk down the street or pass the receptionist at the office. We're wrapped up in our own worlds, feeding off our own worries and needs and so we miss the moments where God would have us see His hand at work.

As a woman of worth, you want your perceptions to change. You want to become more aware of your sisters in Christ and your family. You want to realize the moment when God wants to speak through you for the good of someone else. You want to be tuned in, alive with His spirit and energy, and fully present to receive His guidance on someone's behalf.

Look around today at those who move in your sphere of influence and offer them grace and encouragement. Help them to face today with more joy.

*Be on your guard; stand firm in the faith; be courageous,*
*be strong. Do everything in love.*

1 Corinthians 16:13-14 NIV

Lord, I thank You for being with me right now. Help me to let go of anything that keeps me stuck in the past or anything that keeps me fearful of the future. Let me see Your face in the sunshine of today.

Amen.

## The test of beauty

*Characteristics that define beauty are wholeness,*
*harmony and radiance.*

Thomas Aquinas

---

You know what happens to your face when life gets out of balance. You start to see those worry lines that form around your mouth more clearly. You don't feel good about anything you wear and you're just not able to have a "good hair day." Nothing seems to come together. You may even find that you're short tempered or moody and that the people around you move out of your way. Your life is out of rhythm and you have no sense of harmony and peace. Your mind is crowded with worry; nothing feels just right and your beauty fades.

When you sense those things happening, it's time for a new beauty routine. That routine starts by admitting that you are not at peace with yourself and your situation. That routine requires that you ask God to restore you to wholeness and radiance according to His plan and purpose for your life. When you do, you'll feel beautiful again, maybe not immediately, but soon.

*A happy heart makes the face cheerful, but heartache crushes the spirit.*

Proverbs 15:13 NIV

Lord, I haven't been myself lately and I need You
to help me get back on track. Help me to find
the peace and harmony that Your Spirit brings.
Amen.

# *Autumn beauty*

Never lose an opportunity of seeing anything that is beautiful,
for beauty is God's handwriting – a wayside sacrament.
Welcome it in every fair face, in every fair sky, in every flower,
and thank God for it as a cup of blessing.

Ralph Waldo Emerson

The wonder of the autumn is that it brings a crescendo of God's creativity into living color. Leaves on the trees shout with joy for the glory of the season. Fiery flowers bloom on the grassy hillsides and birds feather their nests for the coming winter. Everything is alive with the Spirit of God!

Wherever you live, take some time to appreciate the gifts God has given you in nature. Thank Him for the beautiful sunsets and the triumph of the landscape. Ask Him to keep you fully engaged in all that is beautiful so that you can continue to share your thoughts of joy with others.

God's handwriting is indeed everywhere for those who are willing to read it with hope and expectation; it jumps off of every precious tree limb, bringing a harvest of contentment and joy.

*Shout to the Lord, all the earth. Serve the Lord with joy; come before Him singing.*

Psalm 100:1-2 NCV

Lord, I love the fall leaves and the beauty that surrounds
me at this time of year. Help me to really breathe in the
joy that You offer so exquisitely today.

Amen.

## *Striving to be more!*

Be dogmatically true, obstinately holy, immovably honest,
desperately kind, fixedly upright.

Charles H. Spurgeon

Do you recall what it means to be "dogmatic"? It means that you're unyielding, unwilling to let go and that, like a puppy protecting a bone, you'll growl at anyone who tries to steal your prize. In your effort to become more, you have only one choice: to be dogmatic, stubborn in your pursuit of what God wants in your life. It means that you are so focused on your goal that you won't let anything get in the way. You're immovable and you've barred the door of anything that might prevent your growth.

Your passion for the goal is what pleases God. He sees your heart and how much you desperately want to be more like Him in ways that serve Him in this world. He sees that you are devoted to your mission to grow in ways that cause you to radiate His goodness wherever you are.

God wants you to be fixed on your mission, hungry to achieve it, and unyielding in your love for Him. He knows that there's joy in the striving and great blessing in the effort. Keep moving forward.

*Whatever you do, do it heartily, as to the Lord and not to men.*

Colossians 3:23 NKJV

Lord, I know that I am passionate about my desire to please You. Give me the energy and the strength to keep trying, even when I feel weary. Let nothing keep me from drawing closer to You.

Amen.

## Continuing to grow

*There is nothing that is more dangerous to your own salvation,
more unworthy of God, and more harmful to your own happiness
than that you should be content to remain as you are.*

François Fénelon

---

God gives us a restless spirit that simply won't rest until it rests
totally in Him. He gives us a fresh insight into the Scriptures so
that words bounce off the page in ways that never had that kind
of meaning before. He makes it hard for us to simply remain as
we are.

If your spirit is restless, it may mean that it is beckoning you
to move faster toward the next goal. Your own spirit strives to
give you an inner sense that God has work for you to do; work
that can't happen until you get to the next point of growth and
are prepared for His call. Today, consider the things that are not
entirely settled in your life, those areas where you still question
whether you've gotten as far as you intended or whether you
need to set some new, clear and intentional markers. Ask God to
show you when you have reached a level where He can use your
greater light for the good of others.

*"I tell you, whatever you ask for in prayer,
believe that you have received it, and it will be yours."*

Mark 11:24 NIV

Lord, thank You for challenging me to grow, for making
it hard for me to simply rest on my past efforts.
I want to always grow in Your light and love.
Amen.

# Sorting out foolishness

*If a million people believe a foolish thing, it is still a foolish thing.*

Anatole France

---

Do you remember some of the popular fashion designs from when you were growing up? Maybe you lived through the era of bell-bottom pants, or short shorts. You might have worn your hair the same way that everyone else did or had fashionable glasses. Whatever the case, you probably thought you looked good and everyone else chimed in to encourage and support you. Looking back at your photos of those days, you may now have a different sort of reaction! You probably wonder what you might have been thinking when you made those fashion choices.

The difference is that you were going along with the crowd and trying to fit in. It didn't matter that nobody actually looked good in those funny glasses; they simply were the style of the day. Now that you're an adult, you don't have to follow the crowd. You don't have to wear styles that aren't flattering for you, or to keep up with somebody else's attitudes and opinions. Foolishness will always be foolish, but God has given you a spirit of wisdom and discernment so that you can get away from the crowd and simply follow Him.

*Treat wisdom as a sister, and make understanding your closest friend.*

Proverbs 7:4 NCV

Lord, thank You for keeping me so connected to You that I can make wiser choices. Help me to remain in Your care and grace all my life.

Amen.

## A believer's heart view

*I believe in Christianity as I believe that the sun has risen, not only because I see it but because, by it, I see everything else.*

C. S. Lewis

As much as we might benefit from the "seeing is believing" approach to life and matters of faith, we probably gain greater insight and awareness from the opposite side of the coin: Believing is seeing. Believing is like looking through the lens of a telescope and discovering that things that were there all the time are now clearly in view. You couldn't see them before, because you had no idea how to look for them, no idea they were even out there.

Your faith is a matter of believing and the more you are able to believe that God has plans for your life – that He's personally involved in the things that make a difference to you – the more you'll look for Him and the more you'll see His hand at work in your life. Like the stars that can only be seen through a telescope, God is there in a multitude of ways. He doesn't disappear from your view, He simply waits for you to seek Him.

Look for Him in everything you do today. He'll help you believe and He'll help you see Him more clearly.

*Seek the Lord and His strength; seek His face evermore!*

1 Chronicles 16:11 NKJV

Lord, thank You for guiding me toward Your light. Help me to see more of You and to move beyond those things that are not of You.

Amen.

# At the end of the day

Make it a rule, and pray to God to help you keep it, never,
if possible, to lie down at night without being able to say:
"I have made one human being at least a little wiser,
or a little happier, or at least a little better this day."

Charles Kingsley

---

Whether we're aware of it or not, we have influence on others and
we can affect their lives in positive or negative ways. Sometimes
it's simply your willingness to intentionally do good that makes
all the difference.

Think through the conversations and interactions you've
had in the past few days. How many times did someone say just
the right thing, offer the kind of encouragement you needed or
thank you for a kindness? How many times did you offer praise, a
smile or a helping hand just when it was needed?

You naturally do good things because you have the spirit
of Christ in your heart and it prompts you to do what you can
to be a positive influence. You are an ambassador of the living
kindness and expression of God. Do what you can to make it a
better day for someone today.

*"A good man brings good things out of the good stored up in him."*

Matthew 12:35 NIV

Lord, I am grateful for what You've done to make my life abundant
and joyful. Let me always be willing to share that joy with others.

Amen.

## *True confidence*

Confidence thrives on honesty, on honor,
on the sacredness of obligations, on faithful
protection and on unselfish performance.
Without them it cannot live.

Franklin D. Roosevelt

---

The more you understand your value and worth in the eyes of God, the more confident you become in the world. Your confidence rises because you are faithful to the goals you've set to become a woman after God's own heart.

Any time you've done something through your best effort, you want to share it with others. When you make a great meal for your family or you bake a fabulous dessert for your friends, you love to share what you've done. You want them to feel the joy in receiving the efforts of your hands as much as the pleasure you felt in the preparation.

The same is true of your efforts to sustain a living and loving faith: The more you prepare in joy to do the Lord's work, the more fun it will be to share it with those around you. You'll move forward with confidence, knowing you've done your best to honor the God of your heart.

*Whatever your hand finds to do, do it with your might.*

Ecclesiastes 9:10 NKJV

Lord, I do want to honor You. I want to offer you to others
with a confident heart because of all we share and all I know
of You. Thank You for being with me today.

Amen.

## What your heart knows

*God never made a promise that was too good to be true.*

Dwight L. Moody

---

What would it mean to you to truly wrap your arms around the idea that you are not in control? Does it mean you have no responsibility for your actions or your life? No! It simply means that you cannot know the mind of God. You cannot know exactly what plans He has for those around you and how He wants to help them to see who He is and how He desires to love them.

If God is truly in control of your life and everyone else's, which He is, then what is your role? What part should you try to control on any given day? You can be in control of yourself, of the behaviors you exhibit, and of the actions you take. You can be in control of your heart, staying prayerfully connected to the Source of your life so that you can know more of what He wants for you. You can control the effort you put into your work and the willingness you have to share your gifts with others.

You have a lot of control when it comes to the things you can choose from day to day. God gives you that control because He knows you'll grow from it and become stronger. Thank Him each day for caring enough about you to be in control of your life.

*There is no authority except that which God has established.*

Romans 13:1 NIV

Lord, I am grateful that the world does not depend on me.
I praise and thank You for being the God of this universe
and of all that is past, present and future.
Amen.

# *Just for today*

He who gives you the day will also give you
the things necessary for the day.

Gregory of Nyssa

Most of us assume that when we go to sleep at night that we'll awaken to a new day. We assume that life goes on and that we don't have much effect on the daily workings of the world. Sometimes we even assume we are at the mercy of forces beyond our control and that there is nothing we can do to make our lives feel better or more positive.

If you can, just for today, no matter what your circumstances might be, imagine that God sees you, walks with you and desires only to make your life better. Imagine that He aches to have you feel His presence and to realize that He won't let anything bad happen to you. Rest in His care! Let Him soothe you with His promises to love you and to be with you always. Just for today, breathe Him in and give Him room to reside with you.

The more you feel His presence, the more you'll come to trust that He is with you always, providing for your needs and loving you beyond measure. Serve Him in joy today.

*God did this so that they would seek Him and perhaps reach out for Him
and find Him, though He is not far from any one of us.*

Acts 17:27 NIV

Lord, thank You for walking with me and providing so well for me
even when I don't seem to notice. Help me to understand that I am
never alone here, that You see me and love me always.

Amen.

## *Facing the darkness*

*I would rather walk with God in the dark than go alone in the light.*

Mary Gardiner Brainard

———————

How do you experience darkness? Do you feel nervous if you don't have a nightlight on in your bedroom or bathroom? Do you tremble when you think of walking alone on a darkened street or camping out in the woods at night?

Most of us have a fear of the darkness, a fear of not being in control or not being able to react quickly enough to danger. Of course, we know that once we're tucked into our beds and fast asleep, we have to let go of those fears and trust God to take care of us, or we'd never sleep well.

You can trust God even in the darkness, for He is always light. He always sees clearly what you need and what is happening in your life. He protects your heart and mind, both day and night. Whenever you sit on the edge of darkness, wondering if you are alone and vulnerable, imagine God sitting next to you as a brilliant and shining beacon of love and protection. He'll be your nightlight.

*God is light; in Him there is no darkness at all.*

1 John 1:5 NIV

Lord, thank You for beaming Your light over me. You know I need You always, even when I temporarily allow the darkness to prevail.

Amen.

# A delightful thought

All earthly delights are but "streams." But God is the ocean.

Jonathan Edwards

---

Remember those paper chains you made as a kid? Maybe you used them to decorate a Christmas tree, or simply to hang in your room for fun. You made them from brightly colored paper bands and stapled each end together until you just couldn't do any more.

Sometimes you do the same thing with your worries. You start putting them together one by one, letting them loop around your heart and mind and hanging them in the corners of the places where fear lives. You keep creating them as though you're afraid you'll run out of paper and won't be able to make any more.

It's time to break those chains. It's time to let go of worry and to trust that God is bigger than any concern you might have. In fact, no matter how many streams of worry you pin together, they all run to the same place, to the ocean that is God, the One who takes all your worries upon Himself.

*Cast your burden on the Lord, and He shall sustain you;*
*He shall never permit the righteous to be moved.*

Psalm 55:22 NKJV

Lord, help me to stop worrying and making chains
out of the things I worry about. I hang my worries up
like trophies. Today, I want to break that chain.
Amen.

## *Never talk defeat!*

Never talk defeat. Use words like hope, belief, faith, and victory.

Norman Vincent Peale

---

When the coach comes out before the big game, he doesn't talk to his team about the possibility that they may not win. He doesn't remind them that they could be defeated. He spurs them on toward the goal and gives them hope that victory is just ahead.

You may need to give yourself pep talks from time to time with the same goal in mind. Remind yourself that victory is at hand and all you have to do is get into the game and give it your all.

We need positive self-talk every bit as much as any team in a sport needs it to face an opponent. You have an opponent in the world who will proclaim your shortcomings and mistakes to anyone who'll listen. He'll work to make you think you don't have what it takes to move ahead and win the day.

He lies! He knows that if you believe in the victory, it will be yours. He knows that God is on your side every step of the way. Get out there and win!

> *We are not those who turn back and are lost.*
> *We are people who have faith and are saved.*
>
> Hebrews 10:39 NCV

Lord, thank You for calming the voices that seek to defeat my spirit today. Help me to believe in You and the work we're doing together, and help me move on to the victory I have in You.

Amen.

## The true goal

Heaven is one's destiny. Becoming like Jesus is one's goal.

Anonymous

When you know where you're going, it's easier to get there. God promises eternal life, a place in heaven when your work here is done. He's already outlined your destiny. The one part of it that you can create in your own way is what you'll accomplish by the time you get there.

Not everything you do on earth matters in the realm of heaven, so it's important to understand what actually makes a difference. According to the New Testament, everything rests in receiving Jesus into your life and working to become more like Him in the things you do each day. Jesus really is the goal; your reason for striving.

You may have other goals today. You may be planning to get in a thirty-minute workout, eat fewer calories, write a report or something else. Those are good objectives for the day, but as you list your intentions, see if there's any way you can strive to become more like Jesus. How can that desire become a goal for you to achieve each day? The more you learn about Him, the more you communicate with Him in prayer, the more you'll understand what it means to be like Him. You're on the way!

*"Remain in Me, as I also remain in you."*

John 15:4 NIV

Lord, thank You for teaching me more about You and helping me to take steps to walk more closely with You.

Amen.

## Become more worthy

It is still one of the tragedies of human history
that the "children of darkness" are frequently more
determined and zealous than the "children of light."

Martin Luther King

Striving to become something more than you are now takes
work. You have to be steadfast in your effort in order to see
results. If you're trying to get in a regular exercise routine, you
start with a twenty-minute workout, move to thirty and keep
going until you can do an hour with relative ease. You know the
outcome you want and you go after it.

We aspire to have the same resolve when it comes to
improving our spirits, trying to become more enlightened or
more perceptive to the things of God. We might start with
twenty minutes of Bible reading and prayer, move to thirty, and
then an hour. We do it because we know that the battle rages
in the world between those who bear the light and those who
would keep themselves and others in darkness. We know that
we need to be strong if we're going to make a difference and
encourage the light for all to see.

*"I correct and discipline everyone I love.*
*So be diligent and turn from your indifference."*

Revelation 3:19 NLT

Lord, forgive me when I don't do the things I know would give me
more opportunity to grow as a child of light. Help me desire to do so
and to follow through for the sake of those who might need me.

Amen.

# When conflict emerges

*You will have no test of faith that will not fit you
to be a blessing if you are obedient to the Lord.*

A. B. Simpson

———

Few things are born without struggle. A mother labors to bring her child into the world. A seedling must work to send its tender sprouts above the ground. The human spirit struggles to get through one more difficult life experience. It's friction that makes sparks fly and causes a fire. It's conflict that teaches us that we can survive the hard things and be better for them.

How are we better? We're better because we understand more about how fragile life can be and how important it is to trust God's guidance and provision. We're better because we know that we have inner strength built on a foundation of belief that will help us get through the darkest hours. We're better because we know that God is with us in anything we face and that He will never leave us.

We don't like conflict. We avoid difficulty as much as possible, but God, in His wisdom, seeks to help us understand the strength we can find in Him as we grow through the obstacles of life. God does not seek to test you, but rather to mold you and help you grow into a stronger woman of faith.

*When I am weak, then I am strong.*

2 Corinthians 12:10 NKJV

Lord, thank You for being with me through difficult times.
Help me to be faithful to You in the midst of conflict.

Amen.

## *Live courageously!*

Take courage, and turn your troubles, which are without remedy, into material for spiritual progress. Often turn to our Lord, who is watching you, poor frail little thing as you are, amid your labors and distractions.

Francis de Sales

What are the things in your life that have caused you to act courageously? Maybe it took courage for you to pursue your career because your parents wanted you to go in a different direction. Perhaps you had to be strong to continue in a relationship with someone others didn't think was right for you. Maybe you have had to be courageous in your faith walk.

Courage is not a one-size-fits-all kind of thing. One person may easily get up on a stage and talk to a large room full of people. Another may stand up for justice and participate in a rally for a cause. Each of those things takes courage for some and just seems natural for others.

God wants you to have courage. Each time an angel appeared in the Bible, even with good news, the first words spoken were usually ones of "fear not" or "take courage." Live today fearlessly, knowing that God sees you and is prepared to fight any battle that comes your way.

*Be strong in the Lord and in His great power.*

Ephesians 6:10 NCV

Lord, help me to be strong in the work I do
and in the faith that keeps me close to You.
Amen.

## Ponder this!

We find comfort among those who agree with us –
growth among those who don't.

Frank A. Clark

It's nice when people agree with your views of life, encouraging your direction and supporting your efforts. It's nice and it's necessary, but it doesn't usually add anything to your understanding. Agreement keeps you right where you were before.

Discord causes you to define your thoughts more clearly or to defend your position. Either way, you benefit from the insights gained through the challenges. Does that mean you have to be challenged on every level and resist people who readily agree with your views? No, but when you want to learn something, you will go to the those who cause you to reflect on your decisions and dig deeper for direction.

God doesn't give you the answers you want every time you pray. He challenges you to think something through and weigh up the possible outcomes.

Enjoy the times that you share with friends who love everything you do, but when you want to learn more about yourself, seek out those who cause you to think twice before you act.

*"Present your case," says the Lord. "Bring forth your strong reasons."*

Isaiah 41:21 NKJV

Lord, thank You for helping me through decisions
I make and thank You for challenging me to think
again when that's what I need to do most.

Amen.

## In praise of tension

You will never be the person you can be if pressure,
tension, and discipline are taken out of your life.

James G. Bilkey

---

We don't usually ask for stress and tension. We don't beg God to take away our sense of peace and give us chaos. We don't, but maybe we should. Maybe we should welcome the circumstances that cause us to work harder at our tasks, give more time and attention to detail, and strive to move past our comfort zones.

When we think about it, we're motivated by the pressures of deadlines to get things done or the stress of making a speech. Accordingly, we work harder and we practice over and over again. The right kind of stress can cause us to expend more positive energy.

When good stress becomes overwhelming, however, it's no longer serving you well and then it's time to pray again for balance and renewed peace. If you don't strive for anything, you won't suffer a lot of stress … but you may not be truly fulfilled either.

*I was pleased with everything I did, and this pleasure*
*was the reward for all my hard work.*

Ecclesiastes 2:10 NCV

Lord, remind me that I do need some stress in my life.
Please help me to keep everything in a balanced perspective.
Amen.

*Getting distracted*

I neglect God and His angels for the noise of a fly,
for the rattling of a coach, for the whining of a door.

John Donne

Distraction can be a good thing when you've been focused on something for a while and need a break. It can give your mind a rest and even offer a chance to play and imagine and dream.

Most of us are easily distracted, especially when we have a task at hand that we're reluctant to complete. If you have to mop the floors today, you may find all kinds of reasons to put it off; after all, a second cup of tea is more inviting and a phoning a friend is more fun. The problem is that mopping the floors will still be there as a job to be done no matter how much you procrastinate.

It's easy to get off track and get distracted by life in ways that do nothing to help you grow. Today, see if you can stay focused on your goal to read God's Word with greater intention or to pray with complete surrender. When you make that kind of effort, those things that distract you will simply go away.

*Walk worthy of the Lord, fully pleasing Him, being fruitful in
every good work and increasing in the knowledge of God.*

Colossians 1:10 NKJV

Lord, I do get distracted when my heart and mind
are simply not in the things I have to accomplish.
Please help me to stay focused on You today.
Amen.

## Growing in faith

Faith is a living, busy, active, powerful thing;
it is impossible for it not to do us good continually.

Martin Luther

---

Since faith is a living thing, how you experienced it yesterday doesn't really matter. If you were fervent in prayer or diligent in your willingness to serve God yesterday, that's all well and good, but that was yesterday.

Today, God seeks your face again. He needs you to be a living example of what it means to walk in faith and to reside in His presence. He needs your light to shine and for you to actively pursue His strength and His Holy Spirit. You are His arms and legs and His voice in the world and so what you do today is what really matters to Him.

When you live in the present and allow God's Spirit to work through you and in you, then you cannot but help to do good for others. You have such a desire for the people around you to know God as you do, that even without great effort you share His blessings. Your faith is a powerful thing because you stay plugged in to the Source of all things. Live in that faith today!

*Without faith it is impossible to please Him.*

Hebrews 11:6 NKJV

Lord, thank You for loving me so much that You stick
close to me no matter where I am. Help me to stay steadfast
in my love and in faithfulness to You.

Amen.

## God's work in us

Faith is God's work in us, that changes us
and gives new birth from God.

Martin Luther

Do you remember sensing God's presence in your life to such a degree that it literally changed you, guiding your thinking and your heart? It was like you were reborn and it was a glorious moment. You may still rejoice as you think about that realization as you took your first real steps in faith.

The good news is that God did not stop working in you after that first significant experience. He did not leave you to grow on your own. God has been changing you since the beginning, preparing your heart and mind for each new step, each new opportunity to build your faith. He loves to see you take a leap of faith and realize that He has been there all along and that you could always count on Him. He loves for you to know that He is with you always.

God's work in you is not finished and it won't be completed until the day He calls you home to be with Him again. In the meantime, thank Him and praise Him, and let others know what He has done in your life. You are a new woman!

*He has committed to us the message of reconciliation. We are therefore Christ's ambassadors, as though God were making His appeal through us.*

2 Corinthians 5:19-20 NIV

Lord, thank You for Your mercy and grace.
I know that I am nothing without You.
Amen.

## Affection for God

*We do not walk to God with the feet of our body,*
*nor would wings, if we had them, carry us to Him,*
*but we go to Him, by the affections of our soul.*

St. Augustine

You know what it feels like to be in love. Your mind easily wanders to the one who holds your affection. You find yourself wondering what else you could do to please the one you love, how you can become more for that person. Nothing delights you than being able to create special moments for the two of you, times that you share in loving and warm conversation. Your heart flies to your loved one at a moment's notice, brought there by a song or a memory or a sweet word that comes to mind.

Those feelings are not unlike the love God has for you and the way He sees you all the time. His thoughts are all about what you need and what else He can do to show you His love. The wonderful thing is that He responds to your love for Him. You say a prayer and He's there; you sing a song of praise and love to Him and He smiles. Let God know of your affection every day and it will be a great blessing to you always.

*My flesh and my heart may fail, but God is the*
*strength of my heart and my portion forever.*

Psalm 73:26 NIV

Lord, I do love You and my heart sings with joy at the things You do in
my life. Help me to live in ways that honor the love between us.
Amen.

# A WOMAN WHO FEARS THE LORD IS
## *to be praised*

PROVERBS 31:30

## *New doors*

*All the doors that lead inward, to the sacred place of the Most High,*
*are doors outward – out of self, out of smallness, out of wrong.*
George MacDonald

You've always been a woman of worth in the sight of God and as you grow stronger in your faith toward Him, you can see how He has shaped you and molded you, helping to sculpt you into a masterpiece of His design. The closer you move in His direction, the more the windows and doors of your soul open.

One of the gifts of our growth is how encouraged we are to realize that we truly have changed in positive ways. We've been tried and tested, but not depleted and overwhelmed. We've been fearful and uncertain, and yet landed on our feet in a place better than we could even have imagined in our fearful state.

God has groomed us so that when we step out into the world in His name, the people who see us are attracted to that light. His light makes us beautiful. His light makes us radiate joy.

You've been opening new doors all your life and the best ones are still to come. God has gone before you and is even now preparing the way for you. Keep following Him and growing stronger in His love.

*Many women do noble things, but you surpass them all.*

Proverbs 31:29 NIV

Lord, thank You for helping me move past the run-down and worn-out versions of myself, opening new doors to a better me.

Amen.

# NOVEMBER 2

## Banking on friendship

Friendship is like a bank account. You can't continue to draw on it without making deposits.

Anonymous

One of the best gifts of becoming a stronger and better you is that you also become a more influential and more joyful friend. You become a person others just want to be around.

Friendships develop because of mutual interest, requiring an investment on the part of all those involved. When you have a close personal friend, you celebrate their joys, lift them up when things are tough, and listen to their dreams. You find fun ways to laugh together and you forgive each other when little foibles occur.

Your friendship with God requires a similar kind of interest. You make deposits in your friendship account with Him each time you choose to spend time in His presence. When you withdraw from Him, your account does not close, it just doesn't build the same kind of interest it does when you're together. God leaves your account open all the time. He loves it when you choose to build your relationship and spend time together with Him.

*If someone says, "I love God," but hates a fellow believer, that person is a liar. He has given us this command: Those who love God must also love their fellow believers.*

1 John 4:19-21 NLT

Lord, thank You for always being my friend. Forgive me when I walk off and leave You in mid-conversation. Help me spend time with You every day.

Amen.

## A woman of influence

*The serene, silent beauty of a holy life is the most powerful*
*influence in the world, next to the might of God.*

Blaise Pascal

You may not consider yourself a woman of influence, but you are! The people in your friendship circle, your work circle and your church circle look up to you. They listen to your heart, appreciate your time and talents, and seek your advice on things that matter most to them. You influence the way they think about life.

God wants you to be a woman of influence. He knows that you have a gift for sharing His love and light and it pleases Him each time you do so. You're His voice in the world, His smile, His gentle touch that reminds others they are not alone.

Whatever else you do today, remember that you are needed. Your kindness is cherished and your spirit brings joy. Do all that you can to influence others in ways that help them want to know more about God's love.

*Let us consider how we may spur one another on toward love and good deeds.*

Hebrews 10:24 NIV

Lord, thank You for giving me this simple role to play. You didn't make me a great speaker or a celebrity, but You made me a woman who can gently influence the lives of those around me. Thank You for that.

Amen.

## *Tune in!*

*I love to think of nature as an unlimited broadcasting station,
through which God speaks to us every hour, if we will only tune in.*

George Washington Carver

———————

Sometimes it's important to create white noise so that you can concentrate on something you're doing and not lose focus. The white noise is not really noticeable to you; it's just as simple as a fan blowing or rain falling. It helps to remove all the other noises that distract you.

When we're surrounded by noise, we may miss the things that are calming or helpful to us. We may miss the grace and peace that God intends for our lives; the peace that nature can bring to us, for example. In the fall season of the year, the earth displays itself in new ways: It tones down its vibrant colors and prepares to sleep through the winter. It calls us to be more peaceful and serene and to discover the still, small voice of God.

When you tune in to the landscape, you might see God's hand in a new way, or hear His voice more clearly as you allow the noises of life to dissipate and the songs of joy to fill your heart.

Let God into your heart today. See if you can discover Him in the skies above you and the earth around you and feel His love.

*"May the Lord show you His favor and give you His peace."*

Numbers 6:26 NLT

Lord, thank You for the incredible gifts of nature.
Thank You for tuning in to my life in so many vibrant ways.
Amen.

## Advancing through life

*She is only advancing in life, whose heart is getting softer, her blood
warmer, her brain quicker, and her spirit entering into living peace.*

John Ruskin (adapted)

Sometimes we have the notion that becoming more, or
advancing in life, has something to do with a job title, income or
social status. We imagine that it is a reflection of where we live or
who we know. How wonderful it is to realize that none of those
things matter at all. None of those things make a difference to
God. What makes a difference is the way your heart softens at the
very thought of being in His presence, at any opportunity to give
Him thanks and praise, or when you see the face of someone you
love who shines with His light.

When your restless spirit finds a chance to relax in the comfort
of your Savior's arms, you recognize how far you've come and
how much you've grown. Give God the glory for all that you are
now and all that you are yet to be.

*The Lord is good to those who depend on Him, to those who search for Him.
So it is good to wait quietly for salvation from the Lord.*

Lamentations 3:25-26 NLT

Lord, thank You for each tiny thing You've done to remind me of Your
presence, a melody that brings me joy, a smile on the face of a friend,
or a Scripture that comes to mind at just the right moment.
You are my Savior!
Amen.

## Resting in the creator

*You have made us for Yourself, O Lord,*
*and our hearts are restless, until they rest in You.*

St. Augustine

You know what it's like to have a restless spirit. You can't sleep very well. You can't focus on your work. You can't really understand what is happening around you because everything seems blurry and insignificant.

Sometimes life causes your spirit to be vexed, overwhelmed or simply saturated with too many bills, too many worries and too many obligations. When that happens, you have only one choice: You have to create a space for yourself, a space where you can catch your breath and inhale the sweet peace of God.

Be aware, though, that sometimes God fosters your restlessness, orchestrates those things that keep you wound up so that He can beckon you to His side. He knows that you might not create an intention to talk with Him on your own, and so He guides you back to Himself, back to a place that will free your spirit and give you peace.

Take yourself into His presence today and rest there. Surrender your worries to Him and find peace.

*I will always trust in God's unfailing love.*

Psalm 52:8 NLT

Lord, You are my contentment. You are my spirit of peace and joy.
Please be with me today and bless my work and my life.
Amen.

## Eternal connections

Stay connected to your Source of strength and life,
and though you may stumble, you will not fall. That is a promise!

Karen Moore

———— ✦ ————

In the world of the Internet, we find it pretty easy to stay connected. We can plug in to friends and family, our favorite websites and video games, and follow the people we care about on Twitter. Staying connected to planet earth is not a problem. Staying connected to God is sometimes more difficult.

It's not difficult because God is no longer available, or because we have to take a number and wait in line for Him; it's difficult because we're so distracted by everything else, and don't make time for God. When we leave the Source of all that we are, the One in whom we live and move and have our being, we start to grow weak and stumble. We start to find ourselves feeling lost and uncertain.

God wants to connect with you today. He wants you to lean on Him and to find your strength in Him. Go to Him! He is waiting to help you right now.

*"For in Him we live and move and have our being."*
*As some of your own poets have said, "We are His offspring."*

Acts 17:28 NIV

Lord, thank You for being with me all the time.
Help me to stay totally connected to You.
Amen.

## The very fiber of success

Success without honor is an unseasoned dish;
it will satisfy your hunger, but it won't taste good.

Joe Paterno

It's important to most of us to feel successful at the things we do. We are energized by knowing that our work has meaning and that we contribute to the things that make the world a better place. Whether we do something that stands out in the public eye, or if we're a great homemaker, we strive to do things with honor and integrity. We know that when we don't, it hurts our lives and grieves our spirits.

Sometimes, it's tempting to cheat a little. We don't usually do so in obvious ways, but we might find ourselves not giving full credit to someone for the ideas they shared that made us look good, or we don't want to admit that we didn't bake that delicious cake we took to our friend's house. Those are not big things, but they still draw away from the success we feel as our work is complimented.

Make it a rule that you will always acknowledge the part others play in your success, no matter how and where you succeed. When you do, the joy is shared all the way up to heaven.

*As long as Uzziah sought the Lord, God gave him success.*

2 Chronicles 26:5 NIV

Lord, thank You for the people who do so much to strengthen me in my work. Bless their lives in a big way today.
Amen.

## *The more you know,*
## *the more you grow!*

*Use your gifts faithfully, and they shall be enlarged; practice what you know, and you shall attain to higher knowledge.*

Matthew Arnold

---

Did you ever receive a gift that you didn't quite know what to do with? You put it away in your closet and thought you'd probably never use it, but then something in your life changed. You discovered that the gift you received so long before was just perfect, the one thing you needed to move forward.

You have many skills. You may not always recognize how valuable they are. You may not even understand that they could have any real purpose in your life and so you hide them away.

God has blessed you, gifted you in many ways. Look around and see if you have any talents and gifts that you've shelved, not recognizing how important they really are. Pull them out and practice them, because God will call on you to use them before you know it.

*Every good gift and every perfect gift is from above, and comes down from the Father of lights, with whom there is no variation or shadow of turning.*

James 1:17 NKJV

Lord, I don't always think of the things I do as being particularly special or worthy of being called a gift or talent. Help me to appreciate the ways You can use me just as I am.

Amen.

## Try a few belly laughs!

For health and the constant enjoyment of life,
give me a keen and ever-present sense of humor;
it is the next best thing to an abiding faith in providence.

George B. Cheever

---

When is the last time you laughed out loud? If you can't think of a moment of total, uninhibited laughter that you've shared with someone in the past few days, then maybe it's time to look at the reasons why. Most of us have plenty of reasons to laugh at ourselves or to laugh at the comical ways of others because human beings do strange, wonderful and funny things.

Do you ever think of God as having a sense of humor? Do you think He enjoys a good laugh sometimes? The possibilities are good that He does because He designed every aspect of us. He wants us to have a sense of humor just as much as a loving spirit or a devoted prayer life. He wants us to be well-balanced and He likes it when we don't take ourselves quite so seriously.

Today, try to take some inventory on your laughter. Look at what you can do to get out there and play and enjoy the world around you. Perhaps a good belly laugh is just what you need.

*Sarah said, "God has brought me laughter,*
*and everyone who hears about this will laugh with me."*

Genesis 21:6 NIV

Lord, I know that I go about each day doing a lot of things
that I believe are important, but I don't always take time to
laugh and play. Help me to laugh more today.

Amen.

## Writing your own story

Laughter is the most beautiful and beneficial
therapy God ever granted humanity.

Chuck Swindoll

---

Today, as you write another chapter of your life, speaking into the wisdom that helps to determine your steps and mark your actions, check to see if you're being straight with the woman in the mirror. Are there any habits that you keep hoping will simply disappear, even though you know in truth you haven't actually worked to change them? Have you made excuses for not exercising or getting enough sleep at night? Have you forgotten your resolution in the early days of January to be more intentional about telling people you love them?

The first step for any of us to create change is about facing our own truths with honesty. You have many chapters to write in your book of life and God has blessed you with a heart and mind that is willing and open to changing in good ways. If you're going to be honest today, can you think of one thing about yourself you might change?

*You, Lord, are our Father. We are the clay,*
*You are the potter; we are all the work of Your hand.*

Isaiah 64:8 NIV

Lord, You know me so well that I can't really hide those
things I make excuses to cover up. Help me to be honest
with you and with myself and seek to make the efforts necessary
to become more of the woman You want me to be.
Amen.

## Good hearts to grateful hearts

*The first and the great work of a Christian is about her heart. Do not be content with seeming to do good in "outward acts" while your heart is bad, and you are a stranger to the greater internal heart duties.*

Jonathan Edwards

---

God helps you to do good simply from the overflow of love you carry in your heart. A woman of worth strives to do good things for others because she's built that way.

So what makes you grateful or causes you concern about doing good in the world? Perhaps you've given so much that you want to step aside; others need to pick up where you left off. You could be right on some level about that, but do you think there are not still ways that God can use you? Are you truly feeling used up or over-used, or just out of energy for doing good things?

If so, seek God's guidance. Seek His help in filling your heart with gratitude for the gifts you share out of the goodness of your heart. Ask how you might serve Him by doing simple things, loving things, even in small ways. He will bless you with new joy in doing good in the world.

*Let the Spirit renew your thoughts and attitudes. Put on your new nature, created to be like God – truly righteous and holy.*

Ephesians 4:23-24 NLT

Lord, I love doing good things for others,
but sometimes I feel like I need to step back from all that.
Help me to continue to do the things that please You.
Amen.

## The energy booster

*Only love enables humanity to grow, because love engenders life and it is the only form of energy that lasts forever.*

Michel Quoist

Love surrounds you and love helps you grow. Being loved is the one thing that makes life sustainable no matter what else is going on. When your finances are rocky and you wonder if you can make ends meet, knowing that you're connected to a community of people who believe in you and love you makes all the difference in getting through your struggles.

When your marriage falls apart and you think love has deserted you, you discover that others step up to the plate and help you get through the pain. They inspire your hopes and dreams for a better future. That's love.

When you feel like you've messed up in a big way, perhaps so big that you wonder if even God can still care about you, you quickly learn that He is still there, ready to guide you and lead you in a better direction. That's love.

Today, let love be enough. Let love keep your heart smiling.

*Let no debt remain outstanding, except the continuing debt to love one another, for whoever loves others has fulfilled the law.*

Romans 13:8 NIV

Lord, thank You for Your love and for giving me so many people in my life who care about what happens to me. Thank You for showing us what it means to love.

Amen.

## *Healthy habits*

We first make our habits, then our habits make us.

John Dryden

━━━━◦◦◦◦◦◦◦━━━━

We tend to be creatures of habit. That means when we go to church, we often sit in the same section, or even the same pew, Sunday after Sunday. We may even have disciplined habits where we do certain things at the same time every day, such as messaging our spouse at a certain time.

Habits can be a good thing, but they're not the same as being disciplined. Discipline usually implies that we're conscious of doing the work required to meet a goal or deliver a project. We may do the same things day after day to get there, but it's discipline that ensures our success.

Of course, we're all aware of the difference between having good or beneficial habits, and bad or detrimental habits. Today, look at your habits and see if they are doing anything to limit your choices. Maybe changing a habit, even a small one, will bring you a new opportunity and give you a fresh perspective.

*Anyone who loves learning accepts correction,*
*but a person who hates being corrected is stupid.*

Proverbs 12:1 NCV

Lord, I know I have some habits I should work on, try to break,
or at least change for the better. I also have some good habits,
but I see that those can sometimes cause me not to try new things.
Grant me wisdom in the things I do today.

Amen.

## The Jesus in you

*I will give myself as a sort of Christ, to my neighbor,
as Christ has given Himself to me.*

Martin Luther

Being a "Christ" for your neighbor is an awesome idea. It means that you need a good understanding of who Christ is and what He might do in any given situation. It means that you have to be intimately acquainted with the way Christ thinks and behaves so that you can imitate Him.

Though we often acknowledge that we are to strive to become more like Jesus, we may not actually meditate on that idea long enough to truly understand what it means. You are Christ's body and hands and heart on earth. You are the one who can deliver His love and His message to those in need. You are His ambassador for good, His light to clear the path for others to see.

As you look around at those you would call your neighbors, imagine what they see each time you pass by, and see if you can find a way to be more like Christ for them.

*Put on your new nature, created to be like God – truly righteous and holy.*

Ephesians 4:24 NLT

Lord, thank You for strengthening me through Your Word and through prayer. Thank You for helping me to be a little more like You each day.

Amen.

## Forever faithful

The golden rule for understanding in spiritual
matters is not intellect, but obedience.

Oswald Chambers

Obedience is one of those words that causes most of us to tremble slightly. We have an intention toward obedience, a desire to do what is right, but we seem to fail at it more than we care to admit. We find ourselves unable to remain consistent regarding the things we tell God we will do.

We're probably glad not to be living in Old Testament times where judgment for disobedience was often handed out swiftly, with no opportunity to explain or seek God's forgiveness.

Jesus saved us from those punishments, but He still wants us to live in obedience to our Father in heaven. He wants us to love and respect God so much that we will do the things we say we'll do.

*"If you follow My decrees and are careful to obey My commands, I will send you the seasonal rains. The land will then yield its crops, and the trees of the field will produce their fruit. Your threshing season will overlap with the grape harvest, and your grape harvest will overlap with the season of planting grain. You will eat your fill and live securely in your own land."*

Leviticus 26:3-5 NLT

Lord, I am not good at being obedient in every situation
as You well know. Help me to be more aware of those times
and circumstances that cause me to step away
from what I believe You would want me to do.
Amen.

## *Keep on following*

*The strength and happiness of a woman consists in finding out the way in which God is going, and going that way too.*

Henry Ward Beecher (adapted)

---

Good friends like to spend time together. When you admire a celebrity, say a singer or an actor, you might follow them on Twitter or read up on them in the tabloids.

When Jesus commanded us to follow Him, He wasn't just saying, "Follow Me and do everything I tell you to do." He was saying we should follow Him and go where He was going: "Come along and see where I'm going, be part of what I'm doing, because it's a great place for you to be too."

When we know how to follow Jesus and where to follow Him, we find that life feels a little easier to understand and the circumstances around us don't weigh so heavily.

May your strength and your happiness reflect your willingness to go where God is going today.

*Then He said: "Whoever wants to be My disciple must deny themselves and take up their cross daily and follow Me."*

Luke 9:23 NIV

Lord, thank You for being in the lead. I regret those moments when I get ahead of You or I am so far behind, I can't see You anymore. Help me to find my strength in following You.

Amen.

## *Be bold!*

*There's a difference between knowing God and knowing about God.
When you truly know God, you have energy to serve Him,
boldness to share Him, and contentment in Him.*

J. I. Packer

Boldness is something we usually admire in other people. We appreciate that they know where they want to go and don't let anything get in the way as they move forward. They may not do it with grace and charm, but they get to their destination. It would probably be good for women in general to believe so much in what they want to do and where they want to go that they would be bold in their attempts to get there.

You might argue that you are bold when it comes to standing up for your kids, or you're bold about not being taken advantage of by a salesman. You're bold when it comes to seeking the right work and the right friendships.

You can also be bold in your faith. You can be so bold as to go to God for anything, no matter how big the obstacles in front of you appear to be. You can boldly share your faith with others and give God thanks and praise. Moving the obstacles out of the way may be easier than you think. Act with boldness of faith today.

*Take courage as you fulfill your duties,
and may the Lord be with those who do what is right.*

2 Chronicles 19:11 NLT

Lord, thank You for being with me and helping me see Your strength to lead me past obstacles and act boldly in Your name.
Amen.

## *With an ounce of passion*

Your greatest fulfillment in life will come when you
discover your unique gifts and abilities and use them
to edify others and glorify the Lord.

Neil T. Anderson

If you collect things or have favorite hobbies, you probably do so with a certain amount of passion. Maybe you're passionate about riding horses, or you love creating beautiful paintings or making gourmet delights. Whatever it is that captures your heart and your talents can be said to be your passion.

The same is true for the things that do not draw you. How hard is it for you to complete a task that simply isn't something you do well? Maybe you don't like balancing your checkbook or filing paperwork. Maybe you put off paying taxes until the last minute because it all seems so overwhelming.

The good news is that you have been invited into life with passions that are designed to help you get where God wants you to go. He gave you those desires. He shaped and molded you to fit the things that He knew you would accomplish well in the world. If you've forgotten what your passions are, it may be time to check in with God, and see where He would lead you today.

*Instead, let the Spirit renew your thoughts and attitudes.*

Ephesians 4:23 NLT

Lord, I haven't felt much passion for anything lately.
Renew my spirit and help me remember the things You want
me to accomplish. Guide me to do them with fresh energy.
Amen.

## *Removing mountains*

*We can do nothing without prayer. All things can be done by impor-
tunate prayer. It surmounts or removes all obstacles, overcomes every
resisting force and gains its ends in the face of invincible hindrances.*

E. M. Bounds

Do you have any mountains looming in your path that you
simply wish would get up and go someplace else? Can you
actually imagine those mountains moving at your request?

Though we may not imagine an actual mountain moving
to get out of our way, we can understand that with faith, the
mountains in our lives can literally be turned to little hills. We
have a connection to the Source of all living things and when we
seek His help in overcoming obstacles, He moves toward us and
clears the way.

Today, you may have to rest patiently in His care. You may
need to be more diligent in prayer, but God is ready any time
you need His help. He is there, even to remove mountains. Don't
let mountains of doubt or fear, or any other obstacle, stand in
your way.

*"Truly I tell you, if you have faith as small as a mustard seed,
you can say to this mountain, 'Move from here to there,'
and it will move. Nothing will be impossible for you."*

Matthew 17:19-20 NIV

Lord, thank You for hearing me when I call, sometimes with
great uncertainty about what lies ahead. Please go before
me and remove the mountains in Your grace and mercy.
Amen.

# Harvesting the seeds

A harvest of peace is produced from a seed of contentment.

Indian proverb

Human beings find it difficult to be satisfied with life. If one area of life starts to feel okay, we quickly move to another one that we aren't happy about. The sad part of our thinking is that we don't move to the things we're not happy about and try to fix them, we move to them and simply try to assign the blame. We are restless, trying to find reasons why things haven't worked out according to our plans. We imagine that even God is standing in the way.

Imagine if you uprooted yourself from that kind of poor soil and moved to a space where you would be free to grow in grace and joy. Let yourself plant a seed of contentment, thanking God for all you have right this minute, even if you are still waiting for other things. Praise Him for all He has done in your life and let Him know how much His love sustains you. When you do that, you will reap a harvest of peace, born out of love and able to flourish and grow.

*Better to be patient than powerful;*
*better to have self-control than to conquer a city.*

Proverbs 16:32 NLT

Lord, thank You for loving me and planting new
dreams in my heart. Help me to be patient about where
I've been planted, and to seek Your guidance as I look for the
greener pastures that only You can produce in my life.

Amen.

# NOVEMBER 22

## *Making progress!*

There is no such thing as completed or perfect
holiness in this life. Progress, yes! Perfection, no!

Erroll Hulse

---

Every day you're becoming more of the woman you want to
be. You may even see yourself differently now, speaking more
tenderly to yourself when you make mistakes, loving yourself
into believing in new possibilities, and turning to God more
regularly for all that you need. You've definitely grown and God
is pleased with your progress.

Are you there yet? Chances are that being "there" is only the
hope of heaven. Being "there" may mean we've learned all the
lessons and can go back home and rest at our Father's feet. Being
here on earth, though, means that we are always seeking to be
more, to understand more about love and giving, and to do
more for others. You strive for greater holiness with each effort
you make toward sharing your love with God or with any of His
children.

Keep on the path. You are making remarkable progress!

*Even before He made the world, God loved us and chose us in
Christ to be holy and without fault in His eyes.*

Ephesians 1:4 NLT

Lord, I don't always feel very holy. I know there is a lot more
work to be done in me and so I ask You to stay with me through
this process and bless my life so that I can bless others.

Amen.

## God's protection

*In perplexities – when we cannot tell what to do,
when we cannot understand what is going on around us –
let us be calmed and steadied and made patient by the thought
that what is hidden from us is not hidden from Him.*

Frances Ridley Havergal

---

If you've ever been to a funhouse with lots of crazy mirrors, you probably saw yourself in all kinds of odd shapes and sizes. You may not have even recognized all the shapes of yourself as you looked into the mirrors. What a strange feeling to see yourself in all those variations!

Chances are that if you could see yourself in several mirrors all at once, just regular mirrors, you might see new things about yourself from different angles and perspectives. You still might wonder who that woman is that is reflected back at you.

God sees you from every angle. He wants you to see the beautiful and joyful aspects of yourself. Even though you are a complex person, He sees you at your best. Stay calm and steady in God's guidance and at the right time He'll reveal more of what you need to grow even stronger in Him.

*Search for the LORD and for His strength; continually seek Him. Remember the wonders He has performed, His miracles, and the rulings He has given.*

Psalm 105:4-5 NLT

Lord, I know You must see me in a lot of different
ways since I change and shift all the time.
Please keep me always in Your care and protection.

Amen.

## The joy of thanksgiving

Thanksgiving is a good thing; thanksliving is better!

Anonymous

---

If you were given one minute to write down everything you're grateful for, how many items would be on your list? Would you be surprised to see that you had written so quickly you could hardly read the list, but you had written nearly sixty things? Or did you struggle because you're going through a difficult time and you've forgotten what you have to be grateful for.

Whether you write six things or sixty, or any number in between, the point is to stop whatever you're doing right now and realize how much you have to be grateful for. You have been living the good life far more than you may recognize. If you do genuinely appreciate the many good things in your life, thanking God is one thing, but the greater blessing is living in a way that shows your gratitude.

When you are conscious of "thanks living," you respond to life with more joy and you offer it your best. You show up when you're needed and you share from the heart. Living in gratitude makes all the difference.

*The eyes of the Lord watch over those who do right,*
*and His ears are open to their prayers.*

1 Peter 3:12 NLT

Lord, help me to live in gratitude to You and to
those around me who love me and support my life.

Amen.

## The streets of life

*I learned that one can never go back, that one should
not ever try to go back – that the essence of life is going forward.
Life is really a one-way street, isn't it?*

Agatha Christie

---

Did you ever have an amazing vacation somewhere, carrying the memory of that place and that experience in your heart and then, some years later, hope to recapture the event? Did it turn out to be everything you remembered? On returning, did it feel that the reality of it matched your first experience?

It may be possible to go back and revisit portions of our lives, but it is seldom the same when we do. Part of the reason is that we're on a continual path of growth and change. We're becoming more all the time and what we're becoming is reflected in our thoughts and actions.

What God wants for you is to build new experiences, seeing them with the new eyes of joy you have because of Him and with a heart made new by His love.

*Jesus said, "No one, having put his hand to the plow,
and looking back, is fit for the kingdom of God."*

Luke 9:62 NKJV

Father, I do sometimes wish I could go back and
relive a perfectly wonderful experience from years ago.
I ask that You would give me the desire to keep carving
out new experiences as I walk more closely with You.
Amen.

## *Winning the battles*

You may have to fight a battle more than once to win it.

Margaret Thatcher

In a boxing ring, the champion might just knock his opponent out with the very first punch. A golfer may hit a hole-in-one on the first swing, and you may win a lottery by buying just one ticket. These things could happen, but they aren't likely. The point is that most things don't work out with just one attempt.

No matter what kind of battle you're in, you probably need to go a few rounds before you get to the winning punch. Life has a lot of different battle grounds. Sometimes they revolve around finances, sometimes around addictions, and sometimes around feelings like depression and sadness. Overcoming anything is hard, but the more you try, the more God can help you win.

If you remember that you aren't the only one facing battles, you'll have more sympathy for those around you. Everyone is fighting something. Everyone has to trust God for the future.

Whatever you can do to keep making an effort for yourself, or to help someone else win a battle, will make God proud. Suit up, because someone needs you today.

*Make every effort to give yourself to God as the kind of person He will approve.*

2 Timothy 2:15 NCV

Lord, please help me remember that I'm not the
only one trying to overcome obstacles and win at the
game of life. Thanks for being with me today.
Amen.

## Loving the questions

*Be patient with all that is unresolved in your heart
and try to love the questions themselves. Do not seek
the answers that cannot be given you because you wouldn't
be able to live them. Live the questions now.*

Anonymous

Women are good at asking questions. We want to know how things work, why they work, and who is responsible if they don't work. We have inquiring minds and that's a gift from God.

Sometimes the questions we have, especially those about our life purpose and direction, or those about unanswered prayers, can feel so important we grow restless waiting for the answers. We wait, but we don't always wait patiently. We wait and we worry.

When worry enters in, then all we think about is the future. The future is just a few minutes past where we are now, but we have not noticed where we are because we need answers.

Be intentional. Look at the questions you have for God and speak them, write them or pray them aloud. Explain your desire for closure or for answers. Then stop everything, surrender the questions at the cross and give God a chance to answer.

*To everything there is a season, a time for every purpose under heaven.*

Ecclesiastes 3:1 NKJV

Father, thank You for hearing my prayers and for letting
me ask questions. Help me to rely on You for the answers
and to be at peace in the process.
Amen.

## Why were you born?

*I was not born to be free. I was born to adore and to obey.*

C. S. Lewis

Probably all of us have thought about why we were born at some point or other. Maybe we had that thought when we were trying to discover our life purpose, or maybe it was simply a question posed to God in a more philosophic way. Whatever the reason for the question, it's a good one for us to ponder. After all, the more we recognize why we are on this planet, the more we will find our way toward our destiny. You know you were born for a reason and by God's grace, after some diligent searching, your heart will speak to you and help you understand His purpose for your life.

In God's wisdom and providence, He gave us the chance to discover our purpose. He exposes us to options and hopes we make good choices. That freedom not only helps us find out who we are and what we're supposed to do, but it also helps us to adore our heavenly Father. It reminds us that we are incredibly blessed by the One who designed us to do a great work.

Give Him adoration from the depths of your heart today.

*The Lord is great and worthy of our praise; no one can understand how great He is.*

Psalm 145:3 NCV

Lord, I do love You and I appreciate all You have done
to help me discover my real life purpose. I know that
I can only achieve my purposes through You.

Amen.

# *Encouraging others*

The applause of a single human being is of great consequence.

Samuel Johnson

---

The first time someone commented on the work you were doing and said something like, "Good job!" was probably the first time you started to realize that you have some impact on the world around you.

We learn a lot by positive reinforcement. We learn when loving words are said or when caring comments are made. We not only learn, but we strive, trying harder the next time to earn those encouraging words again. We need approval from each other and from God. We need to know that our efforts matter to someone.

Today, wherever you are, see if you can find an opportunity to notice the work of someone else. Then go up to them and offer them praise and encouragement. Most likely, it will be the best thing that happens to them all day. You have the power to make someone else's life better, simply by offering a little recognition.

*People enjoy giving good advice.*
*Saying the right word at the right time is so pleasing.*

Proverbs 15:23 NCV

Lord, I know how much I appreciate it when
someone compliments me. Help me to share that kind
of encouragement with those around me.

Amen.

## The spirit of prayer

Prayer obtains fresh and continued outpourings of the Spirit.

J. C. Ryle

---

Does your prayer life ever get a little parched? Maybe you feel like you've prayed for and about the same things for a long time. Maybe you're running dry on what else to say or you're simply not feeling motivated about your prayer life lately.

If any of this is true for you, there are a few things you can do to shower yourself with more joy in prayer: You can scrub up on your reading of God's Word and let His Word speak to you in a new way. Try a new translation for your favorite passages – this may well bring new insights to what you need right now. Expect God to deliver His messages in all kinds of new ways.

He may speak to you very clearly through a good friend or a chance acquaintance on the street. He may seem to rise up out of the pages of Scripture in words you never realized were there before. He may share a story with you during your morning shower or commute to work. The more you are willing to have an outpouring of His Spirit, the more He is able to fill you up and inspire your life again.

Go ahead and drink Him in with the joy that makes your spirit come alive.

*Hope deferred makes the heart sick, but when the desire comes, it is a tree of life.*

Proverbs 13:12 NKJV

Lord, thank You for being with me through the dry times,
those moments when I need You even more than I realize.

Amen.

FOR ALL THAT
HER HANDS HAVE DONE
AND LET HER WORKS
BRING HER PRAISE

PROVERBS 31:31

## God works through you

Prayer is not a matter of getting what we want the most.
Prayer is a matter of giving ourselves to God and learning His laws,
so that He can do through us what He wants the most.

Agnes Sanford

Most of us probably regard prayer as our way of connecting with God to share our hearts and tell Him what we want, what we're missing, or what we don't understand. How often, though, do we use prayer to learn more about what God wants from us?

It's good to put your needs list in front of God on a regular basis. It's even better to pray for those around you and to put their needs before God. It's best, though, to wait patiently and pray expectantly for God to reveal His heart to you, His desires for your life. You're walking this road together and sometimes you need to simply be willing to listen for His voice.

Check in with the One who knows everything you need to understand and ask Him to be with you and to help you with every prayer.

*I pray that you, being rooted and established in love, may have power, together with all the Lord's holy people, to grasp how wide and long and high and deep is the love of Christ, and to know this love that surpasses knowledge – that you may be filled to the measure of all the fullness of God.*

Ephesians 3:17-19 NIV

Lord, I am Your daughter, but I know I come to You a lot more often with my requests than I do with my desire to know more of what You want from me. Help me to wait to hear Your voice.
Amen.

# The one who listens

Prayer is the burden of a sigh,
the falling of a tear,
the upward glancing of an eye
when none but God is near.

James Montgomery

One of the best ways you understand that you're loved is when you feel listened to about anything that is on your mind. When a good friend takes the time to help you reflect on your concerns, offering sympathy and advice, you feel loved. When your spouse shares conversations with you that are filled with a genuine and heartfelt "give-and-take," you feel loved.

God is a good listener! He hears you when you sigh, when you pray, even before you speak. He holds your hand and considers the things that affect your heart. He knows you better than anyone else and is always there for you.

Whenever you're feeling unsure about life, or you have situations that are simply not easy to figure out, then go to the One who wants to hear from you at any time, day or night, and share what's on your mind. God is near you right now and finds joy in all that you are. Go to Him when you need a good listening ear.

*Let the wise listen and add to their learning.*

Proverbs 1:5 NIV

Lord, thank You for being there for me and listening to me.
I know that You will consider my thoughts and prayers
and do what is best for my life and my soul.

Amen.

### DECEMBER 3

# Here comes the future

The surest method of arriving at a knowledge of God's eternal purposes about us is to be found in the right use of the present moment.

Frederick W. Faber

We've talked about living more intentionally in the present. This means that you try to be fully aware of the things you do, the people you connect with, and the very words that come from your lips. You want to be in the moment, because it is the only way you actually live and appreciate the present.

If you were ever a daydreamer as a kid, or are still one, you may well have benefited from the time spent imagining what things could be like. The dreamers of the world do contribute in wonderful ways to all that can be. The only problem is that you can't be in two places at once. You can't daydream and still live in this very moment. You can't be conscious of the now, if everything you think about is linked to the past, or is concerned with wondering what will happen to you in the future.

God knows that we don't do well when our attention is divided. We miss out when we try to serve two masters. If you want to get the most out of today, then be intentional about the things you're doing and give your best to the present.

*LORD, make me to know my end, and what is the measure of my days, that I may know how frail I am.*

Psalm 39:4 NKJV

Lord, I am so happy to have this day. Help me to use it wisely
and to pay attention to all the matters in front of me.
Amen.

## *The dance of time*

Time is your friend. That's right. It is your companion and influences everything you do. You do a lot of things according to a schedule and you do your best to simply keep up.

Sometimes it seems to move slowly, while at other times you can't understand where it went. You were sixteen and, without blinking it seems, you were thirty-six.

You are blessed! God has divine moments planned just for you and He knows the number of your days. He knows the plans He has for you to see that you live a fulfilling life.

The time is at hand for you to give God thanks and praise for your moments and your hours. He wants you to make the most of each minute you are given. It's your day to create with Him!

*"I know the plans I have for you," declares the Lord, "plans to prosper you and not to harm you, plans to give you hope and a future."*

Jeremiah 29:11 NIV

Lord, help me to use my time wisely, to cherish the moments, and to do my best to live in the hope of all You've planned for me.

Amen.

## Who you are speaks volumes

*People should not worry so much about what they have to do,*
*they should consider rather what they are.*

Meister Eckhart

It's good to have a lot of activities that demand your time and attention. You may be a volunteer or a Sunday school teacher. You can spend your time in a lot of ways and be a woman who is constantly doing, always busy.

Parents are often stressed by how much time they spend driving from one event to the other either for themselves or their kids. They are going strong all the time and though they may love it on one hand, it's exhausting on the other.

Consider what it means to be so involved with the "doing" that it lets you ignore other aspects of your life. You are worthy of praise. You are a woman with a tender heart and a loving voice. You are the daughter of a King and He adores you. What you are is good and worthy and kind. Remember that it's great to do good things, but give God the praise He is due for creating you to be the amazing woman you are!

*It takes wisdom to have a good family,*
*and it takes understanding to make it strong.*

Proverbs 24:3 NCV

Lord, I am always running from one thing to the next, and usually I find myself feeling inadequate because I can't do everything. Thanks for reminding me that You already see me as valuable and worthy, because of Your love.

Amen.

# Standing on God's promises

Every promise God has ever made finds its fulfillment in Jesus.

Joni Eareckson Tada

---

Making someone a promise may be one of the scariest things we ever do. It's scary because a promise means that we make a commitment. Sometimes we even make promises to ourselves. We know that no one else knows we made that promise so we can break it without hurting anyone … except ourselves.

We stand on the promises of God! We stand because He keeps His promises and He won't ever change His mind. He won't ever decide we weren't worth His effort or that the sacrifice of Jesus no longer counts. We stand because God values us so much that He is steadfast and immovable, constant in His love and mercy and in keeping His promises.

If you have trouble keeping the promises you make, or if you wonder how it is possible to actually keep promises, keep going back to God. Keep trusting and believing that He loves you beyond measure and that He will never break His promise to be with you for now and forever.

*The Lord is not slack concerning His promise, as some*
*count slackness, but is longsuffering toward us, not willing*
*that any should perish but that all should come to repentance.*

2 Peter 3:9 NKJV

Lord, I am not always good at keeping my promises.
Please help me to be better and thank You for
being so steadfast with the gifts of Your promises.

Amen.

## The great eraser

We serve a gracious Master who knows how to overrule
even our mistakes to His glory and our own advantage.

John Newton

---

Erasers have nearly become a thing of the past. After all, few of us use a pencil anymore and even grade schools are beginning to issue computerized tablets to kids these days. The fact remains, though, that all of us make mistakes and sometimes we'd love to have a big old eraser to blot them out. We'd like a clean slate so that the pages of our lives are no longer marked up or scribbled on, not making sense to anyone at all.

How amazing it is to realize that God Himself has provided an enormous eraser, the kind of tool that can give us a whole new start, a brand-new page to turn. He has seen to it that none of our mistakes, from the little silly ones to the great big serious ones, will ever show up on heaven's blotter when we get to the door. God provided His only Son to take care of our careless ways and our contrary hearts. Now that takes a very big eraser indeed!

Sure, you will continue to make mistakes. You'll be less than perfect from one day to the next, but you will always have a clean slate.

*"You are already clean because of the word I have spoken to you.
Remain in Me, as I also remain in you."*

John 15:3-4 NIV

Lord, I am so grateful that You provided a way to erase my sins.
I know that I live according to Your grace and mercy.
Amen.

## Blessing of give-and-take

Blessed are those who can give without
remembering and who can take without forgetting.

Elizabeth Bibesco

Some people look at the things they do for others as a way of creating a giant scorecard. They imagine that if they do a favor for you, then you're obligated at some future date to do a favor for them. They like to call in their chips and remind people of their good deeds. In matters of "give-and-take," they are very aware of what they've given and they never let you forget it.

Whew! How blessed we are that God doesn't keep score like this. Odds are it is already way out of balance. He gave you everything you have. He stood by you every second and helped you with each thing you did. He gave you your life!

God gives without remembering, but He receives without forgetting. He remembers everything you do for Him out of love. He rejoices in each kindness you share with others, because He takes it as something you've done personally, just for Him.

We can't begin to out-do God when it comes to giving, but imagine what it will feel like when we stand before Him and He recounts the many things we did just for Him.

*"Freely you have received; freely give."*

Matthew 10:8 NIV

Father, I know that You are an over-the-top giver,
because my life is so blessed. Please help me to be
generous to others the way You are to me.

Amen.

## It takes some doing

"I must do something" will always solve more
problems than "Something must be done."

Anonymous

Did you ever witness an event or hear of a situation that caused you to think to yourself, "Somebody needs to do something. Why doesn't someone help that person?" Chances are when that thought occurred to you, you were not close enough to actually step in yourself to help or you would have, but as human beings we are continually being challenged.

We are made aware of the circumstances of other people's lives so that we can discover opportunities to serve. It's okay to select only a few of those opportunities, because you can't do everything, but each of us is called to do something. The sooner we ask the question, "What can I do?" the sooner we'll know what steps to take.

During the Christmas season, we are made even more aware of the welfare agencies seeking help for food donations and financial support. You can't help them all, but let your heart desire to do good and help in whatever ways you can.

*Each of you should give what you have decided in your heart to give,*
*not reluctantly or under compulsion, for God loves a cheerful giver.*

2 Corinthians 9:7 NIV

Father, there are so many people in need that it becomes difficult
to pick one or two charities that I can serve. Please help me
to use my gifts wisely in the places of Your choice.

Amen.

## *The small things are great*

The smallest things become great when God requires them of us; they are small only in themselves; they are always great when they are done for God, and when they serve to unite us with Him·eternally.

François Fénelon

Did you know you're already the star of your own show? Yes, you're the celebrity in the mirror, the one who is right up there on the marquis, and you're there because God's love puts you there. You have already done great things with your life and they have been noticed. Somewhere you might even hear a little applause.

Maybe you can't imagine you've done anything great, after all, you serve the Lord in little ways all the time. You volunteer in the nursery at church, you serve Thanksgiving dinner at the shelter, and you crochet quilts for newborn babies. Those are the little things that make a difference. Those are the things that make you a shining star in God's kingdom.

Pay special attention to the people who do little kindnesses for you today, and reward them with the gift of your smile and gratitude. It's the little things that mean a lot, the things that truly cause a person to rise to greatness.

*We should serve in the newness of the Spirit.*

Romans 7:6 NKJV

Lord, thank You for the people who do so many little things to help me create a better life. Please remind me of the things I can do for others as well.

Amen.

### The risk takers

Have you noticed that life is a risky business? Most of the things you've ever done or ever will do require a bit of a gamble. You have to set a course and then risk the outcome. You change your hair color and take a chance that others will like what you've done, or even that you'll like what you've done. You move to a new city and hope that you'll settle in confidently, that you'll find favorite restaurants, the right church and make good friends.

Risk! It's simply part of living. The one absolute, the one unchanging, never-ending, no-holds-barred part of life is Jesus. You have no risk there … everything to win, nothing to lose.

It's good to be a risk taker sometimes, though. Risk involves courage and thinking something through so you can obtain the best possible outcome. Risk involves letting yourself be vulnerable and exposing your dreams to others. God gave you the ability to dream and to act on those dreams. Take a risk today.

*Cast your bread upon the waters, for you will find it after many days.*

Ecclesiastes 11:1 NKJV

Lord, thank You for seeing what I need and helping to inspire my direction. Give me the courage to go after my dreams and be willing to take a positive risk for the right reasons.

Amen.

## A loving prayer

*Open wide the windows of our spirits and fill us full of light;*
*open wide the door of our hearts, that we may receive and*
*entertain Thee with all our powers of adoration.*

Christina Rossetti

The closer we draw to Christmas and the beauty of the season, the more our hearts are filled with the desire to adore God. We imagine that beautiful manger scene of an innocent young woman, her committed and supportive partner, and the sweet Baby sent to earth by love. It's the time of year when we truly open our hearts and our spirits and bask in the light.

As you reflect on the gifts of the season, think of what it means to simply offer love and praise to your Savior. Share your heart with Him out of love, more than out of your needs for provision or strength. Just let God know how much you love to be in His presence, to be filled with His Spirit of joy and peace and grace. The light will flow through you, through your house and through every open door and window. Praise God and let His blessings flow through you today.

*Sing to the LORD a new song, because He has done miracles.*

Psalm 98:1 NCV

Lord, I bow down before You in gratitude for all You've done
for me and the people I love. I praise You with my whole heart
for allowing me to experience the light and peace of all that
comes from Your Spirit. Please receive my love.

Amen.

## December grace

True grace grows best in winter.

Samuel Rutherford

In many parts of the world, winter is cold and snowy, and everything goes into hibernation. Those who venture outside do so with caution, watching the icy roadways and the snowdrifts. They take extra time to get where they want to go and dress as warmly as possible.

What's beautiful, though, is that having to slow your pace means you can focus on the simple things and become quieter. It doesn't take long after you begin reviewing all that you are and all that you have to warm up to the idea that you've been living totally under grace. You've had the power of God's love with you every day, but feeling it and seeing it has gotten buried in the snowdrifts of life.

God is with you in the winter and surrounds you with the warmth of His love as surely as if He had given you a matching scarf and hat. He protects you in His grace and grants you peace as sweet as gently falling snow. Bless the winter time, for it will surely help you to keep growing in the spring.

*Give to the LORD the glory He deserves! Bring your offering and come into His courts. Worship the LORD in all His holy splendor.*

Psalm 96:8-9 NLT

Father, I thank You for being with me on cold and frosty days, and for letting me linger in front of a fireplace and sharing my heart with You.

Amen.

## A matter of advice

*Do not open your heart to everyone, but discuss your
affairs with one who is wise and who fears God.*

Thomas à Kempis (adapted)

Some of us process our feelings and our ideas by talking them
out with others. It helps us to hear what we're thinking when
we speak out loud. That can be extremely helpful and healthy.
The difficult thing is that we need to be aware of the people
we choose as our confidants. Some are wise and helpful, while
others would simply put up roadblocks for us.

You have a beautiful heart and God wants to protect it. He
wants you to surround yourself with others that know Him and
can advise you in positive and truthful ways. If you've ever talked
about something important with someone who didn't get it, or
simply cast a negative spin on your ideas, you can recognize the
difference.

When you really need advice, seek God's help in discovering
the right people to talk to about your ideas or concerns. A
kindred spirit can make all the difference and help you move
forward with peace and joy.

*For lack of guidance a nation falls, but victory is won through many advisers.*

Proverbs 11:14 NIV

Lord, thank You for putting people in my life who
would advise me with wisdom and love.

Amen.

## *Older and wiser*

It would be a good thing if young people were wise and old
people were strong, but God has arranged things better.

Martin Luther

---

We sometimes quip that we imagine human beings become wiser as they grow older. Certainly, we would agree that life is a school and there are lots of lessons to be learned. Whether we embrace the lessons and become wiser is not always easy, but the opportunity is always there. Certainly God has arranged things well because we are blessed with an ongoing chance to grow. Fortunately, young people are sometimes wise, and older people are often strong, but overall, each day shines a light on the things we need to know and the ways we need to grow.

You are getting wiser and better, and more radiant each day as you walk with the Lord and as you reflect more of His image to the world. It's a beautiful thing to see, a joy to get older and wiser.

Give God thanks, then, that you're still on the path, growing, being challenged, and learning things He would have you know. He's made you older, wiser and more fabulous!

*A gracious woman gains respect.*

Proverbs 11:16 NLT

Lord, thank You for keeping me on as a student,
a member in training in Your kingdom. I am grateful for
what I've learned and the ways that You have shared wisdom
with me. Help me reflect Your spirit wherever I am today.

Amen.

## To agree or to disagree

The fact that I am a woman does not make me a
different kind of Christian. But the fact that I am a
Christian does make me a different kind of woman.

Elisabeth Elliot

---

The more you know who you are, whose you are, and what
you want to become, the more you'll foster opinions that
simply may not fit with the world. Marketers, advertisers and
media specialists will fight back, doing everything they can to
manipulate your thinking and to accept their views. The world
wants you to join into their song.

God has better plans for you, however. It may not be
comfortable, but it will always serve you well to hold your own
opinion up to the Light and see if you sense God's favor. God
cares what you think and those around you are longing to know
some of the things you have learned. Your opinion matters and if
you've never been told that before, take it to heart now.

You're free to express yourself. Give God thanks and praise for
being able to freely be the wonderful you, and to share heartfelt
and inspired opinions with others.

*Praise the Lord! Sing to the Lord a new song.*
*Sing His praises in the assembly of the faithful.*

Psalm 149:1 NLT

Lord, thank You for loving me, helping me grow,
and shaping me into the woman I am today.

Amen.

## *Doing your best*

From the time you were a little girl, people have encouraged you to "do your best." Sometimes you wanted so much to please someone else that you would make a great effort to do your best to win more praise from them. You discovered that there were certain rewards that resulted when you did your best.

As an adult, the rewards may not seem as immediate. There may not be anyone close by to give you praise when you do something well. In fact, you might feel like no one notices what you do at all. You might wonder if it's worth it to go out of your way to be your best self.

Perhaps you can't see the return on your investment each time you bring your best to whatever you're doing. You may be the best casserole maker at church, or the best singer in the choir, but not really feel recognized for doing those things well.

If you have lost sight of what it feels like to be praised for doing a good job, praise yourself. Reward yourself in a small way so that you'll want to make that effort again. Be assured that God sees your efforts and in His love, you have great worth.

*Whatever work you do, do your best.*

Ecclesiastes 9:10 NCV

Lord, thank You for the people who encourage the things
I try to do well. Help me to remember to praise others too.

Amen.

## You have great impact

*If you think you're too small to have an impact,*
*try going to bed with a mosquito in your room.*

Anita Roddick

---

Mosquitoes are insistent. They are heat-seeking missiles that find a way to buzz around your head any time you give them a chance. Unless you actually send them to the Promised Land, they don't seem to quit. They have a definite impact!

Sometimes as women, we tend to think that if we're not in charge of a meeting, or organizing a group, then our work is not important. We have devalued ourselves because we're playing a game of comparisons. After all, life is a competition.

Think about it. Think about the things you have done for others that might seem small, but had a big impact. Maybe it was the time you picked up your friend's child at school when she just couldn't get there in time. What about the way you prayed for your neighbor when she was having a family crisis? These are all small things, but they are great in God's kingdom. These are the things that show Him your generous heart and loving Spirit. These are the things that matter.

*The LORD's eyes see everything; He watches both evil and good people.*

Proverbs 15:3 NCV

Lord, I know how much it means to me when someone helps me
at a moment's notice. Help me be willing to give what
I can in service to those around me today.

Amen.

## The blessing of angels

*An angel can illumine the thought and mind of a person
by strengthening the power of vision, and by bringing within
reach some truth which the angel himself contemplates.*

Thomas Aquinas

At Christmastime, we embrace the idea of angels. We thank them for sharing the light of our Savior's birth and heralding His entry into the world with joy and praise. We love that they protected Mary and Joseph and helped them escape from evil kings. We are grateful for the role they played in giving guidance to the shepherds and wise men. We love Christmas angels.

The blessing of our lives today is that angels are still with us. They come to our aid, often unseen, protecting and strengthening us. They help us in ways that we may never be able to recount because they've done it as part of God's master plan. It's okay if you don't have any personal experience with angels, but consider that they have a deep and abiding love for you.

It's the season to see angels all around and to thank God for their ministry here on earth.

*Do not forget to entertain strangers, for by so doing
some have unwittingly entertained angels.*

Hebrews 13:2 NKJV

Lord, I know we are blessed to have the help of angels
at all seasons and times and I thank You for the part
they play in the human experience.

Amen.

*The word "angel" simply means "messenger." If angels are messengers, then someone, somewhere must be sending a message.*

Dan Schaeffer

---

You may wonder at how long it has taken the human race to get the message. We've been here for some time and we still don't recognize God's hand at work or see His gracious provision. He even provides angelic messengers to help us when we're in trouble, or deliver something vital to our work here on earth. The fact that angels exist certainly should help us grasp the idea that the King of the universe is still trying to communicate with us.

Today, make it a point to consider the work of angels. Ask God if there's any way you can help in the work they do, even if you simply make others aware of their grand design and intention.

Of course, our main goal is not to seek the message as much as the messenger Himself. Our hope is to always glory in the work of God and in His Son so that we can continue the story of His love forever. You are one His most amazing messengers every time you shine His light.

*Suddenly, the angel was joined by a vast host of others – the armies of heaven – praising God.*

Luke 2:13 NLT

Lord, I believe in angels because I believe that You offer us many miraculous ways to know more about You. Thank You for helping me see Your gracious light of truth.

Amen.

# I know I believe!

The more you trust Jesus and keep your eyes focused on Him, the more life you'll have. Trusting God brings life. Believing brings rest. So stop trying to figure everything out, and let God be God in your life.

Joyce Meyer

---

If you've been gripped by God, you know it. No doubt, no maybe; you have absolute awareness like you've never had before in your life. You believed before it happened to you, but now you know. Now you understand that God is real and that He is heavily invested in your life and the lives of all His children. When you're in His grip, you feel safe and strong. You realize that you're not the same as you were before and that you will never be the same again. You're loved beyond measure and it's wonderful!

As you approach Christmas once again, think about what it truly means to be held in such high esteem, to be found so worthy that God would send His own dear Son in the form of a tiny infant, just so He could meet you one day and love you unconditionally. You have been gripped by a love that is steadfast and true, a love that will hold you forever.

Be strong in His great love today.

*"Be strong and of good courage; do not be afraid, nor be dismayed, for the Lord your God is with you wherever you go."*

Joshua 1:9 NKJV

Lord, I am awed that You have done so much for me and for those who seek Your face. Bless each person who comes to the manger to surrender their lives and their love to You this holiday season.

Amen.

## The wager

*Belief is a wise wager. Granted that faith cannot be proved,*
*what harm will come to you if you gamble on its truth and it proves*
*false? ... If you gain, you gain all; if you lose, you lose nothing.*
*Wager, then, without hesitation, that He exists.*

Blaise Pascal

———————

This wager from Pascal is one that has been discussed philosophically and theologically for many years. It's interesting to note that you could simply choose to be a person of faith with the idea that if you are right, all is well, and if you are wrong, it doesn't matter. It is a function of the mind, not of the heart.

Believing in and trusting God is a matter of the heart. It asks you to be drawn to God for one important reason ... so He can love you, and so you can love Him back. God is love.

Today is your opportunity to let God know with your whole heart that you have chosen Him because of who He is and because you believe in His love. When you approach God in that manner, no wager is necessary, because the love you'll receive is for now and forever.

*I will both lie down in peace, and sleep; for You alone,*
*O Lord, make me dwell in safety.*

Psalm 4:8 NKJV

Lord, I thank You that I don't have any need to speculate about whether You're real or not. I thank You for making Your Spirit clearly visible to the eyes of my heart.

Amen.

## Return to God

When we stray from His presence, He longs for you to
come back. He weeps that you are missing out on His love,
protection and provision. He throws His arms open, runs toward
you, gathers you up, and welcomes you home.

Charles Stanley

As a woman of immense worth in God's sight, and as a person who embraced His love some time ago, you may not relate as well to this. But, if you do, if you're still in awe, still amazed that God continues to make Himself known here on planet Earth, then you are a woman who is truly prepared for the events of Christmas.

You're ready for the coming of the Christ child, ready to have His love be born in your heart. You're ready to leave your ordinary work behind, simply to get a peek at Him, to draw closer to Him.

Move closer to the stable today, because God is making a comeback in your life!

*She gave birth to her firstborn son. She wrapped Him snugly in strips of cloth and laid Him in a manger, because there was no lodging available for them.*

Luke 2:7 NLT

Father, I thank You for coming into my life, not just once,
but many times. You've always managed to find me
when I've been lost and to love me back into the Kingdom.

Amen.

## DECEMBER 24

# The message of Christmas

*The Christmas message is that there is hope for a ruined humanity –*
*hope of pardon, hope of peace with God, hope of glory – because*
*at the Father's will Jesus Christ became poor, and was born in*
*a stable so that thirty years later He might hang on a cross.*

J. I. Packer

As you prepare to celebrate the hope of Christmas, imagine the sweet story of a beautiful baby boy and what a difference His birth made to the whole earth. Find ways to represent hope on your Christmas tree and in your decorations this year.

The Christmas celebration is the beginning of all we can understand of God's love for us, a love so strong that it doesn't even end at the cross, but simply begins again to fill us with more hope of future glory.

It's an exciting time of year and everywhere we see signs of people remembering their humanity and remembering what it means to give to others. May your heart and your home shine with the hope and joy of God's never-ending love all through the season.

*In the beginning was the Word, and the Word was with God,*
*and the Word was God. He was in the beginning with God.*
*All things were made through Him, and without Him nothing was*
*made that was made. In Him was life, and the life was the light of men.*

John 1:1-4 NKJV

Lord, Your love is awesome! I have so much hope
in my heart because of You and all You've done.
Amen.

## Celebrating Christmas

*When we celebrate Christmas we are celebrating that amazing time when the Word that shouted all the galaxies into being, limited all power, and for love of us came to us in the powerless body of a human baby.*

Madeleine L'Engle

---

There's no other season in the year that brings out the best in people like Christmas does. Our hearts are more generous and giving, our spirits are soulful and connected to God, and our lives are more meaningful. We go through endless preparations to get our homes in festive shape, plan surprises for the people we love, and sing Christmas carols from morning to night.

Imagine God's delight that first Christmas when He gazed upon His baby boy, and how much joy He must have felt as Mary beamed at her little child, and angels and shepherds and kings celebrated His spectacular birth. It's the generosity of our Creator, and the giving hearts of those who attended that first Christmas that lifts our spirits and cause us to sing songs of praise. With all the angels of heaven, we see the wonder in what God has done, and no Christmas decoration or gift under our tree can quite compare with that. Glory be to God!

*The Word became flesh and dwelt among us, and we beheld His glory.*

John 1:14 NKJV

Lord, this is an amazing day when I reflect on Your baby Son and on the gift He is to us all. Thank You for Your precious love for all of humanity.

Amen.

## The sunrise

The birth of Jesus is the sunrise in the Bible.

Henry Van Dyke

This beautiful image of Jesus as the sunrise reminds us that when Jesus entered into our world, everything changed. He was the beginning of a brand-new day, of a new direction. Jesus was the start of everything we have today, and with each rising of the sun we can sing His praise.

On this first day after Christmas, think of all the new things that were born the day Jesus came to earth. We were given a new gift of salvation, a new way to reach God and a new understanding of what it means to be God's child. We were blessed with a new possibility to be more like God because Jesus would give us an example, be a role model and an image that we could understand. We were given a new set of rules, ones that encompassed the Ten Commandments and went beyond them. Love God and love each other was the new paradigm.

As you look at the new gifts still under the tree and awaken to the new sunrise, thank God once again for His loving way of sharing His sweet light and drawing us closer to Himself.

*The angel said, "Glory to God in the highest heaven,*
*and on earth peace to those on whom His favor rests."*

Luke 2:14 NLT

Lord, thank You for this day and for being the example of love for all of us today, just as You were all those years ago to the people who reached out to You and followed You. Help me to follow You in joy.

Amen.

## As you become more

*Place your mind before the mirrors of eternity! Place your
soul in the brilliance of glory. Place your heart in the figure of
the divine substance. And transform your whole being
into the magic of the God head itself through contemplation.*

Clare of Assisi

---

It's nearly the end of another year and you have been growing
and changing and becoming even more favored in the sight
of your heavenly Father. You've become more aware of what it
means to be His daughter and to seek your strength through His
love and wisdom. You've given Him your heart and now He can
shape you, comfort you and help you through whatever life may
bring.

You're being beautifully transformed and those who know
you may not be aware of what it is that gives you that special
glow. You know it is all about the connection you have with the
One you love, the divine substance.

You're simply becoming more beautiful every day.

*The Lord bless you and keep you; the Lord make His face shine upon you, and be
gracious to you; the Lord lift up His countenance upon you, and give you peace.*

Numbers 6:24-26 NKJV

Father, I thank You for all that You've done to show me how to be
a better woman in Your sight and how to reflect Your image in the
things I say and do. Help me to keep growing in Your love.

Amen.

# A contented peace

Contentment is a pearl of great price, and whoever procures it at the expense of ten thousand desires makes a wise and happy choice.

John Balguy

---

Maybe you remember the biblical story of the man who discovered a great treasure. he was so excited about it, he took the treasure and hid it in a field. Then, to be sure no one would find it, he took everything he had and bought the field itself so that he could protect his treasure.

Have you ever had something that was so precious to you that all you could think about was the treasure and how to protect it and keep it safe from others? Your treasure may not have been a family heirloom, or anything of great monetary value. In fact, your treasure may not have been a "thing" at all, but more of a feeling or an idea that you thought about and rediscovered with joy each time you considered it.

Real treasures will always be greater than material things, for they will be gifts that remain precious forever. They will be gifts of love, of contentment and peace, and gifts of God's grace and salvation. What is your pearl of great value?

*"The kingdom of heaven is like a man looking for fine pearls. When he found a very valuable pearl, he went and sold everything he had and bought it."*

Matthew 13:45-46 NCV

Lord, I have treasures, those things that fill my heart
with incredible joy, and though they fill my life with gladness,
not one of them is as dear to me as my relationship with You.
Amen.

*An idea of peace*

We should have great peace if we did not busy
ourselves with what others say and do.

Thomas à Kempis

As we reflect on our ideas of what we hope for in any new year,
we often think how nice it would be if the world could be at
peace. We wonder why it is so difficult for people to simply get
along and yet, on further reflection we might catch a glimpse of
ourselves, because even we struggle to be at peace.

For some of us, peace eludes us because we get caught up
in the lives of our family and friends. We're the peacekeeper for
those who cannot seem to find peace on their own, and though
we may do a good job guiding their lives, we end up agitated
ourselves because of all they've shared with us.

It doesn't take long as we read through the community
paper to notice all the newsy bits of the neighborhood and the
fact that they aren't getting along all that well. It's no wonder
the world can't solve the issues of peace, when we can't do it in
our own neighborhoods, our own families and within ourselves!

If you like the idea of peace, see what you can do today to
give peace a chance in your life.

*Seek peace and pursue it.*

Psalm 34:14 NKJV

Lord, I do strive to maintain a sense of peace
and order in my personal life and in the things I do.
Help me to find my peace in Your steadfast faithfulness.
Amen.

## *Beginning again*

Every accomplishment starts with the decision to try.

Anonymous

Most of us start a new year by taking a mental inventory of where we've been and what we've accomplished. We look at the things we think of as successes and the ones we're not as proud to revisit. We think about the things we've achieved and about the issues where we know we need to try harder next time.

You should know there are no restrictions on what you can do, because even if you've tried and failed in the past, you may try and succeed this time. In fact, you may have learned all the ways something doesn't work and be well on your way to understanding what does work.

You've already put in a lot of effort to become more of the woman you believe God wants you to be. Don't give up on those efforts – you have important goals to accomplish.

Will you get tired of trying in the coming year? Maybe. Will you want to quit? Sometimes. But keep trying, because you know it's up to you and that you have everything you need to win. The only thing that can really stop you now is not making a decision to try. Your new year awaits!

*"'Not by might nor by power, but by My Spirit,' says the LORD of Hosts."*

Zechariah 4:6 NKJV

Lord, I do believe I've grown and changed for the
better over this past year. Help me to keep believing,
to keep trusting and to keep trying in the year ahead.

Amen.

## *From here to there*

God has a course mapped out for your life, and all
the inadequacies in the world will not change His mind.
He will be with you every step of the way.

Charles Stanley

It's that time again when you start to consider your New Year's resolutions and then actually write them down or speak them aloud. You set new goals, make new plans and even have a twinge of excitement as you consider all the possibilities. You know you have a lot of things you want to accomplish and it's exciting.

There's only one problem: You have to get from here to there. You have to go from thinking about your ideas and planning your ideas to actually doing your ideas.

The way is not always steady and sometimes you may even feel like you're traveling without a safety net, but the one thing you know for sure is this: Once you step foot on the rope and start to move forward, God will be there with you every inch of the way. He will assure you, keep you steady, and help you get exactly where you want to go. Happy New Year!

*Send me Your light and Your faithful care, let them lead me;*
*let them bring me to Your holy mountain, to the place where You dwell.*

Psalm 43:3 NIV

Lord, please help me move in the direction of my goals
without hesitation or fear. Help me accomplish all the things
that are important to my growth this year.
Amen.